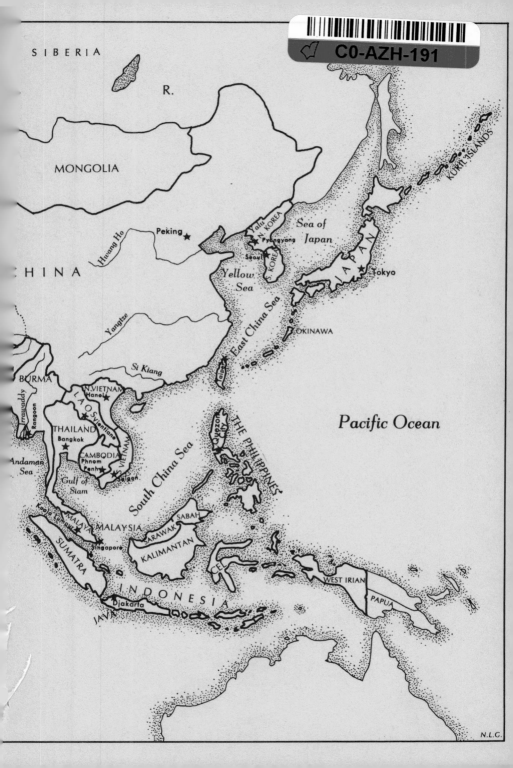

# Unbind
# Your Sons

# Unbind
# Your Sons

THE CAPTIVITY OF AMERICA IN ASIA

**ALEX CAMPBELL**

 LIVERIGHT / NEW YORK

1.987654321

Library of Congress Catalog Card Number: 79–114382

Standard Book Number: cloth  87140-500-8
                      paper 87140-027-8

Designed by Marshall Hendricks

Maps by Nancy Lou Gahan

Manufactured in the United States of America

# Contents

# Unbind
# Your Sons

# 1

# ASIAN FETTERS

As THIS BOOK went to press, the United States
was utterly confused about its policy and purpose in Asia.
This confusion was not new. It did not originate in the Vietnam war. The follies and failures of the war are the dreadful *reductio ad massacrem* of a long process of error, not
its source.

What has gone wrong in Asia began with American policy
in Europe. The Truman Doctrine of March 12, 1947, must
now be seen as the commencement of a very slippery slope.
Down this slope, the United States glissaded into Asia, in a
cloud of misconceptions. The United States had been engaged in World War II, then recently concluded, on two
main fronts, Europe and the Pacific, with two main allies,
Britain and Russia, and against two main foes, Germany and
Japan. But when the war was over it was decided that the
present and future enemy was something called international
communism. This dramatic switch was prompted by events
in Greece. Until February 1947, the British had been militarily supporting a Greek conservative government against
Greek communist guerrillas. But the British Labour government informed Washington that because of Britain's economic
difficulties, the troops in Greece would be withdrawn. President Truman decided that the United States should step into
the British shoes to the extent of affording financial aid to
Greece, and to Turkey as well. The president's decision was
overwhelmingly approved by Congress, which from this time
until the Tonkin Gulf resolution of 1965, and a bit beyond,

constantly gave enthusiastic support to the warlike commitments of successive administrations. Yet only 15 months before the enunciation of the Truman Doctrine, the United States had just as emphatically denounced the presence of British troops in Greece propping up a conservative government there, as a piece of characteristic British self-seeking.

The doctrine offered Greece money, not soldiers. But President Truman made the underlying American resolve quite plain. He told Congress: "I believe it must be the policy of the United States to support free people who are resisting attempted subjugation by armed minorities or by outside pressures."

Was this wrong? Dean Acheson, who was Truman's Secretary of State, nowadays would seem to think so. Mr. Acheson has recently declared that "foreign affairs is trying to adjust the interests of the United States with the foreign activities of other countries. If another country wants to deal with us in a friendly way, so that our interests are protected and their interests so far as we are concerned are protected, that is the end of the matter." No nonsense there about international communism; nor apparently about free people either.

*For years and years we carried on perfectly friendly relations with the government of the tsar. We did also with the sultan in Constantinople. We have done it with dictators and military juntas all over the world. We now take the idea that if a country is comparatively weak, we can be rude to it, we can try to overthrow it, we can try to impose American doctrines upon it. But if it is strong, like the Russians, we are very polite to it. This I think is both stupid and insincere, and contemptible.*

Mr. Acheson seems here to be saying that America ought to content itself with saving itself by its exertions, and the rest of the world only by its example. American foreign policy ought not to make it its business either to abet, or to oppose, revolutions or counterrevolutions. The United States ought not to try to mold the world into its own shape by applying some doctrine or other.

The Truman formula was full of unspoken implications, we now can see. It suggested for instance that a people were free if they had a government system like ours, and unfree if they hadn't. Given that they had a government like ours, therefore were by definition free, then of course "attempted subjugation by armed minorities" must be wrong. However, the world is full of wrongs. If the United States were to seriously attempt to prevent all such wrongs, or put them all right, that would make the United States the world's policeman.

In August 1966, the then Secretary of State Dean Rusk, a thoroughly decent American, told the Senate Armed Services Committee that the United States had treaty arrangements with "more than 40 countries on five continents." Nineteen years earlier, President Truman had assured Congress that "our help should be primarily through economic and financial aid." But then, there came the Korean War and the Vietnam war; and Mr. Rusk had to concede that the Southeast Asia Treaty Organization "commits the United States to a course of action over a vast expanse of the Pacific."

The Truman definition was dubious in its application even to its particular example, Greece. The government that the British had been backing until they decided they could afford to do so no longer was not one that American opinion had favored at first; there had been plenty of American criticism in fact of the British support. When elections were held subsequently in Greece, under the supervision of an international mission that the United States sponsored, the picture did not really become much clearer; the poll was only 49 percent, due to many people besides the Greek communists abstaining. The conservative parties did win most of the votes that were cast, but Greece was obviously a very divided country. (Twenty-three years after, it still is.)

But the real trouble with the new American policy of opposing "international communism" by force and taking sides in other peoples' civil wars began to show in earnest when it was applied to the Middle East, and when it was extended across Asia all the way into Indo-China. Increasingly hard to define, in those unfamiliar Asian settings, were the apparently simple concepts of "free people," "armed minorities" and "outside pressures." The muddle has reached its outside limit in Vietnam, with the indiscriminate wiping out of whole villages, armed guerrillas and unarmed civilians alike, children and women as well as men, in search-and-destroy missions in "free-fire zones" and in bomb and napalm air raids.

In Asia, the United States seems to have locked itself into a whole series of interlinked fetters. Another way of looking at the treaty commitments in this huge region of the globe is that they form a kind of Chinese screen, since their real aim in all cases is to "contain" China. How this occurred (and was accepted and approved by Congress after Congress as well as by successive administrations) is worth a moment's reflection. The initial purpose, as expressed first in the Truman Doctrine about Greece, and then ten years later in the Eisenhower Doctrine about the Middle East, was to fend off "international communism." But both doctrines regarded "international communism" as just a mask for Soviet Russia. Yet, as doctrinal anticommunism marched farther east, the target switched to China; first China apparently indissolubly linked in diabolical conspiracy with Russia; but still China even after Peking was spending more time denouncing Moscow than denigrating Washington. This fairly rapid transfer of the mask of "international communism" from Russia's to China's face was almost a pure accident of American history. The death of Stalin somewhat eased tension with Russia over Europe. But this only reminded America the more forcibly that in each of the three most recent wars in which American boys had died in large numbers, the precipitating incident had been Asian.

Nevertheless, to pin the blame for those aggressions on China was a remarkable confusion of thought. For in the first of those three wars, World War II, the aggressor as far as America was concerned had been Japan at Pearl Harbor, not China; and China was in fact America's ally. In the Korean War, the Chinese did not enter on the side of North Korea until after solemn warnings had been issued from Peking, to attempt to deter General MacArthur's forces coming too close to Chinese territory. These warnings were ignored by both President Truman and MacArthur, though the former subsequently fired the latter, in part for failing to give them due weight. Even so, the Chinese never declared war, but helped North Korea by sending Chinese "volunteers," just as the United States has never declared war in Vietnam. In the Vietnam war, more than a half million American troops in the South never were matched by a Chinese force in North Vietnam, for not a single Chinese soldier or airman was engaged in Vietnam, from first to last.

The Truman Doctrine was targeted on Russia. The Eisenhower Doctrine of 1957 was similarly targeted. In his New Year message to Congress that became the inspiration of the doctrine, President Eisenhower declared that Russia's "announced purpose is communizing the world." Russia was supplying arms to Syria, the way Russia today is supplying arms to Egypt. The Syrians said that they were not communists, as Nasser now says he is not. But Ben Gurion of Israel called Syria a "base for international communism." Congress as well as the President accepted this. The purpose of the Eisenhower Doctrine was to keep Russia out of the Middle East. The doctrine was aimed against "international communism" or any country "controlled by international communism." Overwhelmingly approved by Congress, it was invoked to send U.S. Marines into Lebanon to prevent that country "going communist." Iraq under Nuri Said also sought the protection of the Eisenhower Doctrine. What actually happened in those two countries reveals how irrelevant the doctrine actually proved in practice. In Lebanon, the Lebanese army refused to support a Muslim uprising against the Christian president Chamoun, and the rising therefore failed. In Iraq, the army turned against Nuri Said, and he was killed and his government fell. But nevertheless Iraq did not turn communist.

The American obsession with "communism" had spread from Greece and Turkey to the Middle East. But it was headed for the Far East, where it was to involve itself in its gravest errors. In the Korean War, the real power behind North Korea was universally believed to be Soviet Russia—

with Stalin pulling the strings—even though in the end the Americans found themselves fighting against Chinese not Russian "volunteers." But in the Far East the name of the criminal communist power on American lips quickly became China instead of Russia. The swift pace of events helps explain why. In 1947, when the Truman Doctrine was formulated, China was still ruled, however uneasily, by Chiang Kai-shek, the ally of America and the foe of communism. But by 1949, Chiang's regime had fallen, and he fled to Taiwan with the remnant of his army and supporters; in Peking, Mao Tse-tung and his communists ruled in Chiang's stead. Only a year later, the Korean War broke out. Not long after that, American troops in Korea were killing and being killed by Chinese troops. No Russians were involved. In the American mind, as far as Asia was concerned, Russia somehow got lost in the shuffle, despite everyone's conviction that Stalin was behind the Korean affair. And soon Stalin himself was dead, but Mao Tse-tung seemed very much alive.

Russia today is both communist and an Asian power, as was the case when Stalin lived. However, by the time the current American involvement in southeast Asia had begun, policy-makers in both the State Department and the Pentagon had decided that Russia was "contained" as far as was possible without going too close to the brink of nuclear war. But China it was contended still had to be "contained." To justify this, the "domino theory" was evolved. The phrase was apparently invented by the British prime minister Mr. Harold Macmillan, in 1950, with specific reference to Indo-China, where the French were fighting to regain their colonial possession that they had lost in World War II. Mr. Macmillan said that southeast Asia was like a number of dominoes; if one fell, the one next to it would topple, then the next, then the next again and so on. Mr. Macmillan of course had in mind what happened when the Japanese moved from Indo-China into Thailand, in 1941; as soon as they did this, the way was open to them to march on, through Malaya and Singapore toward Burma and India. President Truman and after him Presidents Eisenhower and Kennedy and Johnson bought the domino theory and simply substituted the Chinese communists for the Japanese warlords, although in fact there was little sign that the Chinese had either the intention or the means of following in prewar Japan's footsteps through southeast Asia. The Chinese leaders, as communists, were perfectly willing to give vocal, and sometimes some limited military support to communist rebels in other countries, for instance in British Malaya; and the Chinese leaders, as representing the national interests of China, had border disputes with other countries, especially India. But none of this had a domino meaning.

Furthermore, the Chinese either fell into or brought on themselves a deadly serious quarrel with Russia, the world's other large communist power and China's biggest neighbor. That quarrel was sufficiently grave to change the whole nature of events in the Far East, and to put all thoughts of pushing over dominoes out of China's mind, even if such thoughts had ever been entertained by Peking. But by now the American obsession with international communism was seemingly impervious to mere facts. The domino theory continued in vogue, as did the corollary need for America to "contain" China. The great schism between the world's largest communist powers was almost ignored, though it was likely to bring far larger consequences for all mankind than the question of whether there ought or ought not to be a communist government in South Vietnam as well as in North Vietnam.

Vietnam has proved to most people by now that the foreign policy that led to it must have something wrong with it. But there is considerable vagueness about what is wrong. To track down the error it is necessary to do what has been cursorily attempted here; to trace the policy back to its beginnings, just after the end of World War II. Looking back, it is plain that the way to hell was paved with what were believed to be good American intentions—though communists whether of the Russian or Chinese variety can hardly be expected to agree. But the hell of it is that the United States has on its hands serious commitments that were freely entered into by more than one administration, backed by several congresses. These commitments must either be kept, or changed. What is to be done? Is the United States compelled to involve itself in the next Middle East war because of the Eisenhower Doctrine, and must it fight "more Vietnams" in southeast Asia because of SEATO? If the reply to both questions is No, as in fact it ought to be, the next question becomes, What then *should* American policy be, toward the tortured lands of the Middle East, and toward the countries of Asia from the eastern shore of the Persian Gulf all the way to the China Sea?

This book attempts answers. To write it, lengthy journeys were undertaken. The views presented are as much those of people in the places visited who were prepared to speak their minds, as of the writer. This then is what the Asians themselves think about their problems, and about American policy.

If the Nixon administration decides that the United States not only need not fight in the Middle East, but ought in addition to pull its military forces off the Asian mainland, as well as getting them out of Japan and Okinawa and the Philippines, such a course seems likelier to please and relieve people in those places than to scare them.

The Vietnam war has frightened them more than an American military withdrawal could. No Asian statesman now wishes to see his country "saved from communism" by American bombs and napalm. Besides, they don't believe this *would* save them, and are quite sure it isn't the way to save them from communism.

The Asian view is that the thrust of American policy in their part of the world has been wrong. The emphasis on "containing" communism by military means was misplaced.

The Asians hope that from now on, they and the United States can do better. Happily, that seems to be American opinion also. "No more Vietnams" has become the watchword of both the great political parties.

There has been more than a touch of "the white man's burden" in American interventions in Asia. The original American intervention in Indo-China was undertaken in support of French colonialism. Many Vietnamese regard Americans as new colonizers. So do other Asians. The United States can help Asian countries, once there is a better American understanding of Asian people, an understanding now lacking. But Americans must firmly reject the notion of taking up the "white man's burden," in the sense that Rudyard Kipling meant when he wrote in 1899:

> Take up the white man's burden—
> Send forth the best ye breed—
> Go bind your sons to exile
> To serve your captives' need.

America must *unbind* its sons from their captivity.

# 2

# ASIA FROM WEST TO EAST:
# THE BIRD'S EYE VIEW

ASIA MAY MOST conveniently be thought of as falling into five geographical boxes. What westerners still largely call the Middle East, but Asians themselves nowadays prefer to call West Asia, extends from the delta of the Nile River, in Egypt, to the waters of the Persian Gulf. Central Asia includes some of the high lands of Asia, and the Muslim states of Iraq, Turkey, Iran, Afghanistan, and Pakistan. South Asia stretches from the Himalayas southward through India to the island of Ceylon and east to include Burma: mostly Buddhist and Hindu lands. Southeast Asia as all Americans now know has for land nucleus the former French Indo-China, ruled from Hanoi and Saigon, but also includes Thailand and Malaysia, and the great island chains of Muslim Indonesia and the Roman Catholic Philippines. But here our categories tend to break down, as categories will; for Vietnam is truly divided, the South being Southeast Asian in culture and temperament whereas North Vietnam belongs in the harder East Asian culture. East Asia is, in fact, what westerners still think of as the Far East; it includes Korea, Japan, and China—if anything as huge and populous as China can be said to be "included" in anything.

So, before we begin a very long voyage from west to east, let us briefly examine our five Asian boxes.

In West Asia or the Middle East, the air sparkles and smells subtly of spice, but also unfortunately of blood and intrigue.

Beirut in Lebanon is sophisticated and so in its own way is Cairo, the capital of Egypt; Beirut is tiny and tortuous whereas Cairo is big and brassy. But intrigue runs swiftly through the streets of both. Riyadh in Saudi Arabia still has a medieval feel about it, while Baghdad in Iraq and Damascus in Syria are both not only very, very old but nowadays seem sinister as well. The frank modern note is struck only in Israel, and Israel is perhaps a little too hard and clear. Can complex problems be fairly posed with the simple clarity that Israeli's hardheaded (and very articulate) spokesmen pretend? In Israel's own case, one can't forget, an estimated 69 percent of this Jewish state's 2,500,000 Jewish citizens are "oriental" Jews, mostly drawn from Arab countries. Thanks to their greater prolificity, they may soon be 80 percent of the population of Israel. In addition there are 300,000 or so non-Jewish Arabs living in Israel—within the pre-1967 frontiers—and, if Israel retains the areas it occupied after the six-day summer war, that will mean a million *more* Arabs.

The Arab-Israeli feud is to a large extent what the Middle East is all about. But it is not what alone has produced frightening Arab fanaticism, whose most numerous victims have been other Arabs. In Iraq, the Arab leader Nuri Said, murdered and in his grave 12 years, has so far had as successors men who appear like the most murderous caliphs from the history books. Nobody's head is safe in Iraq, which has 12,000 troops in Jordan arrayed against Israel. Damascus in Syria like Baghdad in Iraq is also a city of political terror; and moreover the Syrian and Iraqi Baath socialist parties squabble viciously.

Farther east, King Faisal of Saudi Arabia suspiciously watches both Egypt's Nasser and the Shah of Iran; Nasser is too revolutionary republican, and Faisal and the Shah each wishes to be dominant in the Persian Gulf, whose plethora of Arab potentates seek to dodge such dominance by melding their emirates into a federation, despite their own numerous rivalries.

If sanity prevails, the rich oil revenues of the Middle East will be invested in the development of the entire region.

Israel will withdraw from occupied territories back behind more secure, acknowledged borders, in a first stage of peaceful coexistence with the Arab world. The next stage could be peaceful cohabitation. Israel and Jordan at least could live as tolerably with each other as do the Lebanese, who are half Muslim, half Christian. Palestinian refugees would resettle their old homeland, and Israeli ships freely sail through Suez. Moreover, in a sane Middle East it would soon be apparent that the major answer to the area's population problem is not just the building by Nasser with Soviet aid of the Aswan Dam, and the Euphrates Dam in Syria, but a shift of many Arab families to underused farmlands in Iraq, land that at present is largely wasted by unproficient and uninterested tillers lacking the skill that Egyptians have acquired by reaping 7,000 harvests.

It should never be overlooked that the Middle East really is part of Asia. There are no "boxes" in actuality. The Japanese busily invest in Kuwait's offshore oil; the Chinese view of the Middle East is that the United States and Russia are in a joint plot to rule 100 million Arabs through Israel, their tool—a Chinese opinion that to Russia's chagrin seems to have caught on in Syria.

Central Asia, the high lands above the Middle East's fertile crescent, were named by President Eisenhower's secretary of state, the late John Foster Dulles, the West's "northern tier" against Russia. But the Russians have leapfrogged this ill-considered barrier, into the Mediterranean; the Russians also have warships in the Indian Ocean, and growing trade links with Singapore and Malaysia, in southeast Asia.

For convenience, Pakistan has been put here in Central Asia. About two-thirds of Pakistan's political significance for Asia and also perhaps for this country is Pakistan's enmity with India over Kashmir, a rich lush valley in a lofty Central Asian setting. According to Ayub Khan, the former Pakistan president, India looks ambitiously toward southeast Asia also. "The Indian leaders," he once wrote, "have often stated that their true border extends from the Hindu Kush mountains to the Mekong River."

Both Pakistanis and Indians (not to mention Chinese and Russians) might legitimately inquire if the United States is seeking an empire in Asia. There is the massive American military presence in Vietnam and elsewhere in Asia; and President Nixon in an article in *Foreign Affairs* in October 1967, called Indonesia "by far the greatest prize."

Where in fact does the United States stand in Asia? American policy is supposed to be aimed at the "containment" of China, and also at preventing Russia "communizing" the Middle East and other parts of Asia. But American policy frequently seems to lose all sense of direction amid the Asian thickets. So, fortunately, does Soviet policy often seem baffled by Asian complexities. And Peking stumbles quite as much as these two do.

The key factor in Asia is not communism, whether of the Russian or Chinese or the North Vietnamese or North Korean varieties. Nor is the key factor American imperialism. The two chief clues to the Asians and their thinking are a rapidly rising tide of nationalism, coupled with a strong desire by those countries to modernize themselves. These are the two main plots on which the entire drama turns, and those who do not understand this, whether they are Americans or Russians or even Chinese, are bound to lose their places, miss their cues and confuse their lines.

There are plenty of examples ready to hand.

In an apparent riposte to the presence of Soviet warships in the Mediterranean, the U.S. sent destroyers with antisubmarine missiles into the Black Sea in December 1968. That action involved Turkey in a hassle with the Soviet Union, for Turkey is the keeper of the Montreux convention which governs passage of warships through the Bosphorus. Russia protested, and subsequently young Turks demonstrated against the Sixth Fleet and against U.S. bases in Turkey. They were still doing so at the end of 1969.

There are Soviet bases in Egypt, and in Algeria. The Egyptians strongly dislike their Soviet drillmasters. The Russians' bases are sure to be the targets of demonstrations, sooner or later. For in Asia, demonstrations have become the rage.

Egyptian students have demonstrated even against Nasser; Persian students against the Shah, in Iran as well as outside it; and in India there are nearly always demonstrations being staged against the ruling Congress Party. Demonstrations overthrew Pakistan President Ayub Khan. An attempted communist coup in Indonesia backfired and led to the overthrow of President Sukarno.

Asia's demonstrations often threaten to produce only confusion or even anarchy. They may unseat a strong ruler, only to have him followed by another autocrat. Additionally, India, Pakistan, and Indonesia have some reason to fear actual dissolution, as nation-states. Pakistan consists of two quite separate areas, over a thousand miles apart, separated from each other by Indian territory. East Pakistan has always bitterly resented domination by West Pakistan, and much of the successful opposition to Ayub Khan's 10-year regime came from East Paskistani religious and political leaders. Indonesia consists, as Mr. Nixon pointed out in his *Foreign Affairs* article, of over 100 million people, living on a 3,000 mile arc of islands, many of which are opposed to (and on past occasions have rebelled against) Java's predominance. India is nominally a unitary not a federal state; the central parliament can theoretically abolish existing states, or create new ones, by a simple majority vote, and the president of India can and does take over the administration of states in an emergency. But, in practice, India's sheer size makes it very difficult for the central government or parliament to rule the states. Thus, Pandit Jawaharlal Nehru outlawed caste and instituted land reform; the fact remains that in most or all of the states caste continues, and big landlords rule the roost. Everyone periodically expresses puzzlement that India and Indonesia, each of them very large and with large military forces, seem to play such ineffectual roles in the affairs of Asia. The reason well may be that they have all their work cut out to avoid breaking up—or down—into a number of separate countries. There is usually enough regional tumult to threaten administrative paralysis.

China is by no means immune from such a threat. One

aspect of the Cultural Revolution is that China, like India, has run into turbulence in the relations between the central government and provinces that are displaying distinct rebellious tendencies. The Chinese communists have proved no better able to deal with such situations than anyone else in Asia.

The rapid rise and spread of competing nationalisms in Asia raises the question whether the Asians are doomed to repeat Europe's nationalist wars—and whether the United States is doomed to be involved in them, as it was in Europe's. The undeclared war in the Middle East between the Arab states and Israel is only one of Asia's conflicts. There are the Saudi Arabian, Iraqi, and Iranian claims to oil-rich portions of the Persian Gulf (which the Arabs insist on naming the Arabian Sea). Farther east, the Philippines claims Sabah, in Borneo, from Malaysia. The Catholic Philippines simultaneously fears Indonesian seduction of the Muslims who live in the southern Philippines. Tunku Abdul Rahman, the ruler of Malaysia, wants to buy French Mirage warplanes, because the Philippines has U.S. Sabrejets, and because Indonesia has Soviet MIG and TU-16 jets.

Why can't these countries and the others pull their weight in their own collective defense? The answer is, of course, that they are all too busy arming against one another.

The supposed riches of Indonesia could become real instead of merely potential, if attention were concentrated on developing Sumatra, and shifting people from fearfully overcrowded Java.

In the Middle East, if the rulers of Iraq stopped murdering political opponents, they might have energy to spare to implement the plan for the development of the Tigris-Euphrates Valley, which would enable Iraqi agriculture to flourish to the point where it could produce an estimated annual income of about $2,400 for every Iraqi.

In South Asia, India and Pakistan have approved, in principle, the world's largest irrigation scheme, for the Indus basin. The scheme is to harness the 1,900-mile-long river to irrigate an area almost as big as New Jersey, and to share between the two countries a six-river system capable of supporting

50 million people. Both India and Pakistan, however, prefer, in practice, to go on squabbling and sometimes going to war over Kashmir.

In Southeast Asia, the Mekong, 2,500 miles long, is one of the truly great rivers of the world. Fifteen hundred miles of it flow through South Vietnam, Cambodia, Laos, and Thailand. This part of the world could easily become a huge granary, if there were dams and irrigation projects. But local rivalries still block the way.

Japan, relieved by the United States of the burden of self-defense (Japan's spending on arms as a portion of GNP approximates to that of Luxembourg), achieves and maintains a rate of real economic growth of between 9 and 10 percent annually. In most other places in Asia the vast gap between the wealthy West and the impoverished East steadily widens, whether measured in terms of modern armaments or of human welfare.

Into this vast brew of race and politics, we now proceed to plunge.

# 3

# WEST ASIA:

# SUEZ CANAL TO PERSIAN GULF

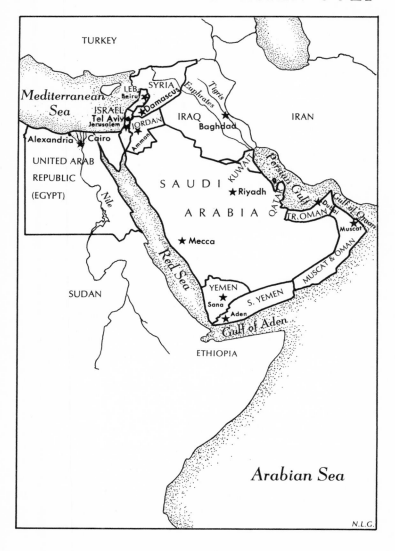

## THE EGYPTIAN SPHINX

WHEN YOU STAND at the Suez Canal, James Morris says, Europe with its cathedrals is behind you. In front of you are the crags of Arabia and bottomless blue seas all the way to China. The Nile Delta is where Asia begins. Here the traveler for the first time encounters the water buffalo, the creaking wheels, the mud and mud huts, the mosquitoes, and the thick human populations which he will be encountering again and again on his way through Asia.

But today the ruler of the ancient land of the pharaohs is Gamal Abdel Nasser who replaced King Farouk, the obese last Egyptian king. Farouk was mainly interested in women, gambling, jewels, palaces, and black marble bathrooms. Nasser, the son of an Egyptian minor civil servant whose father was a peasant from a remote village, has a more focused interest than the former king. Nasser is interested in power.

After almost twenty years of power, Nasser still lives very simply. His home is little more than a cottage. His family life is simple, too; Nasser is said to be a devoted husband and father. He boasts of serving the best coffee that Egypt can produce—but he lives mainly on white cheese, bread, and black olives. Reading is one of his great passions, but not literature—he devours American newspapers and magazines.

Nasser's problem with Egypt is, in a nutshell, that the population of 30 millions is increasing at a rate of about a million a year, and that Egypt has no mineral or other natural wealth save the Nile's fertility. (Egypt has, for example, found no oil.) The population of the United States was much this size at the time of the Civil War. Nasser plainly hopes for rapid economic as well as political progress for Egypt, by his revolutionary tactics. Unfortunately, much of Egypt's endeavor has been diverted to war, with Israel and also in Yemen in south Arabia. When the feudal Arab state of Yemen fell into civil war between republicans and royalists, Nasser backed the republicans and King Faisal of Saudi Arabia backed the royalists. Too many Egyptian soldiers have died in Yemen, just as too many Americans have died in Vietnam.

All the 60 pyramids of Egypt are on the west bank of the Nile and the Aswan Dam is Nasser's 61st pyramid. But the new Cairo, a brassy, enormous city of gray concrete and river bridges, is on the other side of the Nile from the pyramids and the Sphinx. This is a city of intense and incessant politics. There have been frequent "spontaneous" demonstrations of mobs, roused by Nasser against somebody. For example, an American embassy official who looked from his window saw a crowd gathering outside and a TV truck drawing up, simultaneously. He went out to inquire what was going on. The Egyptian TV man looked at his watch and said crisply "There is to be a spontaneous demonstration of the people here against American imperialism in 27 minutes."

Nasser has been assisted by the Russians with arms ever since 1956. With the Soviet aid, and also with the aid of old Nazis from Germany, Nasser has written for Egypt a rabble-rousing scenario that reads like the diaries of the late Joseph Goebbels set to Wagnerian music.

Nasser is a born plotter and intriguer. His targets and victims have varied from time to time in his restless quest to create some sort of empire for Egypt. For example, in 1958 he created the United Arab Republic with Syria, that only lasted 3 years until Syria broke it up. Then, Nasser began to have African ambitions and for a time all Egyptians were solemnly informed and reminded that Egypt after all is part of Africa and therefore they were Africans. It proved impossible, however, for Nasser to convince the easygoing but highly sophisticated Egyptians they had much in common with any of the people who lived far to the south, or even with the neighboring Sudanese. But Nasser has never ceased plotting against somebody. The plotters come into Cairo from everywhere. There are men who are exiles from their own countries in Africa. There are political exiles from Jordan. There are exiles from Saudi Arabia and Yemen. They all gather in Cairo, they are all subsidized by the Egyptian government, and they are all agog to destroy their own governments back home. This is one reason why Nasser is scarcely a popular figure with any of these governments in any of these countries, including even Arab ones, like Jordan and Saudi Arabia.

There are, of course, plotters in Egypt who plot against Nasser himself, but they get short shrift, for the government has set up a very tightly controlled police state. This is not new in Egypt. Centuries ago, Nestorius was exiled to Kharga in the Libyan Desert for preaching the heresy of the Logos. Today, Kharga is still a place of exile for heretics, including Egyptian communists who are sent there and kept in captivity in spite of Nasser's apparent increasingly close association with the Soviet Union.

Nobody can doubt Nasser's sincere ambition to raise Egypt and transform her into a great power. He has done many things in many ways to improve life in Egypt for the common man. The Aswan Dam is only one scheme that is bound to lead to a great change for the better in the conditions of Egyptian life; and yet Nasser's restless plotting has involved him in some costly failures. In 1969, half a million embittered Egyptians had to be evacuated from the Suez Canal zone because of Israeli attacks which Nasser was apparently powerless to repel or to avenge.

The Middle East presents a serious problem for the United States. Here are 100 million Arabs—and some 2.5 million Jews in Israel; obviously the heart of the United States is largely with the Israelis, and yet the Arabs cannot be ignored, especially (so State Department officials argue) in view of Nasser's close connections with the Soviet Union. But even if the United States were to switch, and to choose the Arab side, it would be perplexed to know which Arabs to choose: the revolutionaries like Nasser or the oil kings like Faisal of Saudi

Arabia? These dilemmas have never been resolved by the United States, and do not appear to have an easy solution in sight now.

## ISRAEL, HOPE AND SHIELD

IN MAY 1970 the independent sovereign State of Israel was 22 years old. It has no written constitution, but its flag has the blue shield of David in the center, and its national anthem is called Hope.

Israel is a tiny land, of not many more than 2.5 million people, which is besieged by more than 100 million hostile neighbors. Since the 6-day war of 1967, Israel's stated position has been that a durable peace between it and its Arab neighbors can be found only by meeting with them face to face. This condition has been refused as unacceptable by the Arab nations who are unwilling to recognize that Israel as a state properly exists.

The Israelis fought a fast war in 1967 mainly because the government is unable to maintain complete mobilization for more than a short period without the economy of the country going to pieces. This is not the only military headache from Israel's point of view. Its aircraft are old compared with Egypt's Russian supplied MIG-21s. By the standards of modern warfare, the Israeli armored forces are also fairly obsolete in their equipment.

At the end of 1969, Israel, although militarily successful against the Arabs, was facing a serious financial position. The country was spending about 15% of its GNP on defense and the strain of this was beginning to show very visibly. The prime minister, Mrs. Golda Meir, who visited Washington to ask President Nixon for aid and especially for arms, was born in 1898 in Kiev, in Russia, but she grew up in Milwaukee. She has two children and five grandchildren, and is not likely to remain prime minister of Israel long, because of her health and her age; twice in the past she quit jobs that were too demanding. She was once foreign minister and she has once before been leader of the Israel Labor Party. Mrs. Meir's successor might be the hero of Israel, General Moshe Dayan.

On the Suez Canal, Israel supplements its air power with deeply entrenched artillery and with networks of bunkers. So the Arabs have learned to concentrate their attacks on the "east front"—the Jordanian, Syrian, and Lebanese frontiers. From Jordan, the Arab guerrilla movement Al Fatah and the Palestine Liberation army attack Israel. The Israelis respond to these attacks with air strikes and they try to keep the Arab guerrillas out of Israel by means of border patrols, fences, and mine fields, especially in the Jordan Valley, north and south of the Dead Sea. The continuing war is one of constant movement and constant incidents. For example, on August 10, 1969, the Israelis did what they said they would do if the Arab raids continued: they smashed Jordan's precious East Ghor Canal. On August 21, an Australian, apparently a religious fanatic, set fire to the Aqsa Mosque in Jerusalem. And on August 29, 1969, Arabs hijacked a TWA airliner to Damascus where the Syrians detained the Israeli passengers.

As time has gone by, and as incidents have multiplied, it has become progressively more difficult, because of domestic politics and the mutation of doves into hawks, for the Israeli government to seriously consider giving up secured areas, such as the Golan Heights belonging to Syria, the Gaza strip belonging to Egypt, the valuable coastal belt running from Eilat to Sharm El Sheikh—and, of course, Jerusalem. Almost forgotten are the solemn promises of the former Israeli prime minister, the late Levi Eshkol, on the first day of the 6-day war of 1967, that Israel desired not one inch of Arab territory.

And, also, of course, the Arabs have been no less intransigent. It became clear, for instance, that should Nasser pass from the scene for any reason, his successors were quite unlikely to desist in Egypt's efforts to bombard Israel into retreat.

## THE LEBANESE VICE

THE REPUBLIC OF Lebanon is about the size of Connecticut and about 2.5 million people live very pleasantly there—the population of Lebanon is roughly the same as that of Israel. But though the Lebanese are few in number their religious diversity is bewildering. There are, for example, Sunni and Shia Muslims; Druses; Maronites; Greek Orthodox and Armenian Orthodox Christians; Latin, Greek, Syrian, and Armenian Catholics; Jews; Nestorians; and Protestants. Of all of these, the most interesting may be the Druses, though they are only about 6 percent of the Lebanese population. Their 11th century founder advanced the claim that Hakim, the 6th Fatimid caliph, was the final incarnation of God; and from other religions, including both Christianity and Judaism, he freely borrowed various beliefs to which he added some of his own, such as the transmigration of souls. At the beginning of the 19th century, the Druses unexpectedly acquired an English queen. The eccentric Lady Hester Lucy Stanhope abandoned her job as secretary and housekeeper to her uncle William Pitt, England's greatest prime minister and, after making a pilgrimage to Jerusalem, settled among the Druses on Mt. Lebanon, practicing astrology, claiming to be able to see into the future, and involving herself deeply in political intrigues of which there never has been a shortage in Lebanon. Her boyfriend had been Sir John Moore, the Scottish general who fell mortally wounded in the moment of victory over the French at the Battle of Corunna, in Spain, and who died with Lady Hester's name on his lips.

About a century and half after the passing of Lady Stanhope, Lebanon still seemed to be attracting eccentrics. The

notorious Kim Philby lived in Beirut awhile. This British correspondent, a man of infinite charm whose father had taken an
active part in the politics of Saudi Arabia, turned out to be
a double agent working for British intelligence but also for
the Russians. Subsequently, he fled to the Soviet Union. Another interesting man I once met in Beirut was an American
called Bruce Conde. Bruce had come to Lebanon because he
was convinced that his family had been Yemenis and had held
a high place in that country. He relinquished his American
citizenship, moved from Lebanon to Yemen, and when last I
heard from him he was playing an active part in Yemen's
turbulent politics and military affairs.

By tradition the population of Lebanon is said to be in exact
balance with 50 percent Christian and 50 percent Muslim. This
is fiction. However, in order to preserve it, and so preserve
political peace, there is a tacit understanding. When the president of Lebanon is a Christian the prime minister has to be
a Muslim, and when the president is a Muslim the prime minister is a Christian. In 1958 it looked as if this delicate balance
might be upset, and President Eisenhower sent U.S. Marines
to prevent Lebanon from becoming a communist satellite. This
possibility was a farfetched one, and when the marines waded
ashore, they were startled to be received not by shots fired in
anger, but by eager salesmen of wooden camels and other
tourist souvenirs who waded out in the surf to meet them and
tried to effect a sale before they had actually touched foot on
shore.

Lebanon is the land of pharaoh's cedars. At Baalbek in the
hills there is still a temple of Bacchus, and, on the coast, the
town of Byblos is the origin of the word, Bible. Many peoples
have passed through Lebanon—Phoenicians, Hittites, Crusaders, Greeks, Turks. The Phoenicians are commemorated by
the resplendent Phoenicia hotel designed by the American
architect Durrell Stone; and the hotel Saint George commem-
orates the legend that Saint George's dragon was slain here.

Lebanon, like Egypt and Syria, has no oil—but it makes up
for the lack by having banks where oil-rich Arabs from the
other Arab countries gladly store their gold—literally gold, in

gold bars—for safe-keeping. The Lebanese bankers do not pay them for the use of this gold which, of course, the banks make the basis of their own credit transactions; they make the wealthy Arabs pay for the privilege of keeping the gold there. Beirut also has tall apartment buildings and splendid stores, all of which represent investments by oil-wealthy Arabs from other countries. And, because these Arabs flock to Lebanon for business and for personal pleasure, on the hills surrounding Beirut there are tall and splendid houses which are staffed by people who are Arabian slaves. Then there are the many Lebanese who emigrated and have come home wealthy from the United States, particularly, and from other countries as well. Cosmopolitan Beirut has, of course, a casino, fabulous restaurants, splendid movie theatres. Everybody rich or poor is able to take advantage of the lush surroundings to go skiing in the morning and to go for a swim in the blue Mediterranean in the afternoon. The traffic is horrendous. Lebanese drivers tend to treat roads as race tracks. The din of Beirut traffic is considerably augmented almost every day by large wedding parties who hoot their way around the town and then speed off for a wedding party in the hills. Unfortunately, they go so fast and the hill roads are so precipitous that a distressingly large number of Lebanese weddings never get consummated, because of fatal road accidents to newlyweds.

A well-known tourist attraction is the holding of colorful music festivals amid the picturesque ruins of Baalbek, high in the mountains. The festivals have been interrupted more than once by gun battles between feuding families living in the hills nearby. These feuds sometimes spread to Beirut itself, resulting in private assassination or indiscriminate shooting in the streets. When the Beirut police regard the situation as having gotten completely out of hand, they carefully wind scarves around their helmets, in order to warn the populace that they intend to shoot to kill.

Beirut has an elegant Corniche, and also has the famous University of Beirut, one of the intellectual centers of the Middle East.

In the Middle East setting, the Lebanese tend to shine like

a good deed in a naughty world. All they really ask from life is to be left alone to indulge their passion to make money. But their airline had its planes destroyed at Beirut airport by Israeli commandoes in 1968. The aircraft were relatively old, and insured, and would have had to be replaced anyhow. The Israelis may have done MEA a financial good turn. However, in August 1969, Lebanese public opinion and the Lebanese parliament were divided about equally about the Palestinian guerrillas using Lebanon as a base from which to attack Israel. President Helou backed the Palestinians but wanted them to fight Israel outside of Lebanese territory. Prime Minister Rashid Karami favored "coordinating" the Palestinians with the Lebanese army, but he may have suggested this in order to have better control over the Palestinians. Former president Camille Chamoun, Raymond Eddie and Pierre Jemeyel and other well-known Lebanese politicians sided with President Helou. Helou was due to quit the presidency in 1970, and Chamoun and General Fuad Chehab, another former president, were the likeliest candidates to seek the post. Chamoun scolded the Lebanese for facing their problems with "negligence, ignorance and demagogery."

The politician who is on the left in Lebanon is Kamal Jumblatt, the parliamentary chief of the Druses. Ironically, the Jumblatts owe their leadership of the Druses since about 1630 to their land holdings, which give them a solid economic base. Kamal Jumblatt has given away a good deal of land to former tenants, nevertheless he is about as much a left-wing extremist as is the Shah of Iran who also is an enthusiastic land reformer; and Jumblatt's Progressive Socialist Party has never been a really serious threat to the delicately balanced interests that compose the Lebanese state. That threat was posed instead by the Palestinians, refugees from land occupied by the Israelis. The Palestinians live in refugee camps in Lebanon, but after the 1967 Arab-Israeli war they joined the newly formed Arab commandos. The Karami government fell through its efforts to prevent the Palestinians using Lebanon as a base for armed raids into Israel, as well as for a sanctuary. In Jordan, the Palestinians had similarly shaken off with impatience the restraining hand of Jordan's King Hussein. It was said that Lebanon, which had managed for so long to stay aloof from active participation in the fight against Israel, had been "Jordanized" by the Palestinians.

# JORDAN'S LONELY KING

KING HUSSEIN MAY be the loneliest king in the world. He has been married twice, first to an Egyptian princess, secondly to the daughter of an English soldier. At his second marriage, there were men with machine guns on guard at the mosque where the wedding was celebrated. The king is constantly in danger of assassination.

One of Hussein's major headaches is that the preponderant number of people who live in Jordan are not loyal to him or to his royal house. They are Palestinian refugees of whom there are now probably one million.

Jordan is a country with no real borders. It has only five miles or so of coastline, near Aqaba, where the Queen of Sheba once landed and where Lawrence of Arabia fought one of his celebrated battles. The capital of Jordan, Amman, is a small country town consisting largely of stone buildings that sprawl over seven hills. The male population of Amman is mostly composed of cheerful young fellows in Arab headdresses, all handsome and looking remarkably like the movie actor Omar Sharif.

Perhaps the most famous product of Jordan is the Dead Sea Scrolls, all of which were found in this tiny country. The scrolls are actually tiny scraps of ancient curling leather which were found scattered about in numerous caves. Other than these, Jordan has produced little. It has no oil. All that can live in the Dead Sea is said to be the tetanus bug.

Near the end of the year 1969, the hard fact of political life in Jordan was that the head of the army, Sharif Nasser (no relation to the Egyptian ruler) disliked the guerrilla commanders who drew their recruits from Jordan refugee camps and got their arms from the communists. But Sharif Nasser was unable to do anything about them. By raiding from Jordan into Israel, the guerrillas drew Israeli fire that fell on Jordanian army posts; also the Israelis avenged the guerrilla raids by preventing, by gunfire, repair of the East Ghor Canal, on which much of Jordan Valley farming depends for its continuance. Neither Jordan nor Israel had ever been able to agree even to install a "hot line" for example at the Mandelbaum Gate. The "gate" was a narrow Jerusalem roadway, infested with barricades and gun posts, and named after a merchant, otherwise totally obscure, who once owned a house nearby. Yet a "hot line" there might have saved several lives before 1967, and might even have averted the Israeli-Jordan war.

King Hussein might now be prepared to try to reach a settlement with Israel, except that such an attempt would almost certainly cost him his throne and even his country, and might well cost him his life. For the only settlement that the Palestinians who now swarm in Jordan might conceivably accept is a Palestinian state, and if this did not include all of Jordan, it would probably include so much of it that the Hashemite kingdom of Hussein would simply disappear from the map.

# SAD, PROUD SYRIANS

SYRIA, LIKE JORDAN, has wide open frontiers. Its five million people have a dangerously splendid past to contrast with their present penury. Consequently, they are very xenophobic. "What would a foreigner be doing in Damascus if he were not either a spy or a Zionist?" they tend to ask. Syria celebrated the opening of the Damascus international fair in 1969 with a new airport where, at the end of August of that year, as we have noted, a hijacked TWA plane from Rome landed and the Syrians arrested its Israeli passengers.

Syria was the headquarters of Turkish power in the Middle East and was ruled by the French who also ruled Lebanon until 1945. From Damascus, Haroun Al Rashid and his wife, Zobedya, *walked* to Mecca *on carpets,* and new castles and palaces were built for them at every caravan station. Here, in or near Damascus, Abraham was born; Cain slew Abel; Moses, Job, and Jesus all lived here, as did Mohammed. Here too Saint Simeon Stylites sat on his pillar in the pious 5th century; the pillar was 60 feet high and the famed Syrian ascetic reportedly sat on it for 30 years.

Damascus nowadays is always jammed with soldiers and their desert-camouflaged jeeps; MIGs screech overhead, while posters on all the ancient city walls cry out that "Zionism equals Nazism," and "The Star of David equals the Swastika." Syrians, and the people of Damascus in particular, are very conscious of the fact that Israeli tanks on the Golan Heights are only 35 miles away, and that Israeli jets are only four minutes away. In this sense, Syria, and indeed the whole Middle East, is a sort of microcosm of our modern shrunken world.

Having broken off its close UAR ties with Egypt in 1961,

Syria later tried to renew them but found that Nasser was rather cool, not surprisingly. President Nuredin Al-Attassi kept trying. But Nasser disliked risking the somewhat tenuous ties he has achieved with the rich, conservative Arabs who subsidize him to the tune of $200 million a year. They wouldn't like Nasser to have close ties once more with the volatile, unstable, and radical leftist Syrians. One Syrian reason for desiring closer union with Egypt once again is Syria's growing conflict with Iraq. Both the Syrian and Iraqi regimes are Arab Baath Socialist Party factions; but the Iraqi faction belongs to the Baathist group that Syria suppressed in February 1966, the year before that same group came to power in Baghdad. There are nevertheless 6,000 Iraqi troops in Syria as well as 12,000 Iraqi troops in Jordan. A joint Arab command of Syrian, Iraqi, Jordanian, and Saudi Arabian liaison officers operates near Dera, in southern Syria, under the command of an Iraqi general. "The enemy of my enemy is my friend, though he be my enemy."

## ARABIAN ARAMCO

THE SAUDI ARABIAN peninsula is almost as large as India but it has hardly more inhabitants than greater London; and these inhabitants include at least a half million slaves, who are mostly Negroes, and who are the last slaves in the entire world as far as is known. King Saud of Saudi Arabia built himself a palace which had homes for his wives as well as for all his retainers and which covered a square mile. The palace still stands, but Saud was in exile in Egypt at his death, and his brother Feisal who rules in his stead is believed to have less expensive tastes. Saud built his palace in Riyadh, but Riyadh today is filled with earnest town planners rather than with kings' wives, concubines, and innumerable princely offspring. Modernization is being made possible by the enormous wealth of the country, due entirely to its oil resources, yielding $1 billion a year which is expected soon to double. Town planners are one aspect of Saudi Arabia's wealth; another more striking aspect is that the few roads of the country are littered with abandoned Cadillacs. Wealthy Saudis rarely attempt to have an auto repaired when something goes wrong; they simply leave it where it has broken down, and purchase another one.

Another main city is Jiddah, a picturesque town of crumbling walls and narrow winding streets. It is also one stage of the pilgrimage to Mecca which hundreds of thousands of devout Muslims embark upon every year. A third Saudi Arabian city is Dhahran, the headquarters of the Arabian American Oil Company and also the place of luxurious captivity of a considerable force of American technicians and their wives. The American wives virtually live in *purdah*, may not drive cars, may not receive letters from Israel, and may run into embarrassing situations if they go about unveiled. The well-paid Americans of Dhahran suffer from another disability; liquor is forbidden by the Koran, and the Americans are not permitted to import any. However, most of them have managed to build their own stills which produce dubious brews with headsplitting qualities. Riyadh, Jiddah, and Dhahran are small clusters of population in an empty land. Saudi Arabia has to the southwest, Yemen; to the south, Aden; and on the east, Muscat and Oman, Qatar, Bahrain, and Kuwait. Between the part of Saudi Arabia known as the Empty Quarter and the ocean are hidden valleys—and even hidden "cities" of primitive cave dwellers who speak a language which is not Arabic and which has not been identified; and there are still lingering traces of the ancient merchandise trade in frankincense and parrots and peacocks, pearls and ivory and ostrich feathers, in places with such romantic names as Salala, Qara, Mukhalla, and Dhufar.

Ancient Islamic laws prevail in Saudi Arabia. For instance, the grisly fate of adulterers and adulteresses is still to be stoned to death. And the punishment of a thief is to have his right hand cut off. However, Saudi Arabians explain that the rigor of the law has been somewhat softened in recent times. The adulteress is said to be chloroformed before being wrapped in a rug at which the mob is encouraged to hurtle stones; and the thief whose hand is to be cut off is generally given some narcotic before the sentence is carried out, and after it is carried out he is rushed to the hospital for immediate medical attention lest he should bleed to death.

# THE GULF ARABS

THE GULF ARABS are a coast people. They are complex. They include the Niems, the Shamis, and Kaabs; the Balushs, Duies, Wahibahs, Janabes, Harasis, and the Shihuhs whom the others believe to be the direct descendants of Sinbad the Sailor.

Bahrain, the big island of the Persian Gulf, has a population of about a quarter of a million. It also has a good deal of oil. Iran claims it because Persia occupied the island in the 16th and 17th centuries. However, the Shah of Iran wants to be on good terms with Faisal of Saudi Arabia who does not wish Bahrain to come under Iran. The ruler of Bahrain, Sheikh Isa, looks to both Britain and the United States for protection. Also, the Jordanians have helped the Sheikh to build up for Bahrain a "national guard."

Abu Dahbi is the newly rich country of the Gulf. It has a population of only 50,000, and by 1970 it is estimated that they will be earning some $250 million from Abu Dahbi's oil. The boss of Abu Dahbi is Sheikh Zayad Bin Sultan Al Nihaian. In 1969, the Sheikh was advertising in the newspapers around the world for a financial adviser who, the ad said, would have to be somebody who was accustomed to handling large sums of money. The Sheikh was prepared to pay the right man a salary of $60,000 a year or up, tax free. In Abu Dahbi, it is said, all you have to do to start an oil well coming up is to put your heel in the ground and twist it a little. The tiny country is deep in a quarrel with Saudi Arabia over the Buraimi Oasis, which Faisal claims.

Dubai fought a little war with Abu Dahbi in the 1940s, but now Dubai's Sheikh Rashid is prepared to live off the trade that comes through Abu Dahbi, plus some traditional gold smuggling to India.

The ruler of Qatar, Sheikh Kahilifa, vies with Sheikh Zayad for recognition as top man of the Gulf. But Sheikh Kahilifa lacks the other's wealth. However, he is prepared to fight his way to the summit if he can acquire the necessary arms; as Qatar is not poor either, he probably will succeed in getting them. But Zayad can outspend him on that. The upshot may be each spending around $90 million on missiles and other such toys. Missiles have fascinated the Arabs ever since the Palestinians began using Soviet-made missiles for firing into Jerusalem and other Israeli towns.

Kuwait has oil reserves which are half as big as those of the United States. This enables tiny Kuwait to dispense full, free welfare (including free telephone calls) to all of its inhabitants, without taxing them, though in the memory of people still living, Kuwait earned its bread quite humbly by building dhows and selling trinkets, and was mainly known as a sanctuary for desert tribes who were unwilling to join either Saudi Arabia or Iraq. Kuwait has built the world's biggest and best guarded water filtration plant, so as not to be solely dependent for fresh water on Iraqi supplies from Shatt-el-Arab, although that is only 50 miles away. And Kuwait also pays large subsidies to Nasser of Egypt.

The Sultan of Muscat and Oman has been until lately, and perhaps still is, too preoccupied with rebels at home to play much part in the external politics of the Gulf.

Of the other Gulf kingdoms—Ras El Khaimeh, Umm Al Qaiwan, Ajman, and Saharjah—Umm Al Qaiwan lives ingeniously, if precariously, by selling commemorative stamps. Its population is only 4,000 people. The others depend upon similar gimmicks for their survival.

The Shah of Iran likes to be thought of as the protector of the Gulf, in addition to his specific claim to Bahrain.

If the conservatives win the next British elections they may reverse the proposed British withdrawal from the Gulf, to the extent of sending in a military band—whose token value might not be totally negligible. But nobody yet knows what the role of the United States is going to be in the Persian Gulf, or the shape of its future relations with the Gulf federation that the quarreling oil emirs recently sought to set up. The federation would exclude both Kuwait and Bahrain.

## AMERICA AND THE MIDDLE EAST

THE MIDDLE EAST is a boiling pot where wars are brewed. One day, World War III could bubble out of it. Both Israel and Egypt have recruited German scientists. Israel has nuclear capability, and may have already created and secretly cached untested nuclear weapons. These deserts seem to foment a heady recklessness. In 1956, when French warships gaily joined in the Israeli attack on Egypt, Vice-Admiral Berjot reported to Paris that he thought he had crippled an Egyptian destroyer. "But not entirely sure Egyptian. If this should turn out an error it is not a deliberate attack . . . on the Sixth Fleet." As if to cap this, the Israelis in 1967 crippled an American navy ship, with much loss of life.

Other than the fearsome possibility of a local conflict erupting into a world war, it is not easy to detect vital American national interest in the Middle East. There is heavy American investment in Arab oil, but not in Egypt (or in Israel); and Europe depends far more than the United States for its continuing industrial existence on Middle East oil. Russia in 1969 advised the eastern European countries to turn to the Arabs for their oil, because the Soviet Union apparently is going to need its own oil supplies to develop Siberia. But the notion of communist as well as western customers for Middle East oil ought to please and not alarm Americans. American oil companies should make money.

In May 1950, President Truman's time, a Three Power Declaration by the U.S., Britain, and France stated that if the three governments found that either Israel or an Arab state "was preparing to violate frontiers or armistice lines," the powers would "immediately taken action, both within and outside the United Nations, to prevent such violation." This committed the signatories to very little.

After France and Britain joined Israel in a military invasion of Egypt in 1956, President Eisenhower drew the attention of British prime minister, Anthony Eden, to the Three Power Declaration. However, he and his secretary of state John Foster Dulles both knew that France had armed Israel, and Dulles was probably the man really responsible for the attack on Egypt, for it was Dulles who did a somersault over Nasser's cherished project, the Aswan Dam. Dulles had offered to finance the dam, then abruptly withdrew. Nasser proceeded to nationalize the Suez Canal and its revenues. This in turn triggered off the French and British into breaching the Three Power Declaration by joining with the Israelis in the attack on Nasser while pretending to be attempting to "halt" Israeli aggression.

The next American step was a strange one. A joint resolution of Congress, the so-called Eisenhower Doctrine of March 1957, was passed to enable the president to use armed force "against armed aggression from any country controlled by international Communism" in the Middle East. Suddenly, there was supposed to be a "Communist threat" among the Arabs, and for that reason "the United States regards as vital to the national interest and to world peace the preservation of the independence and integrity of the nations of the Middle East." The Middle East had to be saved from Communism. The Eisenhower Doctrine was responsible for U.S. Marines wading ashore from warships to protect Lebanon, which was supposed to be in danger of going the way of Iraq where there had just been a violent revolution. It transpired however that the leaders of the Iraq revolt were fanatical Arab nationalists, not communists; and, in Lebanon, the mystified marines were not called on to fire one shot.

Gamal Abdel Nasser, the president of Egypt, is not a communist, either. The Soviet Union has twice heavily armed Egypt (before the 1967 war, and since). But Nasser would have been more than ready to get arms from the United States, if the U.S. had let him have them, the way it armed Pakistan against India. Perhaps Nasser was too honest. The Soviet military aid, reputed by now to have cost Russia about $2 billion, has never done much for the Egyptian Communist Party whose hapless card-carriers Nasser keeps locked up in a prison deep in the desert. On the other hand, Nasser refused to pretend, as Pakistan did, that American arms would be used against "Communism." He always insisted his enemy was Israel.

President John F. Kennedy and President Lyndon Johnson expressed American "support" for the integrity of Israel *and* of the Arab states. Russia was quick to recognize Israel, but the two nuclear powers are now scared to death of finding themselves fighting each other through their involvement with their Middle East client-states' quarrels. They are talking to each other to try to extricate themselves from the Arab-Israeli imbroglio. They are going to find this difficult to do; for the Soviet Union is still strongly supporting the Arabs (probably for the simple reason that there are 100 million of them to only 2.5 million Israelis—and the Russians like to be with the big battalions). The United States tends to throw its sympathy (but not much else, at least officially) to Israel. Both superpowers however would prefer that the Arab-Israeli feud had a political, not a military conclusion.

Russian-American cooperation in the Middle East is limited (but not by America's wishes) to trying to avert possible Russian-American confrontation over that region. If the fighting between the Arab countries and Israel should become another full-scale war, the Russians probably will stay out of it (though their aircraft might defend Cairo and Damascus). Should the Russians join the Arabs in combat, American military involvement might prove inescapable. It is because both sides know this that they continue talking, in order to avoid it rather than with any serious hope of achieving agreed solutions of Middle East problems.

American policy in the Middle East might find itself facing a different dilemma. Suppose in another war between Arabs and Israelis, the Arabs were winning without benefit of active Soviet participation, and in consequence Israel looked like it was being wiped off the map? The Soviet Union faces no such dilemma of policy, as there is no prospect of Israel wiping the Arab countries off the map. The United States would then have to decide whether to acquiesce in Israel's doom, or go to Israel's aid. In such a situation, there is no doubt that the United States would act to prevent the destruction of Israel.

Meantime, American official policy is to continue to seek a Middle East peace that assures Israel's frontiers, in exchange for the substantial return of territory formerly possessed, or administered, by the Arab countries that Israel defeated in June 1967. The U.S. cannot of course compel Israel to return territory; on the other hand, the UN Security Council resolution of November 1967, which Israel (and the Arabs, save Syria) accepted, clearly envisages such return. A possibly more vexing issue is Jerusalem. The Nixon administration thinks Jerusalem should be a unified city, with open access for all nationalities and religious faiths, with Israel and Jordan co-operating. This last is what Israel apparently finds incredible, at least at present.

A grave issue is posed for both the U.S. and Russia by the possibility of either Egypt or Israel achieving nuclear military capability. The Russians are no more likely to hand over nuclear secrets to Nasser than they did to Castro; but Nasser has or has had German scientists as advisers, and the chances are that Israel is already capable of producing nuclear weapons. Nor has Israel consented to sign the Non-Proliferation Treaty (signatories pledge themselves not to acquire nuclear weapons), though Egypt signed promptly. Israel conceivably would use an atomic warhead as a last-resort weapon, if facing defeat and fearing annihilation. Egypt is less likely to resort to nuclear weapons (even if Egypt had any), but if Egypt did, the chances are that the United States would intervene militarily in the Middle East—presumably with the Sixth Fleet—risking simultaneous Soviet intervention and, therefore, Great Power confrontation.

These are hypothetical situations. They are not very likely to arise. For instance, one reason why Egypt probably would not use nuclear weapons against Israel even if Egypt had them is precisely that the Egyptians have a pretty shrewd notion how the United States would react. Putting aside such rather fanciful scenarios, it is reasonable to assert that both the United States and Russia will do everything in their power to save Israel and the Arab countries respectively from final defeat—*if* that is ever the real situation, and *short of mutual confrontation.*

In the Middle East, as in all the other areas of the world that we shall be exploring in this book, the two key factors are a strong nationalist thrust and a strong urge to modernize. Israel is a thoroughly up-to-date state, which is one reason why the Arabs resent it so bitterly. For the Arabs also long to be thoroughly modern but are dismally conscious of being materially backward—and the million and more Palestinian refugees moreover blame their own poverty directly on Israel. The material advancement of the Arabs has to be a key component of any lasting Middle East settlement. Nasser was not only one of the first Arab statesmen to realize this, he was also among the first to do something about it. His reforms in Egypt embrace much more than the building of the Aswan Dam. Nevertheless this is his Great Pyramid, and he knows that he has Soviet, not American, help to thank for it. The Russians similarly are assisting the Syrians to create a great Euphrates dam.

At present, most of the wealth that flows from Arab oil and that should be spent on development runs to waste in Beirut nightclubs or is invested not in the Middle East but in the United States and Europe. Harry Hopkins wrote in *Egypt, the Crucible* (Houghton Mifflin, 1969): "While the underdeveloped world cries out for capital, a vast proportion of Arab oil money drains away to the West, where it can earn most in dividends and capital gains for its owners . . . and into the great golden sump of Beirut drains the flight capital of old pasha and new oil sheikh alike, seeking the comforting anonymity of the numbered bank account and refuge from past, present and projected revolution." And this Arab wealth from oil is enormous. Hopkins says the Saudi Arabian government gets about $1 billion a year in oil revenues, a sum which vast as it is will likely *double* by 1973; and Kuwait's accumulated oil wealth is well over $2,300 millions. Between 1953 and 1963, about $2.5 billion is said to have moved from the Arab world to the West, all of it as oil revenues. This wealth, properly used, could make the desert bloom again.

There is perhaps not much the United States can directly do about the Middle East, except perhaps to try harder to understand the Arabs' terrible pride, as well as rightly admiring Israel for its courage and modern ways. It was after all none other than Ben Gurion who once declared: "Cooperation between the Jews and the Arabs can turn the Middle East into one of the great cultural centers of the world, as it once was. And only they can achieve it. No outside powers, however strong, whether from the East or the West, can do what the Arabs and Jews can do for each other."

*For* each other; not *to* each other.

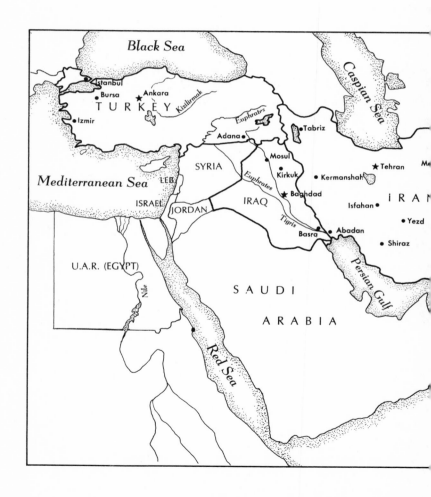

# 4

# CENTRAL ASIA:

# BAGHDAD TO KASHMIR

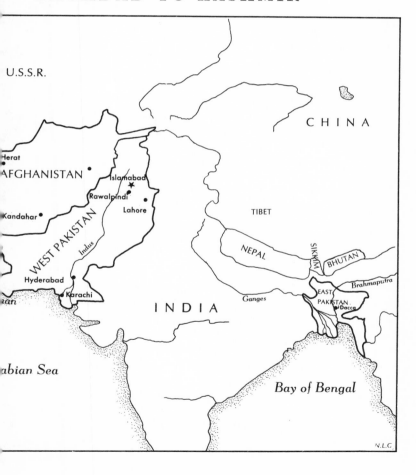

## DEVIL   WORSHIP   IN   IRAQ

IRAQ TOUCHES THE Persian Gulf at Basra, which has oil wells and also rich date farms. But in the northern mountains of Iraq, where the Kurds live, west Asia merges into central Asia. Saladin, the celebrated foe of the Crusaders, was a Kurd. In these hills also live the Yezidis, a strange people who worship the devil; it is strictly forbidden among them to pronounce the sound *Sh*, which begins his name in Arabic; Muslim conquerors slew Yezidis for refusing to eat lettuce, another of their devilish beliefs being that Satan once tried to hide in a lettuce.

Iraq never recovered from Turkish rule, which shrank the population from 35 to 5 million; a solution of Middle East problems would be to transfer Egyptians and Palestinians to those largely unused Iraqi farmlands. With two great rivers and vast oil resources, a couple of decades of political stability could raise Iraqis to Scandinavian levels of material comfort. Nuri Said, the former Iraqi strongman, gave them stability, after a fashion. But, as in South Vietnam, most of the land in Iraq under Nuri Said remained in the hands of a politically powerful and stubborn rich, conservative class—a stopper in the bottle until the bottle exploded in 1958, killing Nuri, killing the king and putting an end to the royal family that had reigned only since 1920. It also put an end to dreams of one day making the southern Mesopotamian Valley from Samara to the sea the cradle of a wealthy and creative civilization. Instead of that happening, Iraq got and continues to endure the rule of Baath Socialist Party fanatics.

Cairo radio often hinted broadly that Nuri Said must be killed. Nuri was, until Nasser, the best politician the Arabs had produced, and he was preaching a Greater Syria, to include Iraq, Syria, Jordan, and Palestine. Fuelled by Iraqi wealth and with no enormous population problem, Greater Syria would have been far stronger a power than overcrowded and oilless Egypt. That, perhaps, is why Nasser decided that Nuri Said had to die.

The ancient capital of Baghdad has some elegant buildings, such as the Palace of Roses where Muslim leaders like to meet from time to time to discuss their common problems. But most of Baghdad is a vast and miserable sea of poverty, and its political life is seamed with espionage and counterespionage. There are few telephones in Baghdad, but it is a safe bet that all of them are tapped. After the murder of Nuri Said, arrested foreigners who had nothing whatsoever to do with politics were massacred on their way from the Baghdad Hotel to prison. They were butchered by mobs in the street. For a while, all power was in the hands of a simple soldier, Kassem, a Hitler with a harelip. More than one attempt was made to assassinate Kassem before one bid finally succeeded. A friend of mine once sought an interview with Kassem and was granted one. The interview was cordial and lasted about three hours. At the end of the time Kassem warmly bade my friend farewell, and presented him with a signed photograph of himself in a silver frame. On returning to his hotel, my friend was accosted by two Iraqi government special police, who arrested him. They said their instructions came directly from Kassem who had ordered that my friend be deported immediately. Their job was to get him to the airport right away, giving him only enough time to pack a bag. He protested that there must have been some mistake, and triumphantly produced the signed portrait of the dictator which Kassem himself had just given to him. The men nodded. "Yes," one of them said, "he told us that was how we would be able to recognize you. You would be carrying his picture."

Kassem was, of course, a madman. But those who have followed him have been equally ruthless and, perhaps, no less mad. The regime that now rules Iraq practices terrorism. The terrorists are a small group of Baath socialists who are as fanatically intolerant as 17th century Puritans. Their intolerance extends to the great majority of Muslim Iraqis, as well as to Jews and Christians. There are about a quarter of a million Christians in Iraq.

In the summer of 1969, the Iraqi government was busy executing "Israeli and CIA spies." The regime declared its firm intention to put on trial for his life a respected former prime minister, Dr. Abdul Rahman Al Zazzaz. The government proudly announced that he would be tried on television. The Soviet Union chose this moment to announce it was going to lend the Iraqi government the sum of $142 million, to develop the giant Rumaile oil field and thus squirt oil in the eye of the Anglo-American Iraq petroleum company.

MODERN   TURKS

TURKEY IS THE only Muslim nation that has relatively normal ties with Israel, though the profile is kept deliberately low. There has been no exchange of ambassadors
between the two countries since 1956; there are only chargés
d'affaires in Ankara and Tel Aviv. Trade talks are held, but
are carefully muffled. The Turks do accept tips on cotton
growing from Israeli technicians, and they may sell Israel a
lot of meat one day; but they don't like to talk about such
things so as not to annoy the Arabs who are an important
market for Turkish products.

There are 30 million Turks, of whom only about 2 million
are in the 20th century. The father of modern Turkey is Kemal
Ataturk, who died in 1938. His name means "father of the
Turks," just as Stalin meant steel. Both Ataturk and Stalin had
essentially the same notion—to catch up with western Europe
and America. Ataturk aimed to bring *all* Turks into the 20th
century. He disestablished the Muslim church, banned polygamy, banned the wearing of fezes by men and of veils by
women. He also put down the fanatical sects of howling and
whirling dervishes.

Ataturk was scrapping the muddy accumulations of centuries. Visit Istanbul today, and you may see the Seraglio, with
its hundreds of rooms and dreadful memories of imprisoned
men and women, kept guarded by deaf-mute eunuchs, who
were trained to strangle condemned prisoners with bow strings
and to toss their bodies in weighted sacks into the Bosphorus.

Nowadays, Istanbul seems to be full of men with gold teeth
eating yogurt, melon, and nuts, and drinking thick black

coffee. They also consume thick sweet pastries in crowded and very expensive restaurants.

Ankara, the new capital, has big buildings of pale stone filled with resolute young military Turks. It also has drab, icy streets, and vast underground shopping areas, for warmth, like Montreal in Canada.

Antioch in Turkey is where Saint Paul lived and where Christians were first called Christians. And, at Antioch, Turkey is only a few miles from Syria and from Aleppo. Also in Turkey is Mount Ararat where Noah's ark came to rest, and where it may be still. Expeditions continue searching for it. Ararat is a lovely cone-shape, like Mount Fuji, in Japan. It is 16,946 feet high. Fuji is 12,397 feet.

Turkey is a country of considerable climatic and historic hardships: freezing winters, frequent earthquakes, frequent invasions and wars, stifling grip of the army because of a constant Russian threat. Yet Turkey, under Ataturk, accepted Soviet aid though Turkey has never been anything but morosely anti-communist. This shows how exaggerated are American fears of communism taking over other countries through aid. Moribund bureaucracy made Turkey the sick man of Europe before World War I; Ataturk changed that image. The Turks who have always been fierce warriors distinguished themselves in the Korean War, under the United Nations command. Their troops' discipline there was as tough as their tactics. Once, a United Nations soldier who was accused of stealing from Korean peasants after a battle for a village was traced to a Turkish unit. A UN officer was prepared to be content with an apology and a promise of better Turkish behavior in the future. But the Turkish commander assured him cheerfully, "It won't happen again; not by this man anyway—we have already caught and hanged him." Ataturk hanged even cabinet ministers with equal promptitude; and in the '60s the Turks publicly hanged a deposed prime minister, Menderes.

Between the years 1961 and 1964, there were four coalition governments in Turkey. Then, in 1965, the Justice Party, based on peasant support, came to power under Prime Minister Suleyman Demirel, himself the son of an Anatolian peasant.

Demirel who is 46 years old and well muscled, is, however, also an economist. In October 1969, he expected to be, and was, re-elected to another four-year term. He claimed to have brought "political stability" which in time would bring "economic expansion." But, said he, "We are just starting" and there would be, he did not doubt, more demonstrations and more strikes by labor unions, because "our people are learning about democracy," and there never were strikes allowed before. The year 1973 will be the "point of economic takeoff." Meanwhile, Turkey gets $100 million a year economic and military aid from the United States, and has 200,000 Turks working in West Germany, who send home $120 million a year. The country still has, nevertheless, a trade gap, a balance of payments deficit, and a fall off in foreign investment, though an international finance consortium is at work trying to improve the latter.

Demirel's opponents are the slightly more leftish Republican Party, Ataturk's heirs, whose leader is Bulent Ecevit. He is 45 years old and draws his support mainly from the towns, though, of course, he too has to appeal also to the peasant majority. To the peasants, Ecevit offers what he calls a "better deal." The peasants are suffering from sagging prices for their exported cotton, tobacco, and olive oil. Sagging prices for exports of primary products are a phenomenon which, as we shall see, also afflicts Pakistan, Ceylon, Malaysia, and other Asian countries that are striving to modernize their economies.

## THE BIG WHEEL IN IRAN

PERSIA WAS THE world's earliest empire under Cyrus the Great (559 to 529 B.C.). One of his successors called himself "Darius, the Great King, King of Kings, King of the Lands and Peoples of all Races, the Land of the Aryans, the Medes, and the Persians." Iran is nearly twice as big as Texas, and it floats on oil and has a population of 20 million. Teheran, the capital, has about 1.75 million people, and 10,000 (rather old) taxis. The city, nestling under the snowcapped Elburz Mountains, features caviar, dance music, and haughty officials who wear gorgeous purple uniforms at the big airport.

Isfahan has the famous blue mosque, and a "palace of forty pillars"—which actually has only 20 pillars, and 20 reflections in a reflecting pool. Isfahan dominates the valley of the Ziandehrud, the richest agricultural area of the country; Isfahan is also the city of Shah Abbas, who started the caravan route to China. The City of Shiraz has roses and orange blossoms and Persepolis' ruins nearby. When winter comes in Persia, the nomad Bakhtiara people move from their high Zagros Mountain fastness, over the Yellow Mountain to the warm desert foothills and the plains of Khuzistan.

In fact, Iran's political secret is that the fabulous country is so diverse and so crisscrossed with different interests that, as the Shah says, "no log can roll" to the extreme right or to the extreme left.

Incidentally, the United States could take a marijuana leaf from the old Persian "Department for the Prevention of Cultivation and Consumption of Opium." The Department in fact controlled the sales of opium as a state monopoly, and made a great deal of money thereby.

In 1936 Reza Shah, a rough soldier who had mounted the Peacock Throne and had founded the Pahlevi dynasty in 1925, after a successful army coup in 1921, copycatted Ataturk. He forebade women to wear veils, as Ataturk had done in Turkey. The present Shah Mohammed took over in 1941, when his father went into exile. Reza Shah died in exile in Johannesburg, in 1944. He had determined to emulate Ataturk's modernization, and to do so he had introduced German technicians into Iran. To avert a Nazi takeover of Iran, the British and Russians occupied the country and seized the oil. One outcome was to speed up modernization—for example, the capacity of the Persian rail and highway system was increased tenfold. Another result was to plant a Tudeh communist party in Iran. Use was made of the communists, or vice versa, by Mohammed Mossadegh, a wealthy landowner who was born in 1881, and who opposed modernization. He never forgave Reza Shah for building railways. Mossadegh was also very xenophobic—he wanted to throw out all the foreigners. Prodded into action by Mossadegh, the politicians nationalized the oil industry, and in 1951 Mossadegh became the prime minister of Iran. He then proceeded to take emergency powers to deal with the grave economic situation created by the closing of the oil wells and the cessation of royalties. The ensuing controversy split the country and the Persian armed forces—and the American CIA, among others, took a hand in the overthrow of Mossadegh. The shah secured an oil agreement with the British companies and sought American military and economic help, but was cautious not to antagonize Iran's great neighbor Russia. In 1946 the shah had actually compelled a withdrawal of Soviet forces, however, from Azerbaijan, which had been proclaimed an "autonomous" republic under Soviet tutelage. The shah then stood firm; the Soviets retreated.

The shah has been married three times. His first wife was Princess Fawzia of Egypt. She produced no male child and the couple were divorced. The shah's second wife was Soraya, daughter of a Bakhtiara tribesman, and a German mother. After seven years there were no children, and another divorce. The shah's third wife Farah, from an old Tabriz family, was born in 1938. The shah was born in 1919. They have children.

No doubt about it, the Shah of Shahs is the big wheel in Iran. The opposition politicians are an ineffectual bunch. From his yellow-green marble palace with a tiled dome, in Teheran, the Shah is constantly supervising the education of the young, the training of the army, the planning of the economy, the conduct of foreign policy, the promotion of sport, and the reconstruction of agriculture. There are about 50,000 villages in Iran; and a few big landowners own up to 40 villages each. The shah, a bit of a Nehru, for years has been in a state of public indignation about corruption, the need for land reform, the need to collect taxes, etc. Unfortunately, many Persian politicians despite the threat of jail and solitary confinement remain corrupt; employers employ thugs against workers who organize; bureaucrats are incompetent; and the big landowners, who include some of the shah's own near relations, oppose reforms. The shah has a palace and a pretty wife, but his job is no sinecure. It's uphill work. But the shah remains confident, handsome, autocratic, and egotistical—a king with up-to-date ideas who at the same time is determined to remain a king.

# UP TO DATE AFGHANS

LANDLOCKED AFGHANISTAN is about 250,000 square miles or rather smaller than Texas. It has no railways but it is entering the 20th century at a fair clip. The population is about 14 million, of whom at least 90 percent are said to be illiterate. However, in September 1964, Afghanistan became a parliamentary democracy with a national assembly of two houses, but with the king appointing the prime minister and the judges of the supreme court. The king is Mohammed Zahir Shah and the prime minister and foreign minister is Nur Ahmad Etemadi.

Only the 680 miles of the Oxus River separate Afghanistan from the Soviet Union. Afghanistan, Marco Polo noted, had the world's best melons—and this is still the case, rightly say Delia and Ferdinand Kuhn in their enthralling book, *Borderlands,* published in 1962 by Alfred Knopf.

This high land is a country of tribesmen, chiefly the six million Pushtuns or Pathans. There are also Uzbeks, Tajiks, Turkmen. Another six million Pushtuns live in Pakistan, and this fact causes friction between the two neighboring countries.

For centuries, political life in Afghanistan was extremely turbulent. Because the royal families practiced polygamy, when a new king ascended the throne he was under strong temptation to hunt out all his brothers, uncles, and cousins and to slaughter them, in case one of them tried to overthrow him. All these royal males tended to feel that they had as much right to the throne as their kinsman who had just ascended it.

The warlike Afghans also threw out British forces on three

separate occasions. The Afghans were probably only prevented from going to war with Pakistan in more recent times by the sobering thought that if the Afghan tribes were mobilized for war, they might pause on their way to the frontier with Pakistan in order to loot the 6,000 foot high capital of Kabul first. To a foreign eye, the high city of Kabul seems to consist mainly of narrow streets and drab, mud buildings. But to tribesmen who live most of the year in black tents looking after their herds of goats and sheep, Kabul looks like a city really worth looting. In the 1920s, King Ammanullah of Afghanistan tried to imitate Ataturk of Turkey and Reza Shah in Persia by modernizing Afghanistan in a hurry. He started to unveil the women and to put them in modern clothes, and he also wanted to build railways and to introduce political democracy. This modernization bid was strongly resisted by Ammanullah's kinsmen and by the tribesmen, and as a result the king was forced to flee the country in 1929. He died abroad, in 1960, but by then he was a forgotten man in Afghanistan. In 1929, the vacant throne was seized by a bandit, a Tajik tribesman, who held it for a few frantic months. Four cousins of Ammanullah, brothers, threw the usurper off the throne and then made one of themselves, Nadir Shah, the king. The other three then took the chief political posts in the country. Nadir Shah was murdered in 1933 and was succeeded by Zahir Shah, the present king of Afghanistan.

A former prime minister, Sirdar Mohammed Daud, was fond of boasting that he "milked two cows." By this he meant that he managed to get aid from both the Soviet Union and the United States all through the years of the Cold War. However, Daud was too shrewd to lean mainly on the two giants. He also sought, as foreign advisors and technicians, Germans, Frenchmen, and other Europeans. But Daud made much the same mistake as the reformers in Turkey did. That is to say, they modernized the country by building roads and textile mills as well as steel mills and hospitals, but education was sadly neglected. The result of that was that neither Afghanistan nor Turkey, until very recent times, produced a middle class or a class of indigenous technicians. Nowadays, that has certainly changed in Kabul, which has modern schools, and the rest of the country seems to be changing too.

Only a few years ago, there were only two hotels in Kabul and neither of them was very good. Unwary travelers were apt to be flattered by being served luscious fruits for breakfast. By the time dysentery had them in its grip, it was too late for them to learn that the fruits they had eaten had been carefully washed in the open drain in the street outside before being served to them. Today, Kabul has modern hotels, including a brand new Intercontinental. Only very recently did the ladies of Kabul quit wearing the *burqa*, a ghastly garment on the lines of a shapeless thick sack, completely covering the head as well as the body, and with only tiny slits for eyeholes. Enveloped in this affair, it was almost impossible to breathe, far less to be able to see. But underneath the *burqa*, the ladies were apt to be wearing the very latest Paris dresses. I once traveled on a plane from Kabul and a fellow passenger was a Kabul lady completely hidden in her *burqa*. However, as soon as the plane took off, she removed the hideous garment, turned to me and demanded, "Do you have a Camel? I am dying for a smoke." Strong man Daud had a ruthless way with political opponents, or indeed with anybody who crossed his path, wittingly or unwittingly. They still tell a story in Kabul about an unfortunate politician, a former cabinet minister, who fell out with Daud and for his pains was thrown into a dungeon, where he remained many years. One day, his jailors removed him from his prison cell, shaved him, bathed him, fed him, clad him in new garments, and led him into the prime minister's office. The poor man was terrified, and his terror was not diminished by Daud coming from behind his desk, shaking him cordially by the hand, pushing him into a large armchair, and tenderly asking after his welfare. Unable to bear the suspense a moment longer, and quite sure that Daud was playing with him as a cat plays with a mouse and was probably about to order his execution, the hapless politician demanded to know, "Why have you brought me here?" Daud replied, "Why, haven't they told you? You are to be our new ambassador to Indonesia."

Now, the politics of Afghanistan are changing. Instead of a strong man, the country has embarked on the hazardous course of parliamentary politics. But some things don't change very fast. In July 1969, Pakistan's President Yahya Khan announced that he was incorporating into West Pakistan the former princely states of Swat, Dir and Chitral. This put Kabul in a rage, because the majority of the inhabitants of the three former princely states are all Pushtuns. The Pakistani press rejected Kabul's protests as "impertinence." However, the Pakistan government rebuffed any notion of holding any kind of referendum to discover what the real wishes of the inhabitants of these states might be, about their own future.

The Pushtun cause has been taken up by India, but almost solely in order to annoy Pakistan. At the time of the celebration of the centenary of Mahatma Gandhi, the Indian government invited to New Delhi, Abdul Khan, a leading Pushtun rebel who had fled Pakistan. Because of his fight for freedom for the Pushtuns, Abdul Khan was known as the "frontier Gandhi." But his visit to New Delhi coincided with religious riots between Hindus and Muslims which made a mockery of the Gandhi centenary celebrations. And Abdul Khan brought no cheer to the Indians. About 1,000 people had been butchered in the religious riots, in Ahmedabad and other towns in Gandhi's home state of Gujerat. Abdul Khan scolded the Indians, saying, "India has forgotten Gandhi." The Indian prime minister, Mrs. Indira Gandhi, said she hoped that Abdul Khan might be able to show her countrymen "the way out of the darkness." (Mrs. Gandhi is the daughter of Pandit Nehru; her late husband was no relation to the Mahatma.) The "frontier Gandhi" was unable to show the way out of the darkness, but he had a warning to deliver to the Indians. He told them, "Nations which are gripped by hatred and communal passions only head towards ruin." This could very well be the epitaph on both Pakistan and India.

Meanwhile, the government of Afghanistan continues to demand the creation of a separate state of Pushtoonistan, to be carved out of West Pakistan, and to include the three former princely states of Swat, Dir, and Chitral. Swat has

614,000 people and the prince Wali Gul Abdul Haq Jehenzeb is the son-in-law of the former Pakistan president Ayub Khan. Dir has 400,000 population and is a very poor state; the Nawab of Dir was installed by Ayub Khan. Chitral is only 12 miles from Russian territory and has 113,000 population. Some of them are fair-skinned descendants of Alexander the Great. They to this day grow grain and fruit, in the Greek tradition. The Pakistan government has now pensioned off the rulers of these small territories.

Apart from his country's strained relations with Pakistan, and its long border with Russia, King Zahir Shah's main problem is still the same as confronted King Ammanullah and which Ammanullah failed to solve. Afghanistan needs to be moved into the 20th century before the 20th century ends; but a pace of change that is still too fast for the tribesmen and the mullahs is maddeningly slow from the point of view of the small but increasing and influential urban educated class. The tribal elders and landowners were so contemptuous of *Democrary-I-Nao* (New Democracy) that they at first ignored the new fangled parliament, but now they are seeking to dominate it and not without success. What they have done is to buy votes wholesale. Meanwhile, modern dams and hydro-electric projects are being built as well as new hotels, but this progress heightens the tension between the traditionalists and the progressives.

High, landlocked, and apparently isolated Afghanistan thus well illustrates a theme that runs through all of Asia from west to east; the theme of modernization and the stresses and strains it engenders. And the innovators look back to Kemal and Reza as well as to the unfortunate Ammanullah, and they look to Nasser as well as to King Zahir and Mrs. Indira Gandhi and Lee Kuan Yew and Park Chung Hee.

## PAKISTAN TODAY AND TOMORROW

IN TERMS OF population the state of Pakistan is one of the largest in the world. It has 125 million people whose numbers are growing rapidly. Only about 20 million of them are able to read and write. In terms of geography, Pakistan is rather an absurdity. It is divided into two wings, West Pakistan and East Pakistan. These two wings are 1,000 miles apart. What separates them is Indian territory. West Pakistan has 55 million people, who are relatively prosperous. They grow cotton, and wool. East Pakistan, which grows jute and tea, has a population of 70 million and is an overcrowded slum. American aid to Pakistan has amounted to some $4 billion and still continues.

Under British rule in India, the Hindu clerical castes adapted to English ways as they had done to their previous conquerors, the Moguls. But the Muslims of India found themselves left out and falling behind. Their discontent was the seed of Pakistan. In East India, the Assamese had cried "better dead than Bengali." In the 1930s, Mohammad Ali Jinnah cried that Islam was in danger, and that "the death of 10 million Muslims is not too great a price to pay for Pakistan." Jinnah was a distinguished Muslim barrister of Bombay, belonging to the Khoja trading caste, and an ex-disciple of G. K. Gokhle, a modern Congress Party leader who humbly preached the doctrine of India achieving its salvation through social service. Jinnah was anything but humble. When in the 1940s the Congress Party, dominated by Hindus, ignored his claim that the one fourth of the population of British India who were Muslims should have one third of the seats in a future independent parliament, Jinnah turned to complete separation.

In the ensuing tumult between Muslims and Hindus, the British viceroy Lord Wavell announced that the British would begin to withdraw politically from India area by area, and that this political withdrawal would be paralleled by withdrawal of military control. The British prime minister Clement Attlee went further. He announced that in any event Britain would withdraw from India by June 1948. The date of British withdrawal was in fact in 1947. When once a decision has been made to get out of a country, the process of withdrawal probably had better be swift.

One important ingredient of the ensuing uproar, and one that was destined to have long-term consequences, was that the Hindu Maharaja of Kashmir was repudiated by the Muslims of Poonch, one of the six components of his polygot princely state. Kashmir consists of the valley of Kashmir, mainly Muslim; Jammu, mainly Hindu; Poonch, Muslim; Gilgit and Baltistan, Muslim; and Ladakh, Buddhist. The warrior caste of Poonch proclaimed an *Azad Kashmir*—free Kashmir government. They were enthusiastically assisted by frontier Pushtuns who advanced within a few miles of Srinagar, the capital of Kashmir. The Maharaja appealed for help to the new Indian government in New Delhi, and Indian planes landed at Srinagar just in time to save the city from the fierce Pushtun tribesmen. Subsequently, the Maharaja was deposed, in June 1949, and a Muslim leader friendly to Nehru became the first prime minister of Kashmir: Sheikh Abdullah. But Abdullah vanished into prison in August 1953, when his appeal for an independent Kashmir became an embarrassment to New Delhi. The Indians, who back the idea of an independent Pushtoonistan state to be carved out of Pakistan, are by no means ready to permit an independent Kashmir.

Jinnah had ordered the Pakistan army into Kashmir in the spring of 1948, to keep Poonch out of Indian hands. A cease-fire on January 1, 1949 left Pakistan in possession of northern Kashmir, a barren hill region stretching towards the Karakorum Mountains, but it is an area that puts Pakistan in a highly strategic situation vis-à-vis China, and to some extent vis-à-vis Russia. This Pakistan area includes Baltistan and Gilgit, but India got Ladakh. China began almost at once to build a road across Aksai Chan, on the Ladakh side. Indo-China relations were disrupted by clashes of border patrols, and also when the Dalai Lama of Tibet received cordial welcome and sanctuary in India, when he fled from Lhasa, the capital of Tibet, in March 1959, after the Chinese took Tibet over. The next big flare up between India and China was the 1962 border war—with Pakistan looking on, but taking no advantage of India's dilemma, because Ayub Khan had publicly emphasized the need for India and Pakistan to combine against a communist threat. Ayub's overture, which could have led to a settlement of the Kashmir problem, was, however, rejected by Nehru.

Perhaps the most crushing consequence of the Kashmir conflict between India and Pakistan was that about half the budget of Pakistan went to defense, instead of to building up the human and natural resources of the infant state of Pakistan.

In the mass migrations that marked partition of British India, Pakistan traded some four million bankers, merchants, doctors, lawyers and teachers for five million poor peasants and poor shopkeepers who quit India and rushed into Pakistan. A Pakistani bureaucrat told me, "in this ministry of mine, there was then not a single desk, not a stool, not a sheet of paper; of course there were no telephones, no typewriters, indeed, not even a pen." Yet somehow refugees were fed, and abandoned crops harvested, banks and mills were kept going. Pakistan retained all British officials who were willing to stay. Three of the four West Pakistan provinces had British governors. West Pakistan got over its difficulties in part by selling jute for foreign exchange which was spent on industrialization. But the jute grew in East Pakistan, and the Bengalis there, of whom about a quarter are Hindus, were exploited harshly but did not share in the development. Also, as in India itself, language problems added pepper to the pot. The Bengalis resented the Punjabis' Urdu. When the prime minister Nazimuddin announced in February 1952, in Dacca, the capital of East Pakistan, that Urdu and Bengali would be the official languages of the whole country, he touched off major riots—

not just in Dacca, against Urdu, but also in Karachi, the capital of West Pakistan, against Bengali being admitted as an official language. Subsequently, all Pakistani civil servants had to pass an examination in whichever of the two languages was not their home tongue.

Jinnah died in September 1948, only eight months after Mahatma Gandhi was assassinated in India. But Pakistan did not achieve a constitution until February 1956. There was no equivalent of the Congress Party of India in Pakistan. Jinnah had been called Quaid-i-Azam, the Great Leader, thus setting a precedent for autocracy in Pakistan. Jinnah was a very autocratic man. Firoz Khan Noon got no appointment in Pakistan while Jinnah lived, because he had once questioned one of the Great Leader's commands. However, after Jinnah's death, parliamentary democracy was tried in Pakistan for about ten years. But it failed. The large landowners dominated the legislature and opposed land reforms. The religious zealots sought a "pure" Islamic state, much the same way as in Israel religious zealots sought an exclusively and strict Jewish state. The Hindus had looked down upon the Muslims and other non-Hindus as unclean—*Mlecches*. Now, the Muslims dismissed all non-Muslims with a disdainful shrug as second-class citizens— *Dhimais*. Moreover, ultra-zealots sought to stamp out Islamic sects which were not deemed orthodox enough, like the Ahmadiyya community. Finally, there was the cleavage between West Pakistan dominated by Punjabis, and East Pakistan (East Bengal) which is entirely surrounded by Indian territory and is also very poor. Above all, the Pakistani politicians turned out to be greedy for money and power and ready to employ blackmail, perjury, and murder to achieve their ends and to put down their rivals. Jinnah's successor Liaqat Ali was assassinated in October 1951, and Dr. Khan Sahib, the Pushtun political leader, was assassinated in 1958. A few months later, in September 1958, the political opposition in Bengal had the speaker of the legislature certified insane. His place was taken by the deputy speaker who was a member of the opposition, but he was killed when a lump of wood was thrown at him in parliament. Power in Pakistan then fell into the hands of two Sandhurst-educated military men, both of them in fact Pushtun. The first was General Iskander Mirza. He was followed into power after only a few months by General Ayub Khan. Ayub Khan imprisoned the politicians, and then dismissed 1,000 civil servants, putting soldiers at their desks in order to get things done, like building houses for homeless refugees and bringing down prices by forcibly dishoarding goods. Ayub took over near the end of 1958, and a year later he introduced his "basic democracy." Village folk were directly elected as members of councils that were called basic democrats. These councils then elected the next upper tier. But these sat with officials who were appointed, and the succeeding tiers were more and more weighted with officials. The basic democrats acted as an electoral college and they elected Ayub Khan president, giving him vast powers. The president appointed all the chief officers of state. He could be turned out of power only by a two-thirds majority of the otherwise feeble national assembly. Or, of course, he could be turned out by revolution. Ayub freely admitted that his own authority was "revolution; I have no sanction in law or constitution," he said. Nevertheless, Ayub in May 1960 accepted as the chief justice of the Pakistan supreme court a Roman Catholic Eurasian, Mr. Justice Cornelius, who had been quite frank in his opinions, many of which were critical of the government. Similarly, in May 1962, Ayub appointed as his minister of law a judge who had been even more outspoken against the military power than Mr. Justice Cornelius.

Ayub Khan was brutally candid in explaining why Pakistan's parliamentary system had failed. "It requires a long period of probation, democracy," he said. "For instance, the British took 600 years of trial and tribulation to reach this stage. So don't let us kid ourselves and cling to clichés and assume that we are ready to work such a refined system, knowing the failure of earlier attempts."

In mid-1969, six months after Ayub Khan had fallen from power, he was living comfortably enough in Lahore, but he had nevertheless become an unperson. His name was virtually banned from mention in the Pakistan newspapers. His successor as president of Pakistan was another military man, Yahya Khan. One of Yahya Khan's first acts was to dispatch his chief rival Air Marshal Nur Khan to Peking. Yahya explained, "We gratefully remember China's wholehearted support during the dark days of September 1965, when we were assailed by a treacherous aggressor." Yahya was referring to the brief war between India and Pakistan that broke out in the summer of that year and ended in more or less of a draw. Yahya also conferred busily with Zulfigar Ali Bhutto, and with Sheikh Mujibur Rahman, the men who had done most to bring Ayub Khan down. There was however no question of attempting to restore parliamentary democracy. One Pakistan newspaper said quite frankly, "Looking at the heat generated over constitutional issues, the basis of representation in the federal assembly, and the question of regional autonomy, it would be futile to hope that the political parties can ever reach an agreement."

Yahya Khan's immediate aims are to get arms from the United States, if possible, and to prevent the breakup of Pakistan, if necessary by using force. It seemed at the start of his regime that the country would be under martial law at least until March of 1970, and probably for a good deal longer. The long suppressed politicians of the country naturally detested this. They were not allowed to hold public meetings or to stage processions. Yahya Khan chose "advisors" from among them, but his word remained law. He appealed directly to the nation for support, made gestures at cracking down on the fifty big families who controlled the industries of the country, and of course kept a vigilant eye on India. Yahya Khan tried very hard to get President Nixon to agree to furnish him with tanks and other military equipment. He saw Mr. Nixon in Pakistan in August 1969, and further meetings were probable.

West Pakistan was being run by Air Marshal Nur Khan, the head of the air force. East Pakistan was being governed by a Vice Admiral who was the commander of the Pakistan navy. East Pakistan presented considerable problems to the new government. The states' rights leader there was Sheikh

Mujibur Rahman, the leader of the Awami league. The national Awami Party was pro-Peking and was headed by Maulana Abdul Hamid Bhashani. Severe contention continued between West Pakistan and East Pakistan, so that it seemed that in the absence of strong military rule they might be at each other's throat, and also there might be feuding between the Sindis and Pushtuns as well as among the Baluchis and Punjabis.

Nur Khan, who had been sent by Yahya to Peking, returned saying that China was "a stabilizing factor for peace in Asia." This was five days after Moscow had accused Mao Tse-tung of planning the conquest of all countries west of China as far as the Turkish border. A new strategic highway that had been built jointly by Pakistani and Chinese engineers was opened, linking Gilgit in Pakistan with Kashgar, the capital of West Sinkiang. Kashgar is the depot of the ancient Silk Road to Samarkand. It looked as if the Silk Road had become an Iron Road, with modern armor. At the same time as this was going on, and as Yahya Khan was trying so hard to get President Nixon to furnish him with American military equipment, the new Pakistan government refused to continue the lease of the United States monitoring station at Badabar, near Peshawar, that had expired on July 17, 1969. The monitoring station had been used to monitor the doings of the Chinese, who now appeared to be the warm allies of Pakistan. Very few western observers acquainted with Pakistan's history were inclined seriously to believe that Pakistan was ever likely to become a satellite of either China or Russia. Nevertheless, Pakistan's tactical friendship with Peking once again underlined the futility of American policies that had striven over many years to make of countries like Pakistan "staunch allies" who would "stand up and be counted" on America's side against "international communism."

## AMERICA AND CENTRAL ASIA

ALL OF THESE five countries, Iraq, Turkey, Iran, Afghanistan, and Pakistan, are essentially Muslim nations. It is not possible therefore to think of them as completely divorced from the great and agonizing problem of the Middle East. Thus, Iraq is fanatically anti-Israel and sometimes seems to be fanatically anti-American as well, mainly because the Iraqi political leaders believe or profess to believe that the Central Intelligence Agency is very active in Iraq, penetrating Iraqi security in order to pass on vital information to Jerusalem and Tel Aviv. And even the sensible Turks, though they quietly do business with Israel, warned the United States not to use its Adana air base in Turkey for any sort of American action in the Middle East, during the 1969 Lebanon crisis.

American policy for the most part respects those central Asian Muslim susceptibilities, but unfortunately does not always behave as properly in regard to other matters, and especially when what is affected is the great American obsession with "communism." Thus, in Turkey, when the government of the great Turkish soldier and statesman, Ismet Inonu, seemed in 1965 to be leaning just a trifle toward the Soviet Union (as a counter to United States policy over Cyprus, which the Turks felt to be insufficiently sympathetic to their side of the case) the United States ambassador made ostentatious calls on the Turkish political parties which were in opposition to the Inonu administration. One of those opposition parties was the Justice Party, that was soon to be led by Suleyman Demirel, who became and remains the Turkish prime minister, the post that Inonu formerly held.

The Shah of Iran is a good if sometimes critical friend of
the United States who however has always been careful not
to be put into the category of "staunch ally." In the reckoning
of some American policy makers, the shah ought to be glad
to stand up and be counted, for did not the Central Intelligence Agency intervene in Iran's internal affairs at a critical
juncture, and work to overthrow the shah's hostile prime
minister, Mohammed Mosadegh? The CIA did, but the shah
was not especially grateful, as he sees his duty as resisting
the attempts of foreign powers to control the destiny of Iran.
The Americans and British tried it during the Second World
War, and the Russians tried to break off a bit of the country
afterwards, as an "autonomous" communist state of Azerbaijan.
The shah has proved well able to fight his own battles, and in
consequence, has wrung respect for his country's independence
from both the United States and the Soviet Union. Both
Turkey and Iran stand on their own feet and are under no
gun. The Afghans seem equally self-possessed. At one time the
geographical proximity of Afghanistan to Russia, with only the
Oxus River for boundary, led American policy makers to toy
with a "domino" theory—should Afghanistan go "communist,"
then Pakistan might succumb also, and if Pakistan fell, India,
etc. This led to a certain rivalry between the Soviet Union
and the United States for the friendship of the Afghans, who,
as we saw, took astute advantage of this in Mohammed Daud's
time to "milk two cows." However, if United States–Russian
rivalry over aid to Afghanistan is still in evidence it has
nowadays almost become a friendly rivalry—even as long as
15 years ago the United States Information Agency in Kabul
was kindly giving tips on request to the Soviet Information
Service as to how to produce give-away literature that would
be tolerably readable despite being obviously propagandist.
The fact of course is that in the unlikely event of the Soviet
Union wishing to extend its rule over Afghanistan, there is
precious little that the United States could do about it, though
the warlike Afghans (who thrice beat the British) might do
plenty. And, as far as any internal "communist" threat is
concerned (of which there has never been the least sign),

Afghanistan's best answer to it must simply lie in good government, not in reliance on United States' or any other foreign arms.

Afghanistan's quarrel with Pakistan over the Pushtuns is no business of any other country besides these two—though India, probably unwisely, has as we saw seen fit to put an oar in, in an oblique but unmistakable fashion. Does the quarrel between Pakistan and India over Kashmir concern the United States, other than as a member of the United Nations, which has had the problem continuously before it since Kashmir became a problem in 1947? Judging by questions that are often asked, some Americans appear to think that the United States should be able to find a formula for Kashmir that would make that problem vanish, and so effect a triumphant reconciliation between Pakistan and India. This is most unlikely. All attempts by the United Nations to resolve the issue have failed. An obvious solution would be to make Kashmir independent of both India and Pakistan, just as Taiwan ought to "belong" to neither the communists nor the Kuomintang Chinese, but to the Taiwanese themselves. However, both Pakistan and India have rejected this solution as stubbornly as the two sets of Chinese have rejected the notion of an autonomous Taiwan. The United States might conceivably have played the part of mediator had it not chosen instead to supply arms to Pakistan as part of a defensive "northern tier" against communism; which arms the Pakistanis of course used not against a communist country—for none had either attacked Pakistan nor had any quarrel with her— but against India. In any case, the role of mediator in the perennial Indo-Pakistan dispute over Kashmir was then preempted by the Soviet Union in the person of prime minister Kosygin, who persuaded the two belligerents to sign a declaration of future peaceful intent, at Tashkent in 1966. This, however, does not mean that Russia will succeed in solving the Kashmir problem or in reconciling Pakistan and India. If the Soviet Union does succeed in doing so, it will fully deserve all the kudos that this miracle earns for it.

What the United States can and should do is to continue

and in all practical ways to improve on its own endeavors and those of the two governments and of the World Bank and other international agencies, including lending consortia, to help harness the great river system that India and Pakistan jointly own, in the service of millions of peasants of both nations whose standard of living can be greatly raised thereby. This is a task not for a year or even a decade but for more than one generation. It is in the great tradition of the good things that the west has occasionally succeeded in doing in middle Asia, to offset the bad. The British created great dams and irrigation systems in Egypt and in British India. American and Russian dam builders and engineers have followed in the British footsteps. The Aswan Dam is a noble achievement which might have owed more to American than to Russian effort, if American foreign policy at the time (1956) had been different. The Indo-Pakistan dam and irrigation system can be a permanent monument to a more enlightened American policy; and, when political conditions are somewhat less unpropitious, a similar Tigris-Euphrates scheme may contribute materially to a genuine and lasting solution of the entire Middle East tangle.

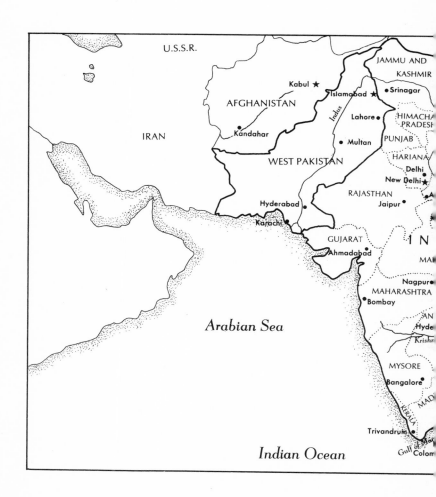

# 5

# SOUTH ASIA:

# EVEREST TO IRRAWADDY

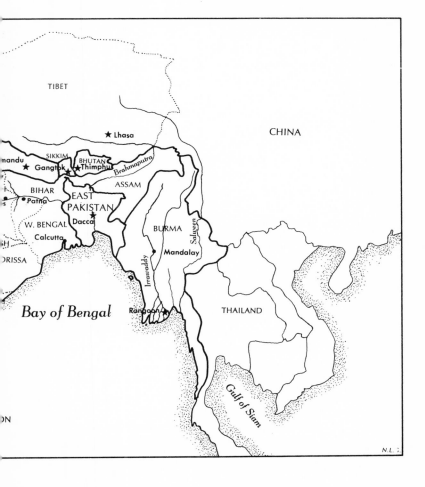

## NEPALESE AND OTHERS

AND NOW WE come to the northern borders of India, the second most populous country on earth. The only country with more people is, of course, China. And on those northern borders, high up in the world's highest mountains, the 570 million Indians and the 700 million—or it may be 800 million—Chinese test each other's strength.

Ladakh, which we have already mentioned, is also known as Little Tibet. Ladakh is a remote Buddhist principality that was conquered between 1834 and 1840 by Gulab Singh, who later became the Maharaja of Kashmir. The Chinese and the Indians fought each other in Ladakh in 1962, as well as fighting 1,300 miles farther east, in the northeastern frontier agency territory (NEFAT).

The land of Nepal was governed by the Rana family of hereditary prime ministers for over a century. The kings of Nepal were sacred but powerless figures, like the Japanese emperors. The Ranas were prime ministers and commanders in chief. But then, in 1949, in Calcutta, India, a member of the Nepalese royal family started a Nepal Democratic Congress Party. Young Nepalese educated in Indian universities flocked to join the new political party. They were secretly supported by Nepal's King Tribhuvane. In November 1950, King Tribhuvane took refuge from the Ranas in the Indian Embassy in Kathmandu, the capital of Nepal. He was then flown to Delhi in an Indian military plane. Indian pressure—and the threat of an internal uprising—forced the Ranas to agree to a coalition government to include the Ranas and the Nepal Congress Party. Now to the political forefront there came the Koirala brothers, one of whom became prime minister. But

King Tribhuvane's son and successor, Mahendra, who ascended the throne of Nepal in 1955, dismissed the Koiralas and dissolved the parliament in 1961. Here we see a repetition of what is by now a familiar story of Asia. Mahendra, young and intelligent, was impatient with parliament and political parties. He preferred to rule his country as an autocrat. And he exiled the Nepal Congress Party back to Calcutta.

Nepal has taken a leaf from the book of the former prime minister of Afghanistan, Mohammed Daud. Nepal also milks more than one cow. In Nepal, it's four cows. Nepal takes aid from India and from China and also from Russia and the United States. The Indians and the Chinese are both busily building roads for Nepal, as well as glaring at one another across its borders.

The Nepalese thought very ill of China's claim to Mt. Everest. However, the Chinese withdrew the claim in 1961, in a formal treaty.

Nepal is 54,000 square miles in size, about the same size as Florida. Its population is 10.5 million. Defense costs Nepal $5 million a year, or about a quarter of the budget. That seems steep. But it has to be remembered that the expenses of the royal household of King Mahendra come to more—$6 million.

Two other Himalayan principalities are Sikkim and Bhutan. Both rely on India for their defense and also for their foreign policy.

After the flight of the Dalai Lama from Lhasa, the capital of Tibet, Bhutan closed its borders with Tibet. It leaned wholly on India for trade and for aid. Stories of religious persecution in Tibet disturbed Bhutan, which is a Buddhist country. There were amiable Chinese suggestions for "peacefully" settling "border disputes between our two countries." This was to be done without reference to India at all, the Chinese explained. The Chinese suggestions were largely ignored by Bhutan. Instead, Indian money went to road building, the building of schools, agricultural programs, public health, and in creating a thin telephone network between Bhutan's few towns. The Bhutanese live off the exports from their fertile valleys; but not placidly.

In April 1964, Jigme Dorji, the brother of Queen Kesang Dorji, was assassinated. Members of his family, but not the Queen herself, fled to Khatmandu in Nepal. There, they accused "imperialist India" of complicity in the assassination. In July 1965, there was an attempt to assassinate young King Jigne Dorji Wangchuk. His attackers were captured, then pardoned, and exiled to a remote village. The identity of the planners of the assassination was known, but it remained a state secret.

Mrs. Indira Gandhi, the prime minister of India, and Mr. Chester Bowles, the former American ambassador to Delhi, both made it a point to visit Thimpu, the capital of Bhutan. In October 1968, Bhutan sent observers to the United Nations, evidently intending to apply for membership. Bhutan is 18,000 square miles in size, and its 800,000 people are mainly Tibetan in origin, but with many Nepalese immigrants.

The Tibetan Chumbi Valley, between Bhutan and Sikkim, is "a dagger thrust at the heart of India." A Chinese thrust here could cut off all northeastern India (15 million people) from the rest of the country. The Chinese have heavily fortified Chumbi Valley. India therefore has 25,000 troops in Sikkim, guarding the strategic passes that the Chinese might try to use. There were artillery duels between India and China here in the fall of 1967. Since then, both sides have confined themselves to using loudspeakers to blast propaganda at each other, a form of cold war that has also been observed in Azerbaijan, between Russia and Iran, and likewise between mainland China and Quemoy.

Sikkim like Bhutan closed its border with Tibet, "with very great disadvantage to us," said the Chogyal (the maharaja) frankly, at the time. "We do not want a quarrel with the north."

In terms of income per head, Sikkim is twice as rich as India. A local distillery makes superb liqueurs. The capital of Sikkim is Ganetok. Sikkim is about 2,745 square miles in area and its population is about 185,000. Most of the people are Nepalese, but the ruling family of Sikkim is Tibetan. And the ruler's wife is an American, Hope Cooke.

# INDIRA'S INDIA

THE HIGH HIMALAYAS are the legendary home of the Hindu pantheon of gods. And this is not surprising. The snow-fed Mother Ganges rises in the Himalayas and fertilizes 1,000 miles of plain.

India is over 1.25 million square miles in size, almost half the size of the continental United States. There are about 570 million Indians, of whom almost 500 million are Hindus, 50 million are Muslims, 12 million Christians, 9 million Sikhs and 4 million are Buddhists. One human being in every seven is an Indian (one in four is Chinese).

India has 63 languages, just one fewer than the Soviet Union. Russia has 18 languages each of which is spoken by over a half million people, India has 25 such languages. However, only 14 of India's languages are recognized by the central government. One language, Tamil, has a continuous literary tradition which goes back over 2,000 years. Kannadu and Telugu are only a few centuries less venerable. There is unfortunately no space here to get into the fascinating linguistic thickets of the complex interplay of Persian, Arabic, Turkish, Urdu, Hindustani, and Hindi. Many non-Hindi speaking Indians fiercely reject Hindi and even prefer English. For instance, a Madras politician always insisted on speaking to the late Mr. Nehru through an interpreter, professing to know insufficient English and professing to know no Hindi at all. The other great feature of India is caste. Manu the great Hindu law giver defined four castes: Brahmins (priests), Kshattriyas (warriors), Vaishyas (traders and farmers); Sudras (servants and menials). According to Manu, everyone else was a *Mleccha* (foreigner or untouchable). But in the course of many centuries the four castes have become something like 2,380 full castes and also many subcastes. The Chitruapur Saraswat Brahmins of Bombay issue their own caste census and directory. When Scheduled Castes (untouchables) and tribes were accorded definite quotas in government jobs and in schools under the Indian constitution, many other castes clamored to be classified "backward." This was so they could obtain similar privileges. But a commission of inquiry in India found that 2,399 communities, representing over 120 million people, could be so classified. For this reason the project was dropped. The castes are learning to act as units, which means that numbers count. This has caused a great depression among the south Brahmins, who are only about 3 percent of the population, and therefore are a discriminated against minority.

Another regrettably outstanding feature of Indian life is illiteracy. Despite its 570 million population, all the newspapers of India together have a total circulation of under three million.

India is divided by jungles, deserts, mountains, and great rivers as well as by religions, languages, and castes. Bengal, isolated in its net of rivers, is perhaps conspicuously different from the rest of the country. We shall see later how Bengal's "difference" has led to a serious political situation.

We have noted how Islam divided India, shearing off the new state of Pakistan. Yet India is linked, through Islam, with those Turks, Persians, and Afghans we have already met. Most of the top officials of the Moguls who ruled most of India for 500 years, from about 1250 to 1750, were Turks, Persians, and Afghans. These men ran a vast bureaucracy that employed many hundreds of Hindu clerks, who learned to shuffle paper, copying and recopying vast registers for the purposes of collecting taxes and administering laws. The typical bureaucrat was the district factotum, or Poo Bah. The British took over this bureaucratic paper maze, and it was inherited in turn by independent India even after English common law had replaced Islamic law.

The battles of Plassey (1757) and Buxar (1764) made

the East India Company the heir of the Mogul empire. But the last Mogul emperor, Bahader Shah, was not deposed until 1858, after the great Indian Mutiny. Persian was the *language* of the Indian law courts until the 1830's.

The British who ruled India divided into "orientalists" versus "anglicists." The orientalists wanted as little interference as possible with native customs whereas the anglicists were reformers who wished to remold Indian in England's image. One of those English rulers, a cousin of the Duke of Wellington, was an anglicist. When he discovered that in the district of India which he ruled it was the custom, after a Hindu ruler had died, that all his wives should be cast alive upon his burning funeral pyre, he sent for a top Hindu. "I do not want to interfere with your customs here," he is reported to have said, "and I am sure that you respect mine. So I shall tell you what we shall do. You may have your suttee (burning of widows). Alongside the funeral pyre I shall erect my gallows. When the widows have been burned, I shall hang those who burn them." This is said to have led to a rapid abandonment of the practice of suttee in that particular district.

The constitution that India adopted after independence in 1947 is the longest in the world. It has hundreds of articles. The supreme court of India holds itself to be "the automatic interpreter and guardian of the constitution," having "the duty to see that its provisions are faithfully observed." Dr. P. Subbarayan told the Indian constituent assembly in 1949: "I think we have provided in the constitution, in the powers vested in the supreme court and high courts . . . for any citizen to have his rights established as against the government of the day."

Certainly, after independence many millions of Indians, despite illiteracy, were successfully registered as voters. And they mostly marked their ballot papers without spoiling them —even when confronted by 14 national and 51 regional political parties who put up 17,000 candidates for 489 seats in the Lok Sabha (India's house of representatives) and for 3,373 state legislature seats, not counting great numbers of independent candidates. The Indian Congress Party on that occasion won 45 percent of the popular vote and thus secured 362 of 489 Lok Sabha seats. The total cost of the 1947 election was about $20 million. By 1967, there were 146 million voters in India, and in that year the Indian Congress Party got 68 million votes.

Mahatma Gandhi, the father and founder of the new nation, was assassinated in New Delhi while at his prayers on January 20, 1948. His assassin was a Hindu who thought that Gandhi had been too kind to Muslims. His assassination did not prevent the new constitution from coming into effect. The 560 princely states of India were wound up with remarkable expedition by Sardar Patel, the minister of interior. A few such states, like Mysore, had had enlightened rulers. But others were "medieval monstrosities where the ruler looked on every female subject as an adjunct to his harem and every male as a potential candidate for his dungeons."

In his book on India, *An Area of Darkness*, B. S. Nipaul says Gandhi failed to change India. "It is as if in England Florence Nightingale had become a saint, honored by statutes everywhere, her name on every lip; and the hospitals had remained as she had described them." Gandhi preached that by reviving village crafts it would be possible to revive village life in an idyllic form, so that India would eventually become a federation of tiny, idealistic village republics, and the state would wither away. Jayaprakash Narayan, perhaps Gandhi's truest follower, essentially repeated this faith in 1959, and also forecast: "As we proceed from the inner to outer circle of communal life and organization, there is less and less to do . . . so that when we reach the circle of the national community it has only a few matters to attend to, such as defense, foreign policy, currency." But in fact the villages of India have not gone that way at all. Here is a recent description by a Chicago professor of a modern Indian village.

Professor Marriott's Indian village is about 100 miles from Delhi and 6 miles from any road. In 1951, there was a shortage of water—it was brought up from wells in leather buckets— and also, the 850 villagers complained that they never really had enough to eat; mainly bread, grain and carrots and a little buttermilk. If you went to the village in the hot weather in the month of May, you would find the leaves cut off the trees, and every blade of grass dug up by the roots and fed to the animals, because fodder was so scarce. It was a traditional village, with 24 different castes. There were very few literate people. Perhaps 20 people in the village had gone as far as the fourth grade, and there were no literate women at all. At Holi, a spring festival, there was a sort of intense saturnalia which lasted about five days, during which the women beat the men, the low castes threw mud on the high castes and, says Professor Marriott, "everybody got high on pot."

Professor Marriott observes, "It was a nice kind of well-balanced social system, and it kind of delighted me as an anthropologist. Others might have said there was a great deal of room for improvement." In 1968 the Professor went back and found that a lot of changes had occurred. Plots had been consolidated and tube wells put in. Production had gone up, improved seeds and fertilizers were being used, and the farmers were getting at least twice as much for their produce as they had been getting. They had begun growing sugar cane, cotton, and lots of vegetables. With more money, the first thing people did was to build five new temples in the village. They were eating three times a day instead of twice, and they were eating a rich diet, with less ghee and more vegetables and grain. There had been a lot of unemployment 16 years before, and now the laborers were all employed and were eating better as a result. As one crop came out of the ground, they started sowing a new one. A lot of people were talking about tractors. Some were talking about getting machines to do fancy things like making ice cream. People were wearing wool sweaters in the winter, whereas before it was all cotton clothing. There were new brick and stone houses in the village that had not been there before. Some of them were very beautiful houses, and they were being lived in; Professor Marriott said that previously such houses were just a false front, and people lived in a mud house, behind. Mud houses, says Professor Marriott, are much better. "They are cooler in the summer and warmer in the winter than brick houses are. But the villagers have parted company with these. They think brick houses are the thing." The village has also become very politically minded. Everybody now votes and an election is a great event. The main public debate is not whether taxes should be collected, but whether the money that is collected should be spent for a school, for improved roads or for lighting the streets. These are nowadays the hot issues. About 50 percent of the villagers are now being educated. This is a great improvement from the previous figure of 5 percent. Only a few are going to high school. These go about six miles, to various high schools. There are about 7 or 8 percent in intercollege, using the village as a dormitory, and coming back every night. There is one lad who commutes 14 miles a day to a university. Every land owning family in the village now has one or two sons in high school. This has become the standard pattern. One son, the eldest, always has to stay on the land because it is so productive. Here, said the professor, "prosperity is working against education." There is a perfect willingness on the part of the boys to come back and spend time in the village and use their education on the land. Previously, people worried about the village a lot, they were hungry in it and they left it. Now they think hard before leaving. There are 9 school teachers in the village, all local boys, previously there were none.

Professor Marriott concludes: "People used to come to me and ask me to get things for them. They used to say, 'You are our mother and our father, you must help us.' Now they're telling me what to do. They say, 'Would you like to get electricity for your house? Well, come along, I know the man who can get it for you.' And they do. Here's a man selling bus tickets in the village, he has more power than any government official because he has given bus tickets to people at the right times. I was told, 'You won't get an electric connection for three weeks.' But that was a government official who told me this. In fact, the bus ticket man got it for me in 6 hours. The villagers know how to get things they want. There are several fixers in the village and they are prosperous. They have learned about technology."

Things, then, haven't gone quite the way that Gandhi and Jayaprakash Narayan and Vinoba Bhave expected. But things may not be as bad as B. S. Nipaul and other critics claim.

In national politics, the Congress Party is still by and large the main political force. The Congress Party's big annual sessions are called *tamashas*, meaning circuses. They really are held in huge tents, but—if one ignores the *dhotis* and *saris*—the Congress Party tent sessions tend to resemble closely an American political convention. All the real work is being done behind the scenes—though not of course in "smoke-filled rooms." The open forum is open to glad-handing and endless speechifying. Indian politics, as in the United States, revolve largely around the pork barrel. Hence, desperate attempts to wrest control from the Congress Party, which still controls the barrel. Employees of the central government have grown in number from 49 thousand in 1939 to about a million today. At the states' level, the castes are becoming like America's Jewish, Polish, and Irish minorities. The ward boss has to look after his supporters by finding them jobs that suit their genius.

In 1955 the Congress Party adopted a "socialistic pattern of society" as its program. But the second five-year plan explained that the "socialistic pattern of society is not to be regarded as some fixed or rigid pattern. It is not rooted in any doctrine or dogma." However, the "public sector" was to expand rapidly and was to "play the dominant role in shaping the entire pattern of investments in the economy, whether it makes the investment directly or whether these are to be made by the private sector." In actuality, what has occurred *is* pretty rigid government control, with regulations bearing down heavily on so many business transactions that for fully a decade the Congress Party regime has been nicknamed "Permit Raj."

Nehru, Gandhi's favorite disciple and India's first prime minister, died in May 1964. His successor, Lal Bahadur Shastri, died in January 1966, and the job of running India went to Indira Gandhi, Nehru's daughter. Indira got the job as a presumed fill-in, but she soon proved that she was indeed the daughter of Nehru (and the granddaughter of the aristocratic and redoubtable Motilal Nehru.) When she was only a school girl, her father, imprisoned by the British, had written her long political letters, many of them enthusiastically extolling Soviet Russia and the Bolshevik revolution. Indira was in the thick of politics and political infighting from her school days. Since, she has travelled widely in Europe and America, and been to Burma, Thailand, China, Indonesia, Japan, and Soviet Russia. Ten years before she became prime minister, Indira was president of the Congress Party for a year, in 1959, and was succeeded by Sanjiva Reddy, the party boss of the state of Andhra. Indira got the Congress Party president's job not just because she was Nehru's daughter, but because she was a leading member of a "ginger group" which was pushing socialism against the party managers. Today, Indira is still surrounded by "young Turks." Reddy had got the Congress Party president's job; in turn, because of strong caste support in the state of Andhra, he was undisputed boss of the Reddys. But he made the error of handing over the Andhra prime ministership to a stooge who, Reddy was sure, would obediently hand it back. But the puppet refused to do that, and actually won re-election, in 1962.

In 1968, the Indian political picture was as confused as hell. Non–Congress Party governments had been formed in eight states. But they found themselves constantly threatened by members of the legislatures who switched parties at the drop of a hat or, as India's former United Nations representative D. N. Chakravarti put it, as easily as changing their coats. These turncoats succeeded in bringing down at least three state governments. Other top state politicians, in a bid to prevent this, enlarged their cabinets so as to be able to offer top jobs to potential defectors. This tactic made defection threats all the more fashionable. In a little over a year, as a result of this sort of political blackmail, Bihar had four different governments. The Congress Party government of Uttar Pradesh, India's biggest state, was brought down by a Congress Party defector who then became the chief minister of Uttar Pradesh with the support of non–Congress parties. But he in turn was overthrown by the communists withdrawing their support from him, at which point New Delhi imposed direct rule. New Delhi also found itself compelled to impose direct rule, that is rule by the central government overruling state government, in Bihar, West Bengal, and the Punjab. All this naturally led in some legislatures to scenes of pandemonium reminiscent of Pakistan before 1958. There was plenty of other violence in India in 1968. Although a new state, pleasingly called Meghalaya (abode of clouds) was carved out of the eastern hills of Assam for the Kshasi and Garo tribes, and seemed to satisfy them, New Delhi continued having trouble with the Naga and Mizo hill tribes, who were assisted with arms and with training in guerrilla fighting by the Chinese. General Kaito, the anti-Peking Naga leader, was assassinated by one of his own men, just as the pro-Peking Burmese communist leader Thakin Than Tun had been. The Nagas' pro-Peking leader was mysteriously kidnapped. Meanwhile, in Orissa, the right-wing Hindu party Jan Sangh was greeted with Maoist slogans when it held its annual conference at Calicut. The Jan Sangh elected as its president a direct-action man, Deen Dayal Upadhyaya, who within three months was found murdered on a railway track near Banaras.

Also in 1968, while Peking continued accusing India of helping "Soviet revisionists and American imperialists to encircle China," India leaned heavily on Russia for arms. The Indian air force's most modern planes were 200 Russian SU-47s; the navy's four submarines were Russian; the army depended on Russian arms and military knowhow. As a consequence of this relationship, no doubt, India abstained in the United Nations voting on the resolution that condemned the Russian invasion of Czechoslovakia. When that vote was out of the way, the Indian defense minister of the day "visited Moscow to do some more shopping." Construction of a huge steel plant at Bokaro began in 1968, with Russian assistance. India had become Russia's largest trading partner. But there was an embarrassing moment at Bokaro when the government-owned steel plant's managing director was menaced by tribesmen with bows and arrows. They all wanted him to give them jobs.

In 1969, Indira may have cleared the decks for "democratic socialism" by putting down the so-called "syndicate." However it threatened to put her down instead. The syndicate was a powerful cabal of Congress Party leaders, most of them very ambitious to become the prime minister. Indira put down the syndicate by firing deputy prime minister Morarji Desai from his post of finance minister, and by nationalizing India's 14 big commercial banks. Then, Indira successfully backed for president of India the former vice president Varahgiri V. Giri, instead of supporting the Congress Party's candidate Sanjiva Reddy. In taking this action, Indira was backed by the Congress Party's left-wing "young Turk" faction. The man in the middle, who was trying to prevent a complete right-left split in the party, was the home minister Yeshwantro B. Chavan. Giri is an old friend of Mahatma Gandhi and Pandit Nehru, but Indira seemed to be looking forward to a leftish political victory in the elections of 1972. She therefore figured that if she did not give the Congress Party a left twist, the country might reject the party in 1972. The chief foe of the left twist was S. K. Patil, the Congress Party leader in Bombay, who alleged that Indira was working in with the communists. She retorted that Patil was working in with India's extreme right-wing parties.

Indira's fight with the syndicate had begun when she had discovered that the syndicate had gotten together and decided that the death of the Indian president Zakir Hussain provided them with the ideal opportunity to elect a new president who would help them get rid of Indira as prime minister. The leaders of the cabal were Congress Party president Kumaraswami Kamaraj, from Madras; Atulya Gosh, from West Bengal; and S. K. Patil, from Bombay. These men had chosen Reddy as one of their own and had got the Congress Party's parliamentary board to push through Reddy's nomination. But, in India, national and state legislatures elect a president; and Indira gained the support of the socialists and communists—and the public—as well as of her own Young Turks in the Congress Party and of other left-leaning members of the party. Indira gained their support by making the two left moves already described: nationalizing the 14 leading commercial banks and dismissing Desai, a leading conservative, from her cabinet. As well as doing this and successfully pushing Giri as the new president of India, Indira also launched a warning investigation of Birla, the great Indian industrial house, and she declared that credit would be siphoned away from rich farmers and big industry, toward small farmers and small business. She chose to interpret communist political successes in West Bengal, Kerala, and Andhra Pradesh as due to peasant dissatisfaction with wealthy high-caste landowners.

An industrial slowdown in India had worsened the position of thousands of persons, some of them unemployed despite having engineering and other skills. They were demanding jobs in industry. Behind these alarmed job seekers there pressed the disillusioned Indian students who, with reason, feared that they would be jobless in their turn. Mrs. Gandhi's hint was that India could go the way of Pakistan, and for similar causes. In Pakistan, under Ayub Khan, the rate of economic growth had been good, but the pace of "social justice" had been a snail's crawl. It would be rash to draw too dramatic conclusions. The total communist vote in India is still below 10 percent. The Congress Party vote is still 40 percent. Indira's aim was not to increase the 10 percent vote for the communists, but to increase the 40 percent vote of the Congress Party. After 1951, the Congress Party shifted a bit to the left. After 1960, it shifted a bit to the right. These are normal tactical shifts.

In West Bengal, the two chief challengers to Congress Party authority have been the pro-Soviet Communist Party of India and, the pro-China, Communist Party of India–Marxist. The CPI and CPI-M formed two cultural alliances in the election of 1967, popularly known as ULF and PULF. ULF included the CPI-M, the PSP (Praja Socialist Party), the SSP (Samyukpa Socialist Party), the socialist unity center, the workers party, the forward bloc (Marxist), and the RCPI (Revolutionary Communist Party of India). PULF consisted of the CPI, the Bangla congress, the forward bloc, and the Bolshevik party. ULF stands for United Labor Front and PULF stands for Peoples' United Labor Front.

In recent years, only eight or ten United States senators and congressmen have visited India each year, and usually only for very brief visits of three or four days. They prefer the fleshpots of Tokyo. But this fact seldom prevents them from professing to be authorities on the huge, complex, and ancient country of India, and predicting its future—for example, "inevitable" communism, or ineluctable flying apart of the states that compose India. American ignorance has produced some poor decisions. The United States decided in 1954 to arm Pakistan, despite warnings from State Department and Pentagon officials—and despite some frank admissions by Pakistanis—that the American arms would be used not against communism but against India. In the summer of 1965 these arms were so used. After the China border attack of 1962, the Indians sought American military aid. After two years of stalling by the United States, India turned to the Soviet Union which then became and remains India's chief supplier of military equipment.

John Hughes of *The Christian Science Monitor* points out that the United States television network men maintain "not a single bureau, resident correspondent or camera crew" in India whose 570 million people constitute a population larger than that of Africa and Latin America combined. Yet United States' aid to India has totaled about $9 billion so far and is still running about $250 million a year, which is a big drop from the previous $400 million a year but is still a lot. It's enough, for instance, to build a railway all the way from Thailand to Persia.

In spite of massive foreign aid, India is still nowhere near the point of economic takeoff. Instead, the problems to be somehow solved still include inflation, budgetary deficits, the need for greater agricultural productivity, and for more exports. The wily and experienced ex-finance minister Morarji Desai had not known whether to attack the forces of inflation by chopping government spending or to increase government spending so as to maintain some sort of economic growth, and never mind inflation. In the upshot, the government did lose control of food prices—but it failed to bring about industrial growth.

At this perilous juncture, India finds itself facing a moment of truth when the inflow of aid will do no more than balance repayments of former loans. In other words, India might conceivably find itself transferring resources to the richer countries, instead of the other way round. The one bright spot in the economic picture was an unprecedented growth of exports of manufactured goods, to which the country pinned its hope of eventual economic development. But continuing exports would call for a check on wage-cost inflation, and that in turn required more stable food prices. Meanwhile, the yearly growth of population of about 2.4 percent means that income per head in India stands just about where it did some four years ago.

The Indian government could plan for all this, and cut its development according to its cloth, provided it knew just how much cloth would be forthcoming. But although the aid-India consortium which met in Washington in May 1968 promised $1.45 billion in aid, about what India had expected, the actuality turned out to be a good deal less. The member governments of the consortium are Austria, Belgium, Canada, Denmark, France, West Germany, Holland, Italy, Japan, Britain, and the United States. The main donor is the United States and the American Congress upset the consortium applecart by voting the smallest foreign allocation in 20 years. India hoped to get $765 million from the United States, President Johnson cut this to $408 million and then Congress sliced that down still farther to $400 million. This was about what had happened in the previous year also. In 1967, the consortium pledged India $900 million, and actual receipts came to about $555 million. Desai came to Washington in September 1968 and tried to convince American fellow conservatives that lending the full amount would be money well spent. In vain. And in 1969 American aid to India was cut once again. Not surprisingly, the Indians are nowadays thinking more favorably than ever of the Soviet Union. Kosygin had visited New Delhi in January 1968, and arrangements were made for consultation between the two big countries' economic planners. In drawing up their own development plans, each country would try to take account of the other's surpluses and of its import requirements.

## INDIRA AND AMERICA

JAWAHARLAL NEHRU was elected president of the Indian Congress Party for the first time in 1929. He followed immediately after his father, Motilal, who was president in 1928. Indira Gandhi became party president exactly 30 years after *her* father.

Indira was born in November 1917, and is an only child. She attended her first political gathering when she was only three years old. Nehru was frequently in jail in British India. Indira has said that as a child, "my favorite occupation was to stand on a high table with servants crowded around me, and deliver thunderous political speeches." The well-to-do Nehru household always had plenty of servants. In 1942, Indira married Feroze Gandhi, a young Parsee. His Zoroastrian faith caused a bitter outcry against the marriage by many Hindus, but these zealots' complaints were ignored by both Nehru and Mahatma Gandhi who liked Feroze. Indira and her husband were soon arrested and put in jail for demonstrating against the British. Feroze's subsequent married life was not very happy. Nehru, his father-in-law, was a widower. Indira who had always been extremely devoted to her father felt her place was by his side as his housekeeper and companion. Consequently, Feroze and Indira both moved in and lived with Nehru. This proved to be a strained relationship for Feroze, who died in 1960 from a heart attack.

His widow visited China and did not like much what she saw. Nehru apparently was still convinced at that time that relations between India and China would continue to be "brotherly," but Indira is said to have been disturbed by the large amount of military preparation and warlike activity that she saw in China, which as far as India was concerned came to a head in 1962 when the Chinese launched an attack across India's northern border.

Indira visited the United States for the first time in 1949 and has subsequently made several visits. On her return to her own country from the United States the first time, she was hotly critical in speeches to the Indian Congress Party of the attitude of the United States Congress towards aid to India. She particularly objected to long congressional debates about letting India have food. "If they do not want to let us have the food, let them keep it," she declared passionately. Feeling between Indira and the United States has since improved, but still has its ups and downs. Whatever she may think of the Chinese, Indira evidently likes the Russians, and seems to have had a soft spot for Ho Chi Minh. This infuriates a lot of American congressmen, and Indira doesn't do much to soothe them by still occasionally letting off blasts at American policies she thinks wrong-headed. Her father used to do exactly the same.

Indira wears a red rose, as her father did before her. She works 16 hours a day, is very aware of the constant political intrigues which surround her and are usually directed against her, and isn't at all sure that the CIA hasn't a hand in some of them. She has had stones thrown at her at stormy political meetings. Her nose was broken by a stone, at Bhubaneswar, in Orissa, in 1967. When she first became prime minister, the politically wise whispered behind their hands that she would not last more than a few months. That prophecy has been proved wrong. Indira knows all there is to know about political infighting. She looks frail; she is in point of fact extremely tough.

Mrs. Gandhi has often given dazzling exhibitions of fast political footwork. Just as soon as she learned that the Congress Party had again performed poorly, in the February 1969 midterm elections in four states (Punjab, Uttar Pradesh, Bihar, West Bengal), she reshuffled her cabinet, firing old favorites and finding new ones, in an apparent bid to grab the headlines to take attention off the electoral setbacks. The

Congress Party's share of the total vote went up, not down, from 42 to 45 percent. The trouble was that the other 55 percent of the votes went to foes of the Congress Party who formed the most unlikely combinations solely in order to defeat it, instead of, as hitherto, fighting one another. After 20 years of national independence and also of Congress Party dominance, even Sikhs and Hindus seemingly were ready to work together just to get rid of the Congress Party incubus.

The main issue of the elections often looked like a familiar American one—demands for states' rights, denunciations of control by the central government. ("The fools in New Delhi" instead of "the fools in Washington.") But there were at least three factors working against a simple victory for the states and a corollary defeat of the Congress Party and of Mrs. Gandhi. The first of these was the lady herself. Since the death of her famous father Pandit Nehru, Mrs. Gandhi had proved to be one of the toughest politicians in a country that's full of tough political wheelers and dealers. She had got the best of every opponent who was rash enough to come out openly against her; and she held in check all those, and they were many, who professed loyalty to her but would actually love to grab her job. The British press lord who remarked, after meeting her, that she had a pretty little head with nothing in it, couldn't have been more wrong. The second factor is that all the Indian states are broke. They have to crawl each year to the central government's feet to beg more money, and are too scared of local lobbies to impose the land and other taxes that would make them less dependent on New Delhi. Finally, the state coalition governments that temporarily eclipsed the Congress Party weren't likely to endure. When they began to break up, each faction was going to be tempted to seek Congress Party support against its rivals, for no single group commands sufficient votes to form a government on its own.

Communalism and regionalism are of course ever present dangers in India, and Mrs. Gandhi, judging by the increasing frequency of her blasts against them, seems to think they're growing. Widespread Bombay riots were touched off by the demand by Bal Thackeray, the leader of the right-wing Shiv Sena, for a self-governing Marathi-speaking state. The Marathis loathe the immigrants who have poured into Bombay the way Negroes and Puerto Ricans poured into New York; but Bombay's immigrants are mostly white-collar intellectuals who grab the top Bombay jobs. In Madras, the Dravida Munnetra Kazhagam similarly longs to oust Brahmins, in order to make room for Tamil-speaking Dravidians. As far away as Ladakh, which is very far north indeed, the nomadic Champas resent the intrusion on their grasslands of 3,000 Tibetan refugees with herds of yaks and goats. The only surprising thing really about Indian divisiveness is that there isn't more of it, considering that one small village of 300 persons may contain as many as 24 different castes, apparently with nothing in common except that as Professor Marriot said at Holi, the Indian spring festival, they all get high together on pot. Yet in politics, at least some degree of collaboration is ultimately imposed on all Indian groups by their knowledge that they have to have allies in order to acquire power, so long as the ballot box prevails, which in India it still very much does. In the Indian Punjab, the Sikhs have had to share power with the Hindu Jan Sangh party, because Sikhs are themselves split into various factions. In every state, the Congress Party still has a big bundle of votes.

In West Bengal—a state that contains a city, Calcutta, as impossible to govern as is New York, and for very similar reasons—the Congress Party will not lose out forever, especially not to the communists. The Bengalis were always India's most active bombthrowers, and they have always resented the power of New Delhi, much the way East Pakistanis, who of course also are Bengalis, resent the political clout of Karachi and Rawalpindi in West Pakistan. The Bengalis proudly regard themselves as an intellectual upper caste, speaking the purest Indian language and boasting of having the best Indian poets, preeminently Tagore, who was a Nobel Prize winner. But the West Bengal United Front was not likely to stay very long united, and either the ensuing breakdown would produce anarchy, as happened in 1967, thus giving the central government the opportunity to reimpose "president's rule," or more probably breakaway factions would seek new allies—and the Congress Party would be a natural. If the Akali Sikhs of the Indian Punjab can form an alliance with the Jan Sangh, in West Bengal even the Forward Bloc (Marxist) probably won't be above turning toward the Congress Party in an hour of need.

India's political complexity is admittedly not easily distinguishable from political confusion. But it isn't unhealthy; to the contrary it is probably a sign of health. There is a lot of political consciousness down now to the village level, by most accounts. In any case, genuine social and economic progress is occurring, if not through the politicians then in spite of them. The younger generation is a much more vigorous, self-confident breed than even ten or fifteen years ago. Usually it's the elders who still moan about too much foreign influence. "Must we continue this British pomp?" fumed the old socialist Acharya Kripalani, in the Lokh Sabha (parliament) recently. He indignantly described how he found himself seated at a banquet next to a bewildered Hindu lady who was so overcome by the unfamiliar array of utensils beside her plate that she ended up eating with two forks.

It remains a harsh truth, however, that neither of the two strongest powers in Asia, the U.S. and the U.S.S.R., is Asian. That may be why Mao gets a big response from some Indians despite China's aggression in 1962. India is still, though to a diminishing degree, dependent on the U.S. for annual shipments of food as well as other aid. An American law that many Americans probably have never heard of, PL 480, is known to at least every Indian who can read, and often they wish they'd never heard of it. It's like being on the dole. Mrs. Gandhi didn't help herself with the U.S. Congress, by sending Christmas greetings to Hanoi, as she once did; or on another occasion choosing a trip to the Soviet Union as the occasion for sounding off on the evils of imperialism, by which she plainly didn't mean the Russian variety. Bowles tried hard to convince the U.S. Congress, and several U.S. administrations, that India is not Peru, but is a strategically placed continent where one-seventh of the human race live; a population as we have noted that exceeds those of Latin America and Africa combined. Nevertheless, U.S. aid to India is at the foot of the U.S. list on a per capita basis—$14, compared to $361 for Israel, $177 for Taiwan and $148 for South Korea. This is not wholly incomprehensible. For, with only 10 percent of India's population, Taiwan and South Korea export 80 percent as much as India does, and therefore appear to be trying harder. India is deep in debt ($7 billion). Yet, though the rupee was devalued, her share of world exports slipped, from 2.4 percent in 1948, way down to 0.8 percent. All other Asian countries were doing better with their exports.

India could be a tourist's paradise, and there are plenty of fascinating and beautiful Indian items of excellent quality that tourists would be glad to spend money on, thus providing India with badly needed foreign exchange. But tourism brings in only $35 million a year, a mere 2.2 percent of India's foreign exchange earnings; tourism by contrast accounts for 43 percent of Spain's. "Tourists are our honored guests" proclaims a big sign at the Delhi airport. But as soon as the honored guest passes into the terminal, he is kept busy filling forms about the exact amount of cash he is carrying. "What is this 'four shillings and ninepence'? It is sterling money? Why do you not write that? And you have *signed* your name but you must *print* it, too!" The incoming tourist is also sternly warned against photographing the airport, as if he'd want to. Later, at a government of India hotel, when the honored guest tries to cash a traveler's check, he finds he has to stand in line, fill yet another form, and produce his passport yet once more.

If, however, one takes the view that Indian villagers are probably more important, or at any rate have more urgent human needs, than foreign tourists, progress seems undeniable (and this applies to Pakistan as well).

In both India and Pakistan, famines probably are past tragedies, but populations continue to grow alarmingly. India has about 570 million people, who very likely will exceed a billion before the growth of people begins to taper off, in spite of the million or so who now have themselves sterilized each year (in return for cash awards or scholarships for their existing children). Condoms, widely distributed through retail sellers of stamps, tea, cigarettes, and matches, as well as by the mailman on his round, have largely replaced the loop, which was not popular. But at the moment, vasectomy is the "in" thing (the Pill just isn't available in India yet). One Indian cabinet minister was so carried away with enthusiasm for sterilization as a means of birth control that he declared in a speech: "The people of India have *embraced* vasectomy." Yet it can cause problems. Many of the doctors who have been performing the operation neglected to tell their male patients that it wouldn't take effect for some months. So, when sterilized husbands found their wives were pregnant, they denounced them for proven infidelity. Snags like that are fairly common in modern India. They are best viewed tolerantly, as part of the price that probably has to be paid for undeniable progress. The United States government and the United States Congress should take the long, tolerant view and not let the occasional tantrums of the lively lady in New Delhi, or her successor, upset them. Anyone whose job is managing India is entitled to an occasional tantrum.

## A CONTINENT'S POLITICS

BOTH INDIA AND Pakistan were visited in 1969 by the Russian defense minister Marshal Andrei Grechko who turned up first in India then in Pakistan, accompanied by an impressive tail of Soviet army, navy, and air force brass. India spends more than $1.5 billion on defense—the 1969 budget pushed it higher, marking a three-fold increase within ten years—Pakistan spends about $520 million. The Indians have twice as many Soviet-made MIG jet aircraft (80) as the Pakistanis; on the other hand Pakistan has some Chinese tanks. After the 1965 Indo-Pakistan war, a fashionably brief summer affair which to the Indians' undisguised surprise ended in a kind of draw, the Soviet Union shared the American inclination to get the hell out of their competition in selling arms to both India and Pakistan. But because the 1969 political upset in Pakistan might push that nation toward China, the Soviet Union was obviously under temptation to get back in the act. Russia conceivably could wind up in an arms supply race with China, selling arms to India to offset Chinese arms sales to Pakistan, the way the U.S. is impelled to arm Israel against Russian-armed Arabs. Alternatively, India and Pakistan could play a game which is very familiar in their part of the world and that the wily Afghans as we noted have played for many years—the game of milking more than one cow. India's armaments are already diversified—British, American, Russian. In the present state of relations, the Indians could hardly hope to add Chinese arms to this ensemble. But the new Yahya Khan government of Pakistan almost certainly hopes to be able to enlarge its supply of

Chinese arms without forfeiting Russian, British or even American sources.

The most spectacular though not necessarily the leading Pakistan politician is probably still Zulfighar Ali Bhutto, the former foreign minister whom former president Ayub Khan first sacked then put behind bars as a political prisoner. The president had power to do that sort of thing under the Pakistan constitution that Ayub himself largely wrote, but in February 1969 widespread rioting forced Ayub to release Mr. Bhutto, and subsequently Ayub was ousted from the presidency which he had held for over ten years, and was thrust into apparently peaceful retirement in Lahore: a Khrushchev-type retirement, rather than a Johnson-type renunciation.

Former foreign minister Bhutto, who is a graduate of the University of California at Berkeley, directed most of his fire at India. Bhutto told wildly cheering crowds of Pakistanis that he was opposed to the Tashkent Declaration that India and Pakistan signed in January 1966 under Russian persuasion, which in effect said that the 1965 war was an unfortunate error and that they would seek in future to settle their differences by means other than fighting. Bhutto however declared that what he looked forward to was "an Algerian-type war of liberation" in Kashmir, which India rules but Pakistan claims. Bhutto accused Ayub Khan of allowing the Kashmir problem to be "scaled down" and announced that he, Bhutto, intended to see the issue "reinstated." That amounted to coolly spitting in the eye of Mr. Kosygin, the Soviet premier, who persuaded Ayub Khan and the late Mr. Shastri, the former prime minister of India, to sign the Tashkent Declaration.

As well as spiritedly offering Pakistanis a new war over Kashmir, Bhutto in his quest for personal power cheerfully proposed tripling the pay of all Pakistan government workers, and nationalizing banking, insurance, and all major industries in Pakistan. He called this "Scandinavian-type socialism in Asian terms." He was eager to work with Maulana Bashani, the 83-year-old but still formidable head of the pro-Peking National Awami Party, and with Sheikh Mulibar Rahman, the leader of the East Pakistan Awami League. Rahman, a hand-some man of 48, had like Bhutto just emerged from jail, having been charged with conspiring to bring about East Pakistan's secession from Pakistan. Rahman was amicably disposed toward the Pakistan Communist Party, and promised to lift the ban that was imposed on it back in 1954, when Pakistani workers tried to seize factories. Bhutto himself headed the left-wing People's Party. Pakistan, as we have already noted, consists of two separate territories, 1,200 miles apart: West Pakistan which covers 300,000 square miles and has 50 million people, and East Pakistan which though it covers only 54,500 square miles has 70 million people. The people of East Pakistan have always bitterly resented their domination by West Pakistan, but their demands for near-sovereign powers have hitherto always been suppressed. Ayub Khan knew very well that if he listened to the East Pakistanis, he would immediately be confronted with similar demands, by the North-West Frontier Pathan leader Khan Abdul Wali Khan and others, for carving up West Pakistan again into four states—North-West Frontier, Sind, Baluchistan, and Punjab.

West Pakistan borders China and is close to Russia; East Pakistan borders Burma. The Chinese are said to have about 1,000 agents active in North Burma and in adjacent Nagaland (in India), training people in guerrilla warfare, in areas where China claims territory from both Burma and India. A Chinese move into Burma would outflank both East Pakistan and India's West Bengal state, as well as Assam (and Thailand). In West Bengal, meantime, there occurred a political upset quite simi-lar to what occurred in Pakistan. The new home minister of the Indian state of West Bengal, Mr. Jyoti Basu, had long been a well-known left-wing agitator for autonomy for West Bengal. He now secured control of police and passports in a new West Bengal government that again was dominated by Indian communists, in a United Front that, as we saw, in-cluded left-wing socialists, the Socialist Unity Center, the Forward Bloc (Marxist), and even a Bolshevik party. The UF, strongly pro-Peking, not pro-Moscow, had strong support among Indian students, who like many students elsewhere are inclined to dismiss the Russian Communist Party as a bourgeois fuddy-duddy, and to go for the Sayings of Mao. For their protesting parents, mostly aging Congress Party pillars, they have only amused contempt, especially when the elders protest that it was they, after all, who achieved independence for India. "You fought for Independence? But we have always had Independence!" As for poor old Mahatma Gandhi, the students seem to have conceived a positive hatred of his memory, for they associate the martyred Father of the Nation with spinning wheels and cottage industries, whereas what they want is a bustling India of mod and modern plants, which Gandhi spent most of his time denouncing.

By overwhelmingly winning a midterm election in the teeth of the Indian Institute of Public Opinion (Gallup) poll, the United Front put an end to the president's rule of West Bengal. Back in 1967, in order to end riots and strikes, the Indian Government had declared an emergency in West Bengal which was thereafter ruled directly from New Delhi, with a Congress Party governor installed in Calcutta. The UF victory was acclaimed by thousands in Calcutta who enthusiastically mobbed the new ministers, demanded the immediate firing of the governor, and drove around City Square in streetcars decorated with flowers and electric light bulbs, exploding firecrackers. The UF ministers' first acts were to fix their own pay at a modest $67.50 a month, and to release all the Naxalites who had been jailed by the previous administration. "Naxalites" are revolutionary Maoists, who according to their own manifesto intend "to unite with our class brothers who are waging heroic struggles in Burma, Thailand, Malaya, and Indonesia." The Naxalite manifesto also welcomed the UF victory as "opening up opportunities for communist revolutionaries to intensify class struggles" in West Bengal, and it called for what it described as "death-defying abandon."

All this might seem to indicate that both India and Pakistan are in for a new period of violence and partition, this time however not a split along religious lines, Hindu and Muslim, but as part of a communist conspiracy inspired if not directed by China; and a good many commentators in New Delhi were quite prepared to say as much. In fact, things very likely are not that bad, or that simple. In Pakistan, the flamboyant Bhutto turned out, at least for the time being, to have much less clout than he claimed or than was claimed for him by cheering crowds swayed by his demagoguery. Bhutto is from Sind, a somewhat peripheral state in terms of political power in Pakistan, and he may be less prominent in future than he himself evidently hoped. As for Sheikh Rahman and other East Pakistan leaders, their demand to have the major voice in the country's affairs was probably just a bargaining counter, to be used to attain their true goal, which is control of East Pakistan rather than striving for a share, even a major share, in the central government of all Pakistan. Ayub Khan's successor as president was just another military man exactly like Ayub. Yahya Khan is a conservative. So for that matter is Air Marshal Asghar Khan, the former head of the Air Force. Pakistan's real testing time might come not in 1970, when theoretically the next elections were due, but after another army-backed administration had revealed whether or not it was capable of introducing and making effective some basic and urgent reforms. For what greatly helped to bring Ayub Khan down was the disclosure (ironically, by one of Ayub's own top economic advisers, attached to the Pakistan Planning Commission) that two-thirds of industry in Pakistan, and four-fifths of the banks, were controlled by only twenty wealthy families. Ayub had encouraged the rapid growth of a wealthy landowning and a wealthy industrial class, urged thereto by American dispensers of aid, who assured him that he must foster "private enterprise." But in Asia "private enterprise" is still apt to be a rank weed. Among other blatant scandals, Ayub's own son Gohar Ayub leaped almost overnight from being a mere army captain to being a millionaire through land deals, and also by selling General Motors trucks to the Pakistan Army of which his father was commander-in-chief. Nevertheless, Ayub's acrid description of his apparently successful political opponents—"five cats tied by their tails"— applied. The cats that had scratched out Ayub probably would scratch one another. Bhutto himself remarked sourly that "a tiger (Ayub) was prowling the jungle, and now that the tiger is wounded, all sorts of inferior animals want to take credit for it."

## BUDDHA'S ISLAND

THE LOVELY, PEAR-SHAPED island of Ceylon, about the size of West Virginia, has mountain peaks and 20 rivers. In the 4,000-year-old Hindu epic, the *Ramayana,* the poet Valmiki tells in lyric verse how Sita the wife of Rama is abducted by Ravana, the king of Ceylon, and how Rama, with the help of the monkey god, Hanuman, invades the island from India and rescues Sita. In history, an Indian prince called Vijaya landed in Ceylon about 500 B.C. and founded a line of Sinhalese kings who ruled the island for almost 21 centuries. The seat of government was Anuradhapura, an ancient capital that ranked with Babylon and Nineveh. Its magnificent ruins still stand.

Under the influence of Vijaya, who was the son of the Indian emperor, Asoka, the people of Ceylon became Buddhists. And today the Buddhism of Ceylon, called Hinayana or Little Vehicle Buddhism (otherwise called Theravada, the doctrine of the disciples), flourishes in Thailand, South Vietnam, and other countries which look towards Ceylon for their religious inspiration.

The Portuguese ruled Ceylon for 150 years, until the Dutch expelled them in 1658; the British in turn expelled the Dutch in 1796. Under British rule Ceylon became the world's chief source of tea, and the city of Colombo was famous as a market for precious stones. Pierpont Morgan bought the world's biggest sapphire here. Tarshish in the Bible is actually Galle in Ceylon, which is where King Solomon and the Queen of Sheba obtained ivory and peacocks. Kandy, up in the hills, is a fairy tale kind of city built around a famous temple.

Though Ceylon is rich in tea, coconuts, and rubber, there

is much landlessness among the peasants, in part because of the rapid growth in population due to the relatively recent eradication of malaria. The tea estates are for the most part foreign owned. The ethnic and cultural picture is confusing. There are about one million Ceylon Tamils, Hindus who do have Ceylonese citizenship. Then there are another million Indian Tamils, Hindus who haven't got citizenship because they emigrated to Ceylon more recently. Together the Tamils come to about 22 percent of the population. There are also some one-half million Arabs; in the 13th to the 17th centuries, Ceylon was the halfway house for trade between west Asia and the Far East, and has indeed been a halfway house for trade between the Persian Gulf and China since the 6th century. And there were Christians in Ceylon in the age of Justinian, according to the Indian seaman and writer Cosmas. The Portuguese made Catholic, the Dutch Protestant, converts and today in Ceylon there are 725,000 Christians as well as six million Buddhists.

The political picture in Ceylon is confusing. A brief rundown on prime ministers since Ceylon gained its independence from Britain:

From 1947 to 1952, D. S. Senanayake.

Sir John Kotelawala, prime minister from 1953 to 1956.

S. W. R. D. Bandaranaike, prime minister from 1956 to 1959, when he was assassinated.

Sirimavo Bandaranaike, his widow, prime minister from 1960 to 1965.

Dudley Senanayake was prime minister from 1952 to 1953, and also since 1965;   Dudley is the son of D. S. Senanayake who was Ceylon's first prime minister. And there are lots of other Bandaranaikes who are also active in politics.

The main parties are the United National Party, conservative socialists who subsequently became what they call democratic socialists, and the MEP (*Mahe Jana Eksathparamuna*), a socialist coalition that was led by S. W. R. D. Bandaranaike. Then there are the Marxist parties. The Ceylon Communist Party, the Ceylon Communist Party-China wing (CCP-CW), the Troskyist LSSP (Lanka Sama Samaja Party). The Bolshevik-Leninist party. The list is not done yet. There is the CDZ, the Ceylon Democratic Congress, which is the Ceylonese version of the Indian Congress Party. The TC (Tamil Congress) and Tamil Federal Party. The two Tamil parties represent the Ceylon Tamils and Indian Tamils and they rarely agree about anything. Yet the Tamil issue dominates modern Ceylon's politics. The Federal Party insists the only solution of Tamil-Sinhalese tension is to have a federal state. As an example of Tamil-Ceylonese differences, in 1948 the minister of local government was suspended and resigned from the cabinet for "appointing a committee to consider the demarcation of the Koneswam temple area in Ft. Frederick in Trincomalee, an area sacred to Hindus." One consequence of the ensuing uproar was that the Federal Party quit the government. Some members of the party would like to see established a separate Tamil kingdom in Ceylon.

Since independence in 1947, Ceylon has had many political alarms and crises and yet, somehow, parliamentary government continues and even seems to flourish. Customarily, the party that obtains power at elections calls itself socialist then proceeds to condemn strikes against it as counterrevolutionary activities. As one prime minister argued—W. Dahanayke, who filled in between the assassinated Mr. Bandaranaike and Madame Bandaranaike in 1959 to 1960—"strikes were justified under the British occupation but now that the government has passed into our own hands, strikes are tantamount to rebellion against the government." A Ceylonese government that indulges in this sort of thing, and most of them have done so, is of course immediately accused by all the opposition parties of striving to become a dictatorship. But in due course elections are held and when they are there is a change of power which is normally relatively bloodless.

The Marxist parties don't grab the peasants, who are a majority of the population. The Marxists derive their political strength mainly from the trade unions in the towns, and get only about 10 percent of the vote. The Marxists are very polite, and communalism is a very much bigger problem in Ceylon than communism. There are quarrels over Catholic parochial schools as well as over Hindu temples, and there are clashes between the Sinhalese and the two sets of Tamils, and between the Hindus, Buddhists, and Muslims. All the politicians speak English, though few of the peasants understand it. And most of the politicians are men of wealth, except possibly some of the Marxists. One former prime minister, Sir John Kotelawala, retired to his estate in Kent, England after his defeat at the polls. The man who defeated him, S. W. R. D. Bandaranaike, was a leader of the MEP "socialist coalition" and was assassinated in 1959. When Mrs. Bandaranaike, his widow, took over the prime ministership supported by Trotskyist and communist allies, the island went into an economic nosedive. Estranged Tamils brought the country close to civil war. In March 1965, a moderate socialist, Dudley Senanayake, with his allies in the United National Party, defeated Mrs. Bandaranaike. However, the seesaw goes on with Mrs. Bandaranaike busily planning a political comeback in 1970.

## THE BURMESE WAY TO SOCIALISM

BURMA HAS A population of 26 million people and is about the size of Texas. General Ne Win seized power in March 1962, less than four years after Ayub Khan had done the same in Pakistan. Like Ayub, Ne Win put the army in charge of the country's economic development. But in Burma's case this was done in order to smash the economic grip of the Indian and Chinese merchants by setting up "people's shops." The result has been admitted economic stagnation—but also severe inflation!—with great shortages of consumer goods as well as a big slump in exports. All the banks, and practically all other enterprises, were taken over by the soldiers. Harassed farmers preferred smuggling goods to growing crops. It took not months, but years to procure raw materials, or even very simple machinery, through the channels of the army bureaucracy. And as for the workers, money rewards such as incentive pay were replaced by "honors for outstanding service." Not surprisingly, not much of the service turned out to be outstanding. Peasants preferred hoarding food to selling it to the state at artificially low prices. Under this "hermit kingdom" policy of Ne Win, tourists no longer flocked to see Rangoon's Shwedagon pagoda, or the temples of Mandole, or the beautiful 11th century monuments of Pagan.

Ne Win tried hard to stay on good terms with Red China, with which Burma has a 1,200-mile border. But when Chinese appeared in his streets waving Mao's little red books, Ne Win cracked down and Peking turned nasty. The Chinese called Ne Win a reactionary racist. Nobody knows whether the Chinese in Burma were encouraged by Peking to yell their slogans or whether their yelling was just an accidental spillover from China's internal upheaval, as happened in Hong Kong. Ne Win's army has held the Burmese communist rebels in check in lower Burma, but in the northern areas bordering China the rebels do better. There they can slip over the border and they can stir up the race minorities, the Karens, Kachins, and Shans. While Ne Win has this kind of trouble on his northeast border, he does not seem to have any northwest border trouble with either India or East Pakistan.

Ne Win took over from U Nu, whom he had in jail for years, but whom he released to be a member of a 33-man advisory board in 1968, to help Ne Win prepare a future constitution for Burma. At the same time, Ne Win released the former chief justice U Mynt Thein; a former president, Dr. Ba Maw, and others he had incarcerated. In the summer of 1969, Ne Win rejected the advice given him by his 33-man advisory board, which was that he should stop bossing the country and return it to parliamentary democracy. Ne Win did, however, permit U Nu to leave the country and, in India and elsewhere, U Nu proceeded vigorously to insist that he was still the legal prime minister of Burma, that Ne Win was a usurper, and that he, U Nu, would not rest until he had restored parliamentary democracy to Burma—if necessary by a coup.

Whether a return to parliamentary democracy as advocated by U Nu would make any considerable change in the state of affairs is a moot question. When I was in Burma in 1955, U Nu's brand of parliamentary democracy was in full flower. Police were everywhere. It took 16 police inspectors to inspect my passport. Getting into the country was very difficult. Getting travelers' checks cashed in the country was almost impossible. And getting out was an extremely tedious and laborious process.

U Nu was a big-hearted man with some remarkable ideas. It was said of him that once while traveling abroad, he excitedly cabled his entire cabinet to meet him at the airport because he had a great revelation to make to them. When he got out of his plane they clustered around him, expecting some dramatic announcement of some vast political or economic change. U Nu excitedly told them he had had a dream in which he had seen a cave where the Buddha had once preached. He knew exactly where it was located and he announced that he would take the cabinet to it forthwith. They piled into the official black cars and drove off. But when they reached the spot indicated in the dream, there was no cave there. "Never mind," U Nu is said blandly to have remarked; "it should have been here, and I'm sure it was once here, and we shall build one." He did, too, and I visited the cave in the company of Khrushchev and Bulganin who were then also visiting Burma. U Nu showed his visitors around, explaining how he had had the cave created and had then dedicated it to the Lord Buddha. Khrushchev's terse comment was, "Very nice; I noticed that the roof leaks; that wouldn't happen in the Moscow subway."

In 1968, the Burmese Communist Party did itself great political damage by running amok, killing Buddhist monks, desecrating Buddhist shrines, and calling Buddhism the "opium of the people." The upshot was that the party split, not for the first time, and its head, Thakin Than Tun, was murdered by one of his own lieutenants.

The party of which Ne Win is the chairman is called the Burmese way to socialism party (BWSP). Ne Win was a member of a group of young nationalists called the 30 comrades, who secretly gained control of the army during the 1942–1945 Japanese occupation of Burma, and who then formed a government that was led by Aung San, who however was assassinated (with most of his cabinet) in July 1947.

Six months later, January 4, 1948, the Union of Burma ended 63 years of British rule as a province of India. But almost immediately Karens, Kachins, Shans and other Burmese tribes returned to the kind of tribal warfare that has marked Burmese affairs from about the 5th century. The latest tribal troubles have brought Ne Win and Indira Gandhi together, for the Chinese have armed the Naga and Mizo tribes of India, as well as arming Ne Win's Karens and Shans, in Burma.

AMERICA AND THE ASIAN

BALKANS

THE COUNTRIES WE have discussed in this chapter
—Nepal, Ceylon, Burma, India, and Pakistan—are in a sense
the Balkans of Asia. That is to say, they have in common
with the Balkan countries of eastern Europe a tendency to
political instability. For instance, the Nepalese political opposition is in exile and it threatens that one day it will seek the
violent overthrow of King Mahendra. And U Nu, the former
Burmese prime minister, is also in exile and has also threatened
to overthrow his successor, General Ne Win, whom U Nu ac-
cuses of being a usurper. Pakistan is Balkanized in the sense
that the western "wing" of this large but cut-up country is
constantly at daggers drawn with its eastern "wing." In India,
there are serious and apparently enduring conflicts among the
component states, for linguistic as well as political reasons;
and there are religious divisions also, mainly but not entirely
between the preponderant Hindu majority, and the 50 million
Muslims who elected to remain in India at the time of partition when the Islamic state of Pakistan was formed in 1947.
Ceylon in spite of serious ethnic, linguistic, and religious differences as well as political ones has managed to retain a parliamentary system whereby power has been transferred more or
less smoothly from one party to another in the process of fairly
held elections; but the island's deep internal divisions nevertheless recall those of a Balkan country of eastern Europe.

American policy toward those five Asian nations has paid
little attention to what these countries themselves obviously
regard as their really serious and pressing problems. Nor is it

even true that United States policy in south Asia has preferred
to concentrate on the problem of giving those countries economic aid, arguing that whatever their internal divisions and
difficulties may be, the prime need is to lift them into the
modern age by helping them to raise their very low standards
of living by means of liberal transfusions of capital and know-
how and technology. What American policy has done for the
most part is to concentrate hard on the alleged problem of
communism that was said to confront all those countries and
to shape the specific policy according to the assessment of how
close the communist wolf had come to closing its jaws on its
presumed victim. Thus, Ceylon has had comparatively little
American aid rendered to it—about $20 million of aid a year
for fertilizer and school lunches—because although Ceylon has
a communist party (in fact, it has several) it has not hitherto
been regarded as in great danger of a communist takeover.
This may change as and when the United States takes a greater
interest in the future of Trincomalee, the island's great harbor,
one of the finest in the world and the obvious counterpart of
Singapore in the Indian Ocean. Nepal, on the other hand, has
received a good deal of American attention, and not just because of the strong fascination that Kathmandu and its quaint
customs seem to have for American tourists. The real reason,
of course, is that Nepal is close to communist China and is
regarded as being in some way as of considerable strategic
significance.

Pakistan is the prime example of American policy being
influenced—one might truly say obsessed, with communism.
Because Pakistan more than India seemed willing to conform
to American patterns of political behaviour and to act as a
"staunch" ally prepared to stand up to the communist challenge, the United States was far more enthusiastic about giving or selling arms to Pakistan than about conferring them on
India. The miserable and disconcerting upshot of this policy
was just what its critics said it would be, only worse. Pakistan,
as the critics foretold, used the American tanks and other
modern weapons against India, not against any communists.
Ironically, the chief mediator in the Pakistan-India quarrel

proved to be a Soviet Russian communist statesman, Mr. Kosygin. And as an extra and unexpected irony, Pakistan the staunch ally against communism decided at a critical juncture that its national interests dictated an alignment with communist China—of course because the communist Chinese were at loggerheads with Pakistan's enemy, India. Even after all those ludicrous errors, a danger still exists of their repetition or their continuation. A strong temptation evidently confronts American policy planners to divide Pakistan politicians into "bad guys" and "good guys." Thus, Bhutto is a "bad guy" because he is supposed to be pro-Peking. Conceivably, Mr. Bhutto could come to power in Pakistan, East or even West; would the United States then frown on him as an unacceptable Pakistan leader? The truth is the United States has made too many enemies of men like Bhutto, quite unnecessarily. And, with some staunch allies like the United States has lately had, who needs staunch enemies?

The Pakistan example spelled out sharply what should have been obvious in any case. This is that though the United States might sincerely think communism was these south Asian countries' chief problem, they themselves never shared the American belief, and certainly have never acted upon it. The Nepalese do, it is true, fear the Chinese; but they fear the Indians also, and try their best to balance off the one powerful neighbor against the other. The Burmese have had both good and bad relations with China. For the moment, they are bad. But the Burmese have never shown much interest in soliciting American help against their internal communists who have kept the country in a sad uproar for 20 years; and still less against Communist China. The fact is that communism is regarded by those countries as only one component, and that by no means the largest, of their complex problems. The American concentration on communism never fails to irritate the Asian leaders and peoples, who feel that they have quite enough real troubles on their plate without the United States making things worse by picking out just one problem, and continually harping on it. When Indians heard the Central Intelligence Agency had allegedly involved itself in their elections, apparently on the theory that American help should be rendered to political parties that the United States deemed to be strongly anti-communist, so as to forestall the chances of communist electoral victories, public opinion in India was not moved toward anti-communism (that is, broadly speaking, its inclination most of the time) but toward at least temporary anti-Americanism. The United States' arms aid to Pakistan naturally produced the same effect, only even more so. If the CIA ever attempts to "save" Trincomalee from the Reds, a Sinhalese swing toward anti-Americanism can confidently be predicted. At the other end of the south Asian continent from Ceylon, Nepal if it indeed presents a strategic problem, poses it for India (or China) not for the United States. And India, or China, can cope with it, better than the State Department can, or the Pentagon.

In the old imperialist days of British India, the prevailing British nightmare was of the Russian bear trying to claw its way over the Himalayas. Now, the Himalayas are allegedly threatened by a Chinese dragon which may or may not be a paper dragon. But would the Russian bear permit the Chinese dragon to do this? It seems inherently improbable that the bear would. That is surely an important factor that ought to be taken into account in all calculations concerning south Asia. There is not much sign that this is being done. In any case, in spite of the movie roles of the late Errol Flynn, it seems a fantasy to imagine Americans replacing the British Bengal Lancers as defenders of the northwest frontier and the Khyber Pass, not to mention the jungles and teak forests of Burma.

## CULTURE CONTRASTS

NEW DELHI IS a city that is less than half a century old, yet its broad, leisurely boulevards and big and spacious buildings of red sandstone have an aura of unchanging, indeed of petrified history. This dead calm is at least in part because of the determination of Mrs. Gandhi's government to make India a socialistic country aiming to come as near as possible to self-sufficiency through practising austerity. The government pursues a puritanical policy of high taxes and of almost no imported luxuries. In his 1969 budget, the then finance minister Mr. Morarji Desai increased the tax on imported automobiles to 100 percent, and wisecracked that this would double an imported car's value as a status symbol. There are in fact very few automobiles, most of them small British and Italian makes. Delhi's broad thoroughfares and huge traffic circles are used by thin trickles of cars; they are like the vast Indian rivers which normally contain only a little water and a great deal of sand. Although New Delhi's Mogul Gardens around the Presidential Palace, with their ponds, orange and frangipani trees, and fabulous blooms, are nowadays thronged by Indians of all classes and castes, and no longer are for the exclusive use and enjoyment of the viceroy and his carefully selected guests, still the Indian capital manages to look as if it were bathing in the refulgent rays of an everlasting imperial sunset.

West Asia, as Asians call the Middle East, has its grotesque brutalities; "study of revenge, immortal hate," as Milton said of a different place. India, God knows, has its absurdities. Where else but in New Delhi (or Moscow) would there be a hotel run by the government and built on the lines of the

Pentagon? The endless corridors of the Asoka Hotel are always filled with turbaned servitors. As you advance the hundred yards or so toward the elevator, the rows of seated servitors rise, bow, smile and place the palms of their hands together in the Indian greeting of *namaste*. But the day we left New Delhi, their lethargic peace was shattered by bemedalled Russian generals as big as oak trees who were wheeling and charging along the miles of hotel corridors like tanks on maneuvers.

Fortunately, the vast Indian subcontinent is too massive to be overturned by huge Russians, however heavily bemedalled, or by Chinese and Chinese-inspired revolutionaries or even by the riptide of western modernization. India and Pakistan, and especially India, stand solidly on their Hindu and Muslim foundations. From the British they imbibed some bad things, like reams of official blanks and miles of red tape, and some very good things indeed, like the western infrastructures of democratic government and due process. But it is now clear that India and Pakistan intend, and have the ability, to adapt those western institutions to their own use, without disrupting the fundamentals of their own way of life.

No such comforting assurance can be derived from the present state of affairs in southeast Asia, to which we now turn. Hinduism at times seems almost too eternal, no more susceptible to change than the high Himalayas are likely to alter their form quickly through erosion; and Islam conceivably will outlast all existing molds of Christianity. But southeast Asia has really no form at all, and consists of lava that is still bubbling, from not one but several volcanoes. The main influences are Hindu, Muslim, Buddhist (two varieties), and modern Western which embraces both Americanism and Marxism (two varieties again). The Americanism is faintly tinted here and there with lingering French and British hues, like striped toothpaste. Moreover, it is very difficult to define the geographical limits of the southeast Asian civilization, if that is what it is. Does the territory that for want of a better name is called North Vietnam belong in it, or is it really part of the east Asian culture that emanates from China, embraces Japan, and one of whose pillars despite the Book of Mao is still Mahayana Buddhism? And, if North Vietnam is really in east Asia, what is to be said of South Vietnam with its million or so Roman Catholics and strong Khmer (Cambodian) element whose tradition is Therevada not Mahayana Buddhism? Whatever its final political fate may be, the Mekong Delta where most South Vietnamese live probably has stronger cultural affinities with Pnom Penh, and Vientiane, than with Hanoi.

# 6

# SOUTHEAST ASIA:
# BANGKOK TO HANOI

## TIES WITH THAIS

THAILAND, THE SIZE of France, has a population
of 36 million. This includes 3 million Chinese, 700,000 Malays
and 200,000 assorted hill tribes. Thailand is the world's largest
rice exporter—by contrast, Ceylon has to import about half of
the rice it consumes—and Thailand also is a big exporter of
rubber and tin.

The country was never a colony. It once had a British
governess, the famous Anna who taught the royal children of
Siam, but it never had a British governor. On the other hand,
in World War II Thailand was an unwilling ally of Japan.
Thailand is an ancient monarchy. The present ruler King
Bhumibol was born in the United States and he became king
in 1946. But 14 years before that, in 1932, ambitious politicians
and soldiers had made the monarchy "constitutional" by revolution. In 1958, another revolution rid the military of the politicians. The present prime minister of Thailand is Thanom
Kittikachorn, who is a field marshal. He held elections in
February 1969 and they may have been fair, for he and his
party did less well than they had expected.

Thailand has 12,000 soldiers fighting on the American side
in South Vietnam, and there were until recently more than
50,000 American military personnel in Thailand. The big U.S.
airbases in Thailand are Ta Khli, Khorat in the center, U-
Taphao in the south, Ubon in the east, and Sakolnakorn Udom
and Hakhom Phanom in the north. Then there is a big naval
base, Sattahip, which is covered by U-Taphao, which is the
airbase that is home to the B-52s which are able to reach as
far as Sinkiang in China, as well as being home to the refuel-

ing KC-135 stratotankers. This almost makes U-Taphao another Okinawa.

For a long time, the Thai government pretended that no U.S. planes were bombing North Vietnam from Thailand. Then, when the bombing became a very open secret, they switched, acknowledged, and sent 12,000 soldiers to South Vietnam. This was done in the hope of binding the United States to Thailand's side. But what the Thais want is not 50,000 United States military in Thailand, it is an old style alliance. When President Nixon visited Thailand he pledged continuing United States support to Thailand Prime Minister Thanom Kittikachorn, and in May of 1969, in Bangkok, the Secretary of State Mr. William P. Rogers reaffirmed the 1962 bilateral agreement between his predecessor Secretary Dean Rusk and the Thai foreign minister Thanat Khoman. None of this however precludes the Thais from trying to reach better relations with both Red China and the Soviet Union. And the Thais have made some overtures to both those quarreling countries, although until recently Bangkok refused to have either diplomatic or trade relations with Peking.

The Thais are naturally worried about Thailand becoming another South Vietnam. And indeed Thailand as of now has three guerrilla "fronts":

1. One thousand men, remnants of the Malayan Chinese communists, operate hit-and-run raids on both sides of the Thai-Malaysian border. Their leader is supposed to be the redoubtable Chin Peng, who first fought for the British and was well decorated by them for valor, then turned around and joined the cause of Peking. The Thai population among whom Chin Peng and his men work are overwhelmingly Muslim.

2. On the northeast Mekong River border, about 3,000 guerrillas are said to operate. And the North Vietnamese have set up near their capital, Hanoi, a special training village for Thai guerrillas, called Hoa Binh. It's a sort of guerrilla warfare Olympic village. In northeast Thailand there are 40,000 settlers from North Vietnam who sought refuge there back in the

days when the Vietminh were fighting the French, but who mostly continued adoring the late Ho Chi Minh. It is not known yet whether they will continue to obey the orders of Ho's successors.

3. The mountainous north of Thailand is the home of about 250,000 Meos and Yaos. On the allegiance of these tribesmen, Buddhism, the religion of Thailand, seems to have no particular hold—nor do they share the emotional feeling that most Thais have toward King Bhumibol. When the Meos first began showing signs of communist influence, the Thai army with typical ruthlessness moved thousands of them to lowland concentration camps, and also napalmed mountain villages. The tribesmen then began to respond to this treatment with Chinese AK-47 rifles instead of traditional bows and arrows.

Thailand is receiving about $200 million a year from the spending of the United States military at the bases and also the Americans' spending on rest and recreation from Vietnam. The Thai economy is growing about 8 percent a year. And some of this income is spent trying to open up the northeast with roads and water.

# SWINGING THAILAND

ARRIVING IN BANGKOK from Delhi is a cultural shock, for the capital of Thailand is frenetic with traffic. The street scenes of Bangkok are consequently very different from Delhi. The importers of Thailand seem to be working overtime, bringing in Japanese, German, and American cars in quantities that are now far in excess of the city's ability to handle traffic. The rush begins in the early morning and after only an hour the main streets are clotted with apparently inextricable tangles of jammed vehicles. What does flow freely is human sweat, for the temperature is at 88° F. well before noon and it is very humid.

Most of Bangkok's traffic fortunately is not by road but by river and canal. The city is interlaced with canals, and housewives go shopping by boat. But the craving to be up to date has also overtaken the canal traffic. The boats that formerly were rowed with seemingly effortless grace get their velocity from racketing outboard motors. Spirited youths go shooting up and down the canals like rockets, sending great waves washing through the waterside wooden homes. Even saffron-robed Buddhist monks, their heads shaved and with the poker faces that presumably connote deep meditation, seem always in a hurry and they too race past in speedboats. The tourists who go by boat to visit Bangkok's famous floating markets willy nilly travel noisily also. The tourist craft are all equipped with ear-splitting engines, as well as with guides whose volubility is a waste of breath as not a word can be heard. The tourist boats are too large and unwieldy to go fast in the narrow canals that are jammed with other craft. The smaller speedboats race around them, impartially soaking everyone with spray. Slowly, but amid enormous mechanical din, the tourists make their wet way up the canals, past floating gardens, hibiscus, coconut trees, flamboyants, orchids of breathtaking loveliness, and other tropical blossoms. It is like traveling through paradise, encased in a private hell of deafening cacaphony.

According to the Thai foreign minister Mr. Thanat Khoman, Thailand is "a paradise threatened by communism." The communists, however, are not in evidence in Bangkok. They are miles off, in the trackless north and northeast, on or near the border with Laos; and also in the extreme south, in the jungles on the Malaysian frontier. What is very much in evidence in Bangkok is American influence. There are 50,000 American airmen in Thailand, and thousands more American military descend on Bangkok from Vietnam for "rest and recreation." The inevitable consequence is a proliferation of Happy clubs, Seesaw bars, and prostitution. Less crude, but perhaps more significant, is the kind of American influence that was mentioned by Under Secretary U. Alexis Johnson, when he was ambassador to Thailand in 1960. Mr. Johnson said then that "Thailand presents an opportunity for American capital to demonstrate what private enterprise can accomplish in the economic development of a country." American capital and know-how have been hard at work ever since, and the demonstration has duly taken place. There is a widening gap between the rich and the poor; an obsession with gaudy consumer goods that so far has benefited Japanese and American exporters rather than Thai craftsmen or manufacturers; rising prices, jangled nerves, increasing crime, and a stampede of people into the towns which are incapable either of employing all the immigrants or of decently housing them. The economists point, with pride, to the 8 percent rate of annual growth of Thailand's gross national product. But about half of this seems to be directly derived from American military spending on such items as the six air bases ($700 million) and a new deepwater port ($150 million). This military spending which has now gone on in Thailand for about a decade, and the presence of the 50,000 American airmen, are of course entirely due to the Vietnam war. When that war ends, neither the Thais nor anyone else have the faintest idea of what will happen to Thailand or to the Thai economy. The plethora of imported consumer goods that is so overwhelmingly visible in Bangkok suggests that the Thais are not taking too much thought for the morrow, and certainly are not copying the Indians' puritanism and frugality, and taxing and denying themselves in the present in the hope of becoming more self-sufficient at some future date, and hopefully as soon as possible.

This is not to say that nothing whatever is being done and that all the American money is passing through reckless Thai hands into Japanese and other pockets. The Thai government talks a good deal about national planning and development, and it has some excellent economists. But Thailand's affairs have always been in the control of a tiny elite that has not been notorious for penny-pinching, and in any case the task of developing Thailand presents serious problems. The 36 million Thais are mostly peasants with hardly any education and few if any skills save those that are traditional and therefore now outmoded. There is not much scope for manufacture and little chance of creating a common market with neighboring countries except, perhaps, Malaysia. Such small industry as exists is dominated by elite families who also run the government bureaucracy, *are* the military, and who are all related to one another.

Thailand's fortune, apart from fortuitous American military spending, lies in its fine rice that it is able to sell abroad to India and other countries. As far as manufactures are concerned, the Thais seem unable to outsell even the Indians, far less the astute and determinedly profit-conscious Japanese. The government planners have not been able to do very much for Thai small businessmen, or for the uprooted peasants who stream into the towns. (They are uprooted in part because, with rising land values, the landowners have wakened to the profitability of more intensive development, and to their ability to dispense with tenants.) Not a great deal has been done, either, for the peasants who are still on the land, who grumble that they are not getting their share of water from the new irrigation schemes.

The government professes keenness to develop the northeast where the guerrillas are causing trouble and where incomes are on the average only half of the average elsewhere. But although about one Thai in three lives in the northeast, so far only about $2 per head is being spent on rural development there. There are said to be about 3,000 guerrillas operating in the northeast, and about a thousand near the Malaysian border in the south. For at least five years, the guerrillas have been bathed in a floodlight of no doubt gratifying publicity, accompanied by horrendous forecasts of Thailand being subverted into another Vietnam. In fact, the guerrillas who have little or no popular support have so far shown themselves incapable of more than murderous assault on local officials and government spies, of whom they do manage to dispose between 100 and 150 each year. This is in a population of 12 million scattered in remote villages. As most of the disaffected are refugees originally from Vietnam, Meo tribesmen, or people of Laotian origin, Thailand's northeast problem is scarcely different from India's endemic Naga and Mizo tribal difficulties. What gives it significance is the Vietnam war, the presence of North Vietnamese troops in neighboring Laos, and anti-Thai rumblings from Peking. The rest of Thailand, and probably not more than a fraction of the northeast itself despite its backwardness, is emphatically not a hay rick that only awaits a subversive match to burst into flames.

Thailand's real problem comes from a directly opposite source, the impact on its way of life of "what private enterprise can accomplish." The impact is already severe, and the question is how the Thais intend to react to it. The Thai tradition is to be flexible, to bend with the wind and bow to the storm, but to make the most of every opportunity to retain as much as possible of Thai values without being forced or maneuvered into open, therefore costly, defense of them. That is how the Thais dealt with the Japanese in World War II; how they would probably deal with a similar Chinese threat if one seriously emerged; and how they appear to be dealing with the current onslaught on them of western modernization. Thus far, in spite of considerable social stresses, they seem to be doing rather well. But the stresses are bound to increase, and the outcome is still uncertain. Recently, after a decade of virtual military rule, Thailand returned to a weak solution of parliamentary democracy. This experiment had been tried before, but was discarded without much popular commotion because of corrupt politicians and ambitious military men. The military caste, led by Marshal Thanom Kittikachorn who prefers to operate in the post of prime minister rather than to appear as a junta leader, and General Prapas Charusathiara who modestly robes his strong-man role in the cloak of minister of interior, ran up a United Thai People's Party on their political sewing machines, and went to the polls with it. The results may have surprised them. They lost Bangkok to the opposition democrats led by Seni Pramoj, and had to maneuver to win or buy the allegiance of 72 elected independents. The military were not dislodged, for they got 76 of the lower house's 219 seats, to the democrats' 57, and on all vital issues the lower house votes jointly with the senate, which is three-quarters its size and is rendered doubly innocuous by consisting of appointees of the executive. Moreover, all the politicians, in government or in opposition, and including the socialists as well as the independents, are merely factions of the Thai upper classes, and mostly related to one another, as the military are. The elections nevertheless removed any fears that ten years of military rule had made Thais supine or had hopelessly brainwashed them. Mr. Pramoj gave the military a good tongue-lashing, and the successful independents as well as the scores of candidates who ran and failed, or who tried but failed to run, were no less outspoken. In the countryside, peasants freely cussed the government for its corruption and its neglect of them. Finally, as soon as the successful candidates of all parties had assembled in Bangkok, bold members of the winning UTPP as well as democrats and independents announced they intended to try to force the government to see to it that poor peasants as well as rich landlords got a proper share of irrigation water, and also that curbs were put on the police, who in Thailand have until now had the power to prosecute as well as to arrest.

The parliament that the military had long promised to restore, and finally did, might still be only a toy; but it was also a model that pointed the way to a stronger legislative branch in a not too far-off future.

Some rich Thais, including ones who made their pile only recently, conscientiously devote a portion of their wealth to schools or to other good causes. Nevertheless, the gap between rich and poor in Thailand is widening. An increasing number of wealthy Thais send their children abroad to school in Switzerland, or elsewhere in the west. An increasing number of the children of the poor do not get any schooling at all. This is because there are very few schools and rapidly rising numbers of school-age children. At higher levels of education, Thailand has so far not shared in the student unrest that is sweeping other countries. This is not because Thai college students are less dissatisfied with a world they never made, but because each time there is a threat of trouble the king of Thailand rushes to the scene and restores harmony, or at least its appearance, just by his presence. King Bhumibol is 43, was born in Cambridge, Massachusetts—as a result of the ups and downs of prewar Thai politics when his mother for safety's sake was out of the country—and he has been on the throne since his elder brother was mysteriously murdered in Bangkok, in 1946. The king has a beautiful queen and is devoted to her and also to the saxophone, which he likes to play alongside leading jazz musicians who visit Thailand from time to time. But, more important to his country, he is extremely popular with youth, especially the students, who will generally do whatever he requests. The ruling military and the politicians are well aware of this, and King Bhumibol uses his influence with great skill both to allay discontent and also to pressure the ruling elite into some concessions and reforms they otherwise might refuse.

# THE THAIS AND VIETNAM

MR. KLAEW NOVAPATI was the member of parliament for Khon Kaen, and also the deputy leader of a mildly socialist political group in Thailand called the Economist-Unity Party. He thought that Senator Fulbright and Professor Reischauer were quite right to question the stationing of more than 50,000 American military in Thailand. As the Economist-Unity Party is only a small opposition faction, Mr. Novapati's view might not be deemed too important. The reason it is of significance is that almost identical views were expressed by the Thai foreign minister Mr. Thanat Khoman, and the powerful Minister of Interior General Prapas Charusathiara. Furthermore, the policy they seem to prefer—depending less on military forces for safety and giving more weight to raising standards of living as a means of warding off both external and internal threats—was also approved by Prince Sihanouk of Cambodia; the prime minister of Laos, Mr. Souvanna Phouma; the prime minister of the Republic of Singapore, Mr. Lee Kuan Yew; and the president of Indonesia, General Suharto. These southeast Asian views were conveyed to Secretary of State William P. Rogers, in Bangkok in May 1969, at the meeting of the Council of the Southeast Asia Treaty Organization, and were not without effect on American policy.

The SEATO treaty was signed in Manila in September 1954, and the United States Senate approved it overwhelmingly, 82–1. This is not surprising. Though the pact led step by step to large military commitments that have since become unpopular, it is mildly worded. All it ostensibly did was to commit each of the parties to "act . . . in accordance with its constitutional processes" to meet a common danger in the event of "aggression by means of armed attack." But the SEATO treaty, and perhaps the fact that Bangkok was the headquarters of the SEATO organization, got American politicians into the habit of making large supportive gestures toward Thailand. Thus Vice President Johnson on May 17, 1961, proclaimed, in Bangkok, "Nothing is more important to the United States than the security of your great country." *Nothing* more important to Americans than Thailand's security? The Thais might well have smiled indulgently at the big American's Texas-style exuberance, and taken his words with a pinch of salt. In fact, they treated them with utmost seriousness, or professed to, because Thailand was then at loggerheads with China and also with Cambodia and Vietnam. On February 18, 1962, the then attorney general, the late Senator Robert Kennedy, confirmed Johnson's pledge by declaring, also in Bangkok, "the United States is dedicated to the security of Thailand." A month later, Secretary Dean Rusk and Thai Foreign Minister Thanat Khoman issued a weightily worded joint statement that was tantamount to a full military alliance between the two countries, save that the United States Senate was never called on to ratify it. Two months later, in May 1962, President Kennedy sent 4,800 American military to be stationed in Thailand. That was still not an enormous commitment. But the subsequent massive American involvement in the Vietnamese civil war automatically led to escalation of the American forces in nearby Thailand. Of the seven American air bases in Thailand, the three major ones at Udorn, Sakolnakorn and Nakhon Phanom are in the troubled north and northeast. But they are not used, nor would they be of the slightest use, for fighting the guerrilla bands who emerge from the northern jungles to murder Thai government officials and informers in remote villages. The air bases were built for the purpose of bombing North Vietnam. They could also be used for bombing China. They are closer to China than Guam is, and the closest the U.S. has so far got to China's nuclear weapons installations. The Chinese may have attempted to speed up their nuclear weapon development because of the implied threat to their installations from the American air bases in north and northeast Thailand.

Possibly the belated realization that the large U.S. military presence in their country, while provoking some discontent among ordinary Thai people, was not really intended to help the Thai government quell jungle guerrillas, was what moved Thai leaders like Foreign Minister Thanat Khoman to take a less favorable view of the Americans than before. More likely, however, they had come to realize that the United States was not only not going to "win" the Vietnam war but that American public opinion would shortly compel a drastic cutback in American forces in southeast Asia, especially Thailand. The Thai government never wished Thailand to become merely a fallback position for the United States, in the event of Vietnam being lost. All it did was to permit the United States to build air bases in Thailand, to help "win" the Vietnam war. But the battle was to be fought, and won or lost, in Vietnam, never in Thailand. As hopes of a decisive American military victory in Vietnam faded, the Thais showed increasing uneasiness about the implications of huge American military installations on their soil. The Thais were also much disconcerted by the *Pueblo* spy ship incident and the way it was handled by Washington. America suffered severe loss of face in Bangkok and indeed in all other Asian capitals by the North Korean capture of the *Pueblo* in January 1968. The line that the Thais are now taking is that there is going to be a western military withdrawal from southeast Asia—the British have already announced they will be out by the end of 1971—and that the southeast Asians must fill this vacuum themselves, but not with military alliances, which have been rendered distinctly unfashionable by the course of events over the fifteen years since SEATO was signed. The new watchword is "regional cohesiveness."

Mr. Thanat Khoman explained to newsmen in February 1969 that the countries of the region, including Indonesia, did not have and never could have the kind of military potential that would protect them from an armed attack by a big country like China. But, he added, if they stuck together, and kept their heads, the chances were that no Chinese armed attack would be launched against them, and if the communists tried subversion, the answer to *that* was to see to it that their people were content and were making too much material progress to be subverted. General Suharto of Indonesia responded the next month to this suggestion by the Thai foreign minister. The Indonesian leader told a group of U.S. publishers and businessmen, in March, that the best deterrent to any expansionist move by China was to make and keep southeast Asia prosperous. "Indonesia," he declared, "opposes foreign military bases, and military pacts." And the keynote had really been struck months before, in December 1968, by the prime minister of Singapore; Lee Kuan Yew had then said: "I would hope that the others around us—particularly to the north of us—don't lose their nerve. I don't believe that Thailand, for instance, can be subverted and destroyed by the same processes which have undermined South Vietnam, because I think basically they are a different type of people. They are Thais and they have a history of their own, a culture of their own. It is a culture which doesn't lend itself to guerrilla fanaticism, which is what is required for a successful guerrilla insurrection. And so, if we don't lose our nerve . . . the rest of southeast Asia will stick and will jell, and . . . we will all cooperate and help each other flourish and prosper, and grow stronger and more secure."

In 1966, Asian countries formed an Asian and Pacific Council (ASPAC) whose members are Australia and New Zealand, Taiwan, Japan, South Korea, Malaysia, the Philippines, Thailand, and South Vietnam. The following year, an Association of Southeast Asian Nations was formed (ASEAN), consisting of Malaysia, Singapore, the Philippines, Thailand, and Indonesia. Hitherto, that kind of regional cooperation in Asia had been just what Lee Kuan Yew once called it—"a thinly disguised exercise in collectively soliciting aid from the wealthy nations." But now that the United States as well as Britain looked like withdrawing the bulk of its military forces from the area, the Asians got more serious about their own cooperation. Thus, Thailand publicly abandoned its longstanding grievances and territorial claim against Cambodia, and Mr. Thanat Khoman explained that the Thais had done this to set an example, in order to persuade other countries in southeast Asia to forget about their feuds with one another. He almost certainly had in mind Indonesia's quarrels with Malaysia and Singapore, and the Philippines' claim to Sabah, the portion of Borneo which chose to join with Malaysia, in a popular plebiscite, instead of joining either the Philippines or Indonesia.

When the war was over, what would the U.S. do? The Thais would not mind having a reduced American force remaining in Thailand, at least for a while, to see what was what. But nothing like 50,000 troops. Most southeast Asians hoped the Americans would continue economic aid, for example by going on with Mekong River development. The Mekong is 2,500 miles long, and for 1,500 miles it flows through Vietnam, Cambodia, Laos, and Thailand. Dams and irrigation works could make the area one of the great granaries of the world, the former World Bank president, Eugene Black, said. However, guerrillas in Laos had attacked Japanese workers who were building the United Nations' Nguyen Dam, 40 miles northwest of Vientiane, the Laotian capital. Clearly, no sustained development was possible until the fighting stopped.

## THE PRINCELY POLITICIAN

CAMBODIA, 70,000 SQUARE miles in area, is about the size of Missouri and has a population of around seven million and is the Belgium of Asia so to speak. Pnom-Penh has been the capital of Cambodia since the 15th century, and the Cambodian monarchy endured from the 9th century, until Prince Norodom Sihanouk abolished it by refusing to succeed his father King Norodom Suramit, who died in 1960. Sihanouk prefers the role of top politician, but in March 1970 was surprised by a cabinet coup. There are no legitimate rivals, only the outlawed right wing Khmer Srei, which allegedly is linked to the American Central Intelligence Agency as well as to South Vietnam and Thailand. There is also a left wing Khmer Vietminh, which is openly allied with North Vietnam and with the Viet Cong in South Vietnam. The 35,000-man Cambodian army spends all its time running around the little country putting out bushfires started by one or another of Cambodia's foes.

The prince, now in his early 50's, has highly ambiguous relations with the United States, China, and Russia, for an obvious reason: He doesn't want his country to cease to exist. Once before, Cambodia retained its existence only by becoming a French protectorate, in 1864. This saved it from being partitioned between Thailand and Annam (Vietnam). That state of affairs ended when Japan chased out the French in World War II. After the defeat of Japan, Sihanouk declined to return his country to French rule.

At the same time, he stayed neutral in the war between the French and the Vietnamese communists. Neutrality has remained Sihanouk's policy and, he claims, his country's salvation—so far. He has had border disputes with the Thais and the South Vietnamese; he resents the armed intrusion on Cambodian territory by the North Vietnamese and the Americans. In July 1968, Sihanouk's little navy captured on the Mekong River an American troop transport with eleven American soldiers and one South Vietnamese soldier. Sihanouk offered to exchange the prisoners for 14 bulldozers which he said he wanted as compensation for 14 victims of an accidental American bombing of a Cambodian village. Meanwhile, the Americans were treated well as the "guests" of Sihanouk and the Cambodian people. Cambodia is that kind of country. Its tradition is Indian, not east Asian. It lives by selling rice, rubber, and maize, but its main resource is tourism. Thousands of people each year visit the famed Angkor Wat and other monuments of Cambodia's past.

Cambodia has never needed convincing that military alliances with larger powers are not the answer to southeast Asia's problems. The Cambodians know from their own history that emphasizing the military aspect is apt to lead to disaster. Between A.D. 700 and 1200, Cambodia was ruled by a military-theocratic complex. The god-king, or *devaraja,* imposed heavy taxes, and a draft, in order to fight a series of wars. These triumphs, which provoked peasant revolts and ruined the country, are commemorated in the vast monuments of Angkor Wat. This, and his own unfortunate experiences at the hands of the United States and others, convinced Prince Sihanouk of Cambodia that "it is force that governs the world, not right or justice." Throughout the Vietnam war, and for the foreseeable future, Cambodia's role is that of the man on the see-saw, striving to retain his balance. The traditional enemies of the Khmers (Cambodians) are the Thais and the North Vietnamese. One of these, Thailand, is an ally of the United States; the other is an ally of China and Russia. The population of Cambodia is about 7 million, of whom half a million are of Vietnamese descent, and over 300,000 are Chinese. Clearly, Cambodia's only hope of preserving its identity during the Vietnam war was to cling to a precarious neutrality, which in a region of uncertain borders was sure to be violated from time to time by one or other belligerent. But for years, it was American policy to frown severely on any southeast Asian country that dared to proclaim itself neutral. Sihanouk however was not the kind of man to remain silent in the face of even implied criticism. For years, he has kept the press of the world busy, printing his lengthy and elegantly sarcastic letters on foreign affairs. The United States was not his only target; he also criticized China, and France. But the United States matched Sihanouk in pique. It virtually accused him of giving aid and comfort to the Viet Cong while laughing up his sleeve at America and only hypocritically claiming to be neutral. There is no doubt that Viet Cong forces trespass on Cambodian territory from time to time, no doubt that Sihanouk knew it, and none that he had no way of preventing it. So the child's tantrums continued in both Pnom-Penh and Washington.

Sihanouk was intensely annoyed because his efforts to keep Cambodian rice reasonably priced, so as to satisfy both the farmer and the consumer, were thwarted by the big money that was offered for it by both the Viet Cong and Saigon which had plenty of dollars to spend. The prince had forbidden such sales, but of course they went on and he couldn't stop them. No doubt there were other sales as well, such as arms. The Cambodian military was accused of ordering from abroad far more arms than it itself could use, and selling off the surplus into Vietnam. The traffic, if it exists, was surely exaggerated. It was said that huge arms shipments passed through Sihanoukville, the Cambodian port. Sihanoukville moved about 750,000 tons of cargo a year. The figure for Singapore was more than 30 million tons.

Plain folk in Cambodia have benefited enormously from Prince Sihanouk's benevolent rule, and not only by his success, so far, in keeping them in peace, though that is an inestimable boon considering the present state of both Vietnam and Laos. But the prince has also managed to enlist his country's Buddhist clergy in exhorting the people to furnish voluntary labor for building roads, dams, schools, and hospitals. And Sihanouk, like King Bhumibol of Thailand, took the greatest care to stay in step with the youth of his country. He exercised his powers in close consultation with the university students, who are organized in an Assembly of Youth.

These powers of the prince were considerable, but he had them granted to him by popular vote (only 10 percent voted No). Cambodia has both a parliament and a cabinet, but the matters with which they can deal are restricted, and there are no political parties, called by Sihanouk "a luxury we are unable to afford at the present stage in our national development." However, the press seemed to be free to criticize the administration, and, said Sihanouk, "does not invariably adopt an indulgent approach." The National Assembly, in spite of its and their limited powers, sometimes lays hell into the cabinet. Sihanouk's system is almost impossible to define; it certainly isn't democracy, as westerners interpret the term. But then, says Sihanouk, the western form of democracy, French style, "was tried out here between 1947 and 1954, and reduced Cambodia to an indescribable state of anarchy." He is too polite to add that more than once it has done the same to France.

Sihanouk believes that the Vietnamese war "will end only when the United States agrees to the complete and unconditional withdrawal of its armed forces from South Vietnam." He also believes that the communist threat to Cambodia will persist and will probably increase when peaceful conditions have been restored to Vietnam. He says he doesn't trust the North Vietnamese communists any more than he trusts the Thais or the South Vietnamese. He is afraid of Communist China. But he says that combating subversion "is an internal problem and must be dealt with as such by the countries exposed to this threat." He has hinted that the maintenance of some American military forces in southeast Asia is desirable following the conclusion of hostilities in Vietnam, in "countries where their presence is welcome." That probably doesn't mean Cambodia.

Sihanouk is proud of the things he has done to improve education and the standard of living in his country. He is correspondingly resentful of what he regards as Western arrogance. "People from superdeveloped and wealthy countries," says Sihanouk, should "try to avoid the chauvinism which causes them to scorn small countries and poor people, even when these countries and peoples work hard." And he added that Cambodia, though small and poor, refuses to be anybody's satellite. "We depend on ourselves, and our modest resources, for building up our country." In fact, Cambodia has accepted modest amounts of aid from France, West Germany, East Europe, Australia, Russia, and China.

LAOS: GET THESE ELEPHANTS

OUT OF HERE!

LAOS IS SOMEWHAT smaller than Wyoming and has a population of about three million. The country was once called Lane Xang, meaning the kingdom of one million elephants. Most of the people are Buddhists, but a great many of them believe in powerful jungle spirits called Phi. As in India, there are numerous village festivals, and fertility ceremonies with singing of ballads and fireworks. Eighteen major dialects are spoken in one province alone.

Like Afghanistan, Laos has no railway. It does however have B-52s that come in from the United States bases in Thailand to drop a heavy rain of bombs on the estimated 40,000 North Vietnamese in east Laos, and on the Ho Chi Minh trail into South Vietnam from southern Laos. Laos also has United States "special forces," who fight on the ground against the Pathet Lao forces who are allied with the North Vietnamese communists.

For a long time, hardly anyone doubted that with a major push, the 40,000 North Vietnamese and the Pathet Lao forces could take over the western, Mekong Valley half of the country. It hasn't happened yet, and Laos continues to be precariously ruled by a government headed by Prince Souvanna Phouma, with the help of massive U.S. economic as well as military aid. Prince Sihanouk of Cambodia has already written Laos off. "The Vietminh have swallowed Laos," Sihanouk said prematurely in the spring of 1968. At the beginning of 1969, the correspondent of the London *Times*, Fred Emery, after visiting Vientiane, the capital of Laos, wrote: "It remains a dismal fact that during the last wet season, June to

September, the Laos government forces did not manage to retake the areas which they traditionally lose in the dry season, October to May." A bright young man in the Laos government service told Emery: "All the people living under the Pathet Lao would probably vote against them if there were elections. However, all the people on our side, who are the majority, would probably vote for the Pathet Lao, just for a change." In 1969, American bombing of communist targets in Laos was enormously stepped up, the CIA enthusiastically propelled its special force of 30,000 guerrilla Meo tribesmen against the Pathet Lao, and even the U.S. 7th Fleet was said to join in battles. As a consequence of this increased American military intervention, the 75,000-man Laotian army was reported to be pushing ahead again on the Plain of Jars, where military activity in Laos is mainly concentrated.

Arthur J. Dommen, in his splendid book *Conflict in Laos* (Praeger, 1964) describes the Plain of Jars in central Laos as rolling, and bright green, resembling the dairy land of southern Wisconsin, with an average elevation of 3,600 feet above sea level. The plain takes its name from scores of ancient stone jars that were found here. They are 2,000 years old and are probably funeral urns. Each jar is big enough to hold a man.

If the Pathet Lao and the North Vietnamese did succeed in overrunning all of Laos—they already occupy a considerable chunk of it—it is said that the Thais might enter the war. That remains to be seen. But what is this fighting in Laos all about?

Prince Souvanna Phouma, the prime minister and also the defense minister of Laos, and his communist half-brother Prince Souphanouvong, are the chief protagonists in this tragi-comedy. They were both brilliant scholars at the University of Paris where both took degrees in engineering. Souphanouvong made his first contact with the Indochina communists courtesy of General Phillip E. Gallagher, who headed a group of American military advisors in Vietnam at the time of the defeat of Japan which ended World War II. Gallagher was impressed by the capabilities of the new Vietnamese president Ho Chi

Minh, and he arranged Prince Souphanouvong's air trip to Hanoi, to meet Ho.

The Americans had failed to anticipate that the French whom they were busy releasing from Japanese prison camps would simply proceed to reoccupy Indo-China, thus falling foul of Ho Chi Minh and of the princes of Laos as well. Souphanouvong led guerrilla forces against the French in Laos, in tandem with the guerrilla war that was being waged against the French by the Vietminh in Vietnam. Prince Souvanna Phouma in 1949 accepted a compromise that was then offered by the French—United Nations membership for Laos, but with French predominance in foreign affairs. Souvanna Phouma went to Paris; but Souphanouvong fought on in Laos. About a year later, the United States position switched. Washington was moved by the Korean War to conclude that the French were, after all, right when they claimed that the fighting in Indo-China was part and parcel of a communist expansion that "must be contained." Congress began voting money to help the French fight the guerrillas in Indo-China, that is, in both Vietnam and Laos. In 1954, the French garrison of Dien Bien Phu, in Vietnam, was surrounded by the forces of General Giap of North Vietnam who then overran it. That was the end of the French effort to reoccupy Indo-China.

However, from Hanoi's point of view, the southern half of Vietnam remained to be liberated following the withdrawal of the French; especially after a promise that had been made in the 1954 Geneva agreements, to hold all-Vietnam elections by 1956, was brushed aside by the new government of South Vietnam of Ngo Dinh Diem. Because of the demilitarized zone between North and South Vietnam, Laos with its convenient jungle "trails" became strategically vital to North Vietnam for penetrating South Vietnam with armed support for the Viet Cong in South Vietnam.

In Laos, meanwhile the guerrilla forces led by Souphanouvong had shown willingness to enter into a coalition with Prince Souvanna Phouma who was now the prime minister of Laos. Souvanna Phouma was agreeable, although the American ambassador in Vientiane, Graham Parsons, advised against it. So Souphanouvong entered his half-brother's government. In subsequent elections, in the spring of 1958, Souphanouvong received more votes than any other candidate, and he became chairman of the Laos National Assembly. But following his electoral success, the United States abruptly cut off the aid it had been giving to Laos, and political power passed in the National Assembly to an anticommunist group, who excluded Souphanouvong from the government, and also packed Souvanna Phouma back to Paris as Laotian ambassador.

The new prime minister of Laos, following Souvanna Phouma, was called, perhaps appropriately, Phoui.

Russia as well as China was snubbed by Phoui, and the nationalist Chinese and the South Vietnamese were made welcome by him. As tension in Vientiane mounted, Souphanouvong was put under house arrest. Phoui was ousted at the end of 1959 by another right-winger, General Phoumi Nosavan, who had fought for the French, not against them, and who was now being supported by the American CIA. The idea was apparently to try to turn Laos into a "strong" state, like Thailand, run by the military.

The king of Laos intervened, on the advice of the British and French ambassadors and supported by the Secretary General of the United Nations—and the Laotian generals drew back to permit general elections, which however were rigged, to insure that the supporters of Souphanouvong would not gain from them. The rigging went a bit far; one Souphanouvong supporter who obviously had massive backing in his province was solemnly declared to have received only 13 votes to his opponent's 6,500 votes. At this juncture, Souphanouvong wisely escaped from his prison; his guards went along with him.

A paratrooper captain, Kong Le, decided that Laos was being led into a new form of colonization, this time under the Americans. Kong Le staged a successful coup. "I am tired of Lao fighting Lao," he told cheering crowds in Vientiane, "and of incompetence and corruption." Souvanna Phouma, back again from Paris, was conveniently on hand to preside over the National Assembly, and then to head a new cabinet and to become prime minister once more. He invited the Russians back to Vientiane to set up an embassy; the Americans were less popular.

The State Department dispatched former ambassador Graham Parsons back to Vientiane, to warn Souvanna Phouma to have no truck with Souphanouvong, else he would get no American aid (again). Souvanna Phouma sought Soviet aid, and proposed a *troika* government (named after the Russian 3-horse sleigh); the *troika* government that Souvanna Phouma suggested was to be headed by himself, his half brother Souphanouvong, and General Phoumi Nosavan. But Souphanouvong refused to deal with Nosavan, whose forces advanced on Vientiane. Kong Le's forces fought them; Souvanna Phouma fled to Cambodia. Nosavan won the battle but lost the war, for Kong Le became an ally of Souphanouvong and the Pathet Lao forces, and both were supplied arms by the Soviet Union, so that the Plain of Jars was rapidly transformed into a vast armed camp. (Arthur Dommen's explanation of why the Russians suddenly backed Kong Le is that "the Soviet Union was acting out of the imperative need to retain the allegiance of North Vietnam in the developing quarrel between Russia and China.")

The Kennedy administration meanwhile (this was early 1961) backed Nosavan's forces. The U.S. had again picked the wrong horse for military as well as political purposes. Nosavan took American guns, grenades, and money, but his soldiers spent all their time fishing. A cease fire was proclaimed May 3, and Kennedy and Khrushchev sought to patch things up.

Souvanna Phouma, back in circulation once again, sent a delegation to truce talks, as did the Souphanouvong–Kong Le forces, and the Nosavan forces. A conference of foreign ministers assembled in Geneva to discuss Laos. Souvanna Phouma visited Hanoi. Finally, his original notion of a *troika* government was fulfilled, with himself as prime minister, and Nosavan and Souphanouvong as the two deputy prime ministers. General Nosavan was also finance minister, and in that capacity this doughty anticommunist was compelled to make business trips to both Hanoi and Peking, because North Vietnam and China had decided to help the new Laotian government and themselves by building strategic roads in Laos.

All three parties to the Laotian government continued to run their own armies, however, and meanwhile, the United States and North Vietnam were getting more involved in the fighting going on inside South Vietnam where the government of Ngo Dinh Diem was approaching the end of its road. The Ho Chi Minh trails through Laos carried increasing traffic from North Vietnam to South Vietnam. A departing American, Major General Ruben H. Tucker, gave his own view of the Laos situation that differed somewhat from the optimism that was then expressed in Moscow, Washington, and Geneva. He called it "a can of worms."

On the Plain of Jars, tension now crackled between the Pathet Lao forces of Souphanouvong and the forces of Kong Le. Fighting between the soldiers broke out in the spring of 1963, and Souphanouvong immediately left Vientiane to join his Pathet Lao at Kheng Khey. The Americans began to supply Kong Le with arms, the Pathet Lao was not so much beefed up as swallowed up by North Vietnamese military units in Laos. In May 1964, the State Department confirmed that American jets were making reconnaissance flights over the Plain of Jars—the Pathet Lao had shot one down and captured the pilot.

By the fall of 1969, after five years of ridiculously inconclusive fighting, Congress was pressing hard on President Nixon to reveal the full extent of American military participation in Laos. And inevitably Prince Souvanna Phouma, still prime minister, turned up in Washington, in October, to ask Nixon to keep the aid coming but to keep it as quiet as possible. At a news conference, President Nixon explained, presumably for the benefit of those Americans who still hadn't taken it in, that "Laos relates very much to Vietnam because the Ho Chi Minh trail runs through Laos . . . we do have aerial reconnaissance, we do have perhaps some other activity." The

United States military aid program to Laos was in fact estimated at $300 million a year.

A new Laos coalition government would be Souvanna Phouma, now 59, and his half brother Souphanouvong, now 57. For the *troika* has clearly broken down, and General Phoumi Nosavan is in exile, in Bangkok. Souphanouvong still has his cabinet title of deputy prime minister and minister of national economy. His political party, the Neo Lao Haksat, his equivalent of South Vietnam's National Liberation Front, still has its headquarters in Vientiane (guarded and staffed by Pathet Lao soldiers). Meanwhile, economically as well as militarily, Laos under Souvanna Phouma is totally dependent on U.S. aid, without which it would collapse.

Most of the country is in the control of Laotian communists, North Vietnamese, or corrupt Laotian generals of no particular ideology who behave like old-style Chinese warlords. The writ of Souvanna Phouma's government does not run far from the capital, Vientiane. The communists probably could capture Vientiane tomorrow, but prefer to use the "neutral" country as a corridor for supplies from North to South Vietnam. The mass of people are sick of both sides and of the continuous inconclusive fighting. Souvanna Phouma would like to see a coalition government in South Vietnam, with the Viet Cong included in it, for he thinks this might enable Laos to have a coalition government also, as it once briefly did. And if the Vietnam war ended in there being a coalition government in Saigon, perhaps the 40,000 North Vietnamese troops in Laos would go home.

A coalition government in Saigon no doubt would be merely a face-saving formula for the United States, disguising a communist takeover long enough to enable the Americans to get out without too enormous loss of prestige. That at any rate was what most southeast Asians suspected. But they really saw no better alternative. President Johnson's decision not to face the American electorate again, and the *Pueblo* snafu, convinced them that the U.S. is on its way out of South Vietnam, and also out of Asia in its role of "policeman." They expected that sooner or later there would appear in South Vietnam a "popular front," perhaps led by Tran Van Don, the former general, or "Big" Minh, another general. Then all the South Vietnamese who had secretly been either neutral or procommunist, people in the South Vietnam bureaucracy, the pagodas, the labor unions, and so forth, would take courage to declare their true feelings. After that, southeast Asians said, it would be fairly easy to arrange an end of the war, for the more prominent members of the popular front would be "top people" who are related, either by blood or marriage, to the top people in North Vietnam. It really was a Vietnamese civil war, after all, they said. This fact of course might not prevent a good deal of bloodletting after the event; and the southeast Asians were prepared to wax indignant if the United States failed to offer sanctuary to those on the American (and losing) side who were in danger of slaughter. Nevertheless, a popular front could, it was believed, end the war. Some time after that, a reunified communist Vietnam seemed likely. For how could the noncommunists in the south hold out against the communists, when the latter knew what they wanted, whereas the former were fragmented into about 80 factions?

## SOUTH VIETNAM: THE

## THIRTY YEARS WAR

SOUTH VIETNAM IS 65,700 square miles in size, somewhat smaller than North Dakota, and has about 17 million people. "The Vietnamese," says the admirable Far Eastern Economic Review, "are first found as a people in South China and the Red River Delta who fell under Chinese control in the 2nd century B.C." The Chinese held the Delta area for a thousand years, calling it Annam, the pacified south; but revolts were none the less frequent. Thus it is seen that pacification programs in Vietnam are nothing new, and rarely successful.

A century ago, to come abruptly to more modern times, Vietnam with Laos and Cambodia composed Indochina, whose masters were the French. In the second world war of this century, the Japanese swept away the French power, but the French returned after the Japanese defeat to fight the new communist government that had declared Vietnam independent and that had set up its rule in Hanoi under Ho Chi Minh. The ensuing war ended in another French military defeat, at Dien Bien Phu, and in the temporary partition of Vietnam along its 17th parallel, which the Geneva agreement of 1954 said would come to an end, and Vietnam would be reunited, by elections to be held in 1956. These elections however were refused by the American-supported government in South Vietnam of Ngo Dinh Diem. In the ensuing years, Diem suppressed all his political opponents, right and left wing alike, and in 1959 a revolt against him by the Viet Cong gained, at first halting and dubious, then increasingly confident, support from the rulers of North Vietnam. This revolt spread so far that the United States finally passed from giving military aid to supplying American military forces to fight in South Vietnam. None of which prevented Diem's fall—he was captured and murdered by his own military who had staged a coup against him in November 1963, a fatal month—in the United States, President Kennedy was killed.

By the fall of 1964, not only had America's dream faded of making Ngo Dinh Diem the "Winston Churchill of Asia," in Lyndon Johnson's immortally unhappy phrase; it had been brutally destroyed and turned to nightmare by Diem's murder, and South Vietnam was on the verge of collapse. The Viet Cong threatened to cut South Vietnam in half and both the South Vietnamese army and the civilian administration had broken down. The Russians falsely concluded that the United States would accept a communist victory now and Soviet Premier Kosygin in February 1965 visited both Hanoi and Peking. The Russians favored finding for the United States a face-saving formula, rather than forcing on the United States a military defeat. Kosygin said he would support a new Geneva conference; this had been proposed by the Cairo conference of nonaligned nations, in October 1964. Hanoi was dubious. Russia at the 1954 Geneva conference had wrongly advised Hanoi that as a consequence of the agreements reached there, not only would the French get out but all of Vietnam would soon be ruled over by Ho Chi Minh. Peking was worse than dubious about the Russian proposal; it was strongly opposed. It declared that it could smell a Soviet-American trap. "We have every reason to think you have ulterior motives," the Chinese insultingly told the Russians. And Peking declared to the world, "The heart of the matter is that the Soviet revisionist leading group has already degenerated into an accomplice of United States imperalism."

The net effect of these crosscurrents and cross purposes was that Hanoi took that part of Chinese advice which related to not negotiating, but tried out its own recipe (which the Chinese had advised against) of a 1968 Tet offensive against the Americans. The heavy Viet Cong losses that Lin Piao had warned against were duly incurred; but Hanoi's confidence that it could keep Saigon off balance and that U.S. casualties in Vietnam would weaken the U.S. will to fight, was not diminished. And President Johnson did halt the bombing of North Vietnam, peace talks were initiated in Paris, and candidate Nixon did foreshadow the United States military withdrawal steps that President Nixon did begin to take in 1969.

After several post-Diem coups, power in Saigon had passed in 1965 to General Ky, who however was forced to share it in October 1967 with General Nguyen Van Thieu who became president of South Vietnam, with Ky as vice president and with little influence.

According to a statement by Averell Harriman in Paris in May 1968, North Vietnam had at that time 85,000 men in South Vietnam. Thieu had 800,000 men, including local militia and police; and fighting alongside Thieu's men in South Vietnam were 538,000 Americans, and 64,000 allied soldiers, mainly South Koreans and Thais.

In 1968, Dr. Phan Quang Dan was fired from the Thieu government for "advocating direct talks with the National Liberation Front" (during a visit to the United States). For the same offense, Trong Dinh Dzu got five years' hard labor. Dzu had run for president in September 1967 and had given Thieu a fright by coming in second as an independent.

There are many thousands of political prisoners in South Vietnam. Their treatment was investigated by an American study team whose members included a former American admiral and the dean of the Boston College Law School. The team reported in June 1969. When they visited Vietnam, the study team were told that "it is not unusual to torture family members, including children, before the eyes of a prisoner, who then tells everything." Saigon government officials meanwhile reported that the North Vietnamese and Viet Cong each year kidnap and murder some 3,000 South Vietnamese civilians.

Other conditions in South Vietnam included:

1. Millions of refugees, perhaps as much as one-third of the rural population; 80 percent of them fled from United States

bombing. Most came to the cities, and as a result, Saigon with nearly three million people has become the world's most crowded city in terms of population concentration (twice Tokyo's).

2. The Vietnam landscape is moon-cratered. B-52's have dropped more bombs in South Vietnam than were dropped on all the Axis powers in World War II.

3. Inflation, blackmarketing, all forms of corruption are rampant.

4. Anti-American feeling is intense.

American *economic* aid to South Vietnam from 1954 to the middle of 1968 totaled more than $4 billion; in the 12 months to June 3, 1969, it was $400 million. A leading South Vietnamese politician said bitterly, "We are beggars from the world in order to destroy ourselves."

Food production barely held steady. Industrial production was pretty much at a standstill.

These conditions were duplicated in North Vietnam.

# NORTH VIETNAM: UNCLE WHO?

SLIGHTLY SMALLER THAN South Vietnam, North Vietnam is 63,360 square miles in area, roughly the size of the State of Washington. Like South Vietnam, the North has about 17 million population, most of them crowded into the Red River Delta. The country is barely self-sufficient in food, but has lots of coal and minerals which, however, are largely undeveloped; development seems to have been brought almost to a standstill by the American bombing. United States planes began attacking North Vietnam in February 1965, and continued doing so with some trifling intermissions until the end of October 1968. Food production just managed to keep up. Industrial production was pretty much confined to maintenance and repair work.

Russian military aid to North Vietnam is estimated at about $500 million a year. Chinese military aid is estimated at $150 million. The North Vietnamese well could echo the complaint of the South Vietnamese legislator quoted in the last section who said that both Vietnams were being destroyed by their allies.

Perhaps some of the North Vietnamese dare to say the same. The ruling party has bitterly attacked writers and artists, and what it called "stubborn elements in the former exploiting classes, landlords and capitalists, reactionary elements profiting by religion (presumably Buddhists and Catholics), the former puppet administration, army elements not wanting to transform themselves, and other reactionary and sabotaging elements instigated by the imperialists, mainly the American ones."

Ho Chi Minh died in 1969, pushing 80. That left as leading

strong men in the North: Pham Van Dong; Le Duan; General Vo Nguyen Giap; and the pro-Chinese hardliner on the war, Truong Chinh.

Hanoi fears China and leans on Russia but distrusts Russia also. Russia played a key role in arranging the 1954 Geneva conference that seemed to promise 1956 elections which Hanoi hoped would result in "Uncle Ho" winning, and reunification of Vietnam speedily following. When in 1956 elections were *not* held, Moscow was almost mute on the subject. And the next year, Moscow blandly proposed that "both Vietnams" be admitted to the United Nations, thus conceding, which Hanoi never has, that there really are two Vietnams.

China's advice to Hanoi—in keeping with Mao's theory of creating the New Man through prolonged severe struggle— was to fight, without seeking much outside help, a long war of attrition in which the Viet Cong should stay on the defensive until the "balance of forces" changed, no matter how long that took. "Serious losses and heavy setbacks" to the revolution would be the consequence of ignoring this advice, the Chinese defense minister Lin Piao warned. Lin of course also condemned any idea of negotiating with the imperialist enemy. Hanoi, however, retorted—for instance, through army speeches in May 1966—that Hanoi and the Viet Cong could defeat the imperialist enemy by taking the offensive. Le Duan, the secretary general of the Lao Dong party, declared proudly: "Since the day the South Vietnamese people rose up, they have continually taken the offensive."

Hanoi's distrust of the Soviet Union relates to 1954; but Hanoi's distrust of Peking goes back at least to 1953, when Hanoi agreed to copy the Chinese land reform program, and brought in Chinese advisers who procured the execution of thousands of so-called "landlords and rich peasants" in the North. Hanoi was later to admit that it all had been a grave error, and Party Secretary-General Truong Chinh was demoted. This bloody debacle made Hanoi very suspicious of Chinese advice.

Should Hanoi fail to win the war in the sense of reuniting Vietnam under Hanoi's communist rule, North Vietnam is likely to find itself in a similar situation to North Korea, which has not managed to conquer the South and is no longer supported by either Russia or China, having quarreled with both of them. In spite of what some American policy-makers think, North Vietnam has never willingly done China's bidding.

If Hanoi did succeed in reuniting Vietnam under its leadership, the united and presumably communist Vietnamese would probably seek to incorporate Laos and Cambodia also, as Ho Chi Minh certainly hoped to be the natural heir of the French in the whole area that used to be called Indo-China. This would re-enact, under somewhat misleading ideological labels, the ancient history of the region which has traditionally taken the form of struggle for mastery between Tonkinese, Annamese, and others. But it is not certain that the Chinese would permit Hanoi to come out on top. Peking might very well dislike the idea of a strong, independent-minded (and traditionally anti-Chinese) Hanoi, the same way as Stalin resented Tito's Yugoslavia. The area, in short, has its own built-in balance of historical forces that make it seem unlikely that Vietnam would attempt or could succeed, to set up an empire on the Mekong.

## AMERICA AND SOUTHEAST ASIA

AT THE END of World War II, the United States plunged all too lightheartedly into an area, bordering China, of almost infinite ethnic and linguistic, as well as political and economic and also religious complexity (French-converted Catholics in Vietnam have been a major factor in that tortured country's politics). The region had a very long history; for example, the Vietnamese could say with almost complete truth that once they were ruled by China for 1,000 years, but that that ended 2,000 years ago.

On examination, the "Vietnamese" turned out to be composed of Tonkinese, Annamese, and other elements, each with strong individuality—like Serbs and Croats or Englishmen, Scots, Irish, and Welsh; yet at the same time there was undoubtedly something, hard to define, that was nevertheless identifiable as a "Vietnamese" feeling and spirit.

The Cambodians were Khmers, but then there were also Khmers in South Vietnam, plenty of them. Many Laotians seemed never to be quite sure whether or not they were really Thais, and some northern Thais had almost no concept of being "Thai" or of owing any allegiance to either the government in Bangkok or to the Thai royal house; while many Thais, and these not the least powerful, politically as well as economically, were really Chinese.

Most of the people in all those countries were Buddhists; but as we have noted, there were Christians, too; and if the culture seemed obviously derived from that of China, in many aspects it was no less unmistakably not Chinese at all, but rather Hindu—hence, no doubt, "Indo-China."

These were some of the myriad complexities and contradictions, paradoxes and subtle interweavings, that were concealed by the bald mention of such uninformative and even misleading labels as "Vietnam," "Cambodia," "Thailand," and "Laos." But in 1945 hardly one American in 100,000 had even heard of those names, far less been even dimly aware of the teeming realities which they concealed.

The United States went to the help of the French who were seeking to reimpose their rule on Indo-China after the collapse of the Japanese who had beaten the French. Why did America do so? Not, in fact, out of any special concern for the area itself or to "save it from communism" or to establish the credibility of the American pledge or because of a "domino" theory or for any of the other reasons that have been advanced since. The United States first held out a helping hand to the French because the then secretary of state Dean Acheson persuaded President Truman that France's friendship was important for the United States' role in *Europe*. Asian considerations hardly entered into it. Had Mr. Acheson been confronted at the time by John Kenneth Galbraith's aphorism, that it really does not matter to America whether some far-off Asian jungle calls itself communist or not, the overwhelming probability is that Acheson would have agreed unhesitatingly to this straightforward proposition.

Six years and a Korean war later, in 1954, the French were beaten on the Vietnam battlefield at Dien Bien Phu, despite having received extensive American military and economic assistance. They were beaten by the North Vietnamese communist forces of Ho Chi Minh, led by General Giap. The action then moved from the battlefields to Geneva where America grudgingly assented, without actually putting its signature, to an international agreement that divided Vietnam temporarily into two parts, north and south, but which looked forward to their reunification by means of elections. This was an improbable hope, as the communists were unlikely to hold free elections in the North, even if elections were held in the South in 1956 as the Geneva accords proposed. And the pious aspiration was made still less plausible by the plain determination of another American Secretary of State, John Foster

Dulles, to keep South Vietnam out of communist hands. Mr. Dulles persuaded President Eisenhower that America should in effect take the place of the French in Vietnam. This was not done, this time, on account of American interest in Europe. It was done because one of the participants at Geneva was Communist China, with whose "volunteers" America had just fought a bloody and costly war in Korea. It was Mr. Dulles's view that if Vietnam went communist, this would mean an extension of the power of China, which would then proceed to take over one Asian country after another, no doubt including Korea, and even Japan. Dulles sold this "domino" theory to President Eisenhower, who passed it on to President Kennedy.

Nine years later, in 1963, American support of the South Vietnam regime of Ngo Dinh Diem ended in the murder of Diem by his own army and a quick succession of military coups which by 1965 had brought South Vietnam to the verge of total collapse and promised a speedy victory for the Viet Cong and a communist government of all Vietnam. Once again an American president, this time Lyndon Johnson, had to decide if it mattered whether or not a small, backward Asian country that few Americans had ever heard of called itself communist; the decision was that it did matter very much, for President Johnson began an escalation of the United States military involvement in Vietnam that finally had well over one-half million Americans fighting there, of which number 10 percent would die before it was all over.

This in brief is the history of the Vietnam war. What lessons does it hold for future American policy in Southeast Asia? An aim of United States involvement in the war was to reassure other Asians that America keeps its pledges. But this may be more a threat than a reassurance to them. The Thais, as we have seen, do not want their country to be another Vietnam, either in the sense of threatening to go communist or of being rescued from that fate by an American army and air force fighting and bombing on Thai soil. The Thais hope to be able to make their own deal with China instead; as also does Cambodia. Laos, like Vietnam, has been heavily bombed as well as fought over, and most Laotians seem to be anxious only for peace under any sort of government. Meanwhile, and quite divorced from United States policy, China has gone through a major internal convulsion and at the same time has quarreled deeply and probably irrevocably with the Soviet Union, so that relations between those two huge communist countries in Asia will never again be the same as they were. This latter development is probably more significant for the future of the region and perhaps the world than anything the United States has done or failed to do in southeast Asia.

America however can take a long view. Having been deeply involved in the region's affairs for over 20 years, albeit disastrously, the United States can do better than merely cut its heavy losses. It can play a vital role in the development of southeast Asia, in cooperation with other interested nations, including Japan, through the Asian Development Bank, the World Bank, and other international agencies. The Mekong River will still be flowing when all the quarrels and crosspurposes have been forgotten. Dams and irrigation projects on the Mekong would be a better monument to American involvement in southeast Asia than the giant military installations that have been created in Thailand, for which the Thais are unlikely to have much use after the American military men leave, as leave they will.

Would spending President Johnson's proffered $1 billion aid to southeast Asia on harnessing and improving the Mekong be just throwing good money after bad? Even if it were, it would represent only about one thirtieth of the economic cost of a year of war in Vietnam. If, however, it succeeded in its purpose, it would be a war memorial of a not ignoble sort, erected in memory of 50,000 Americans who otherwise may have died in vain.

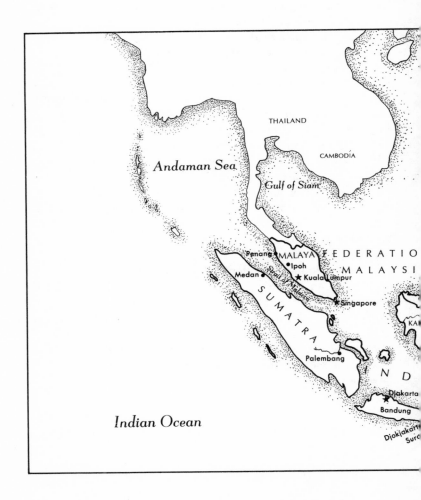

# 7

# THE CHINA SEA:

# MALACCA TO MANILA

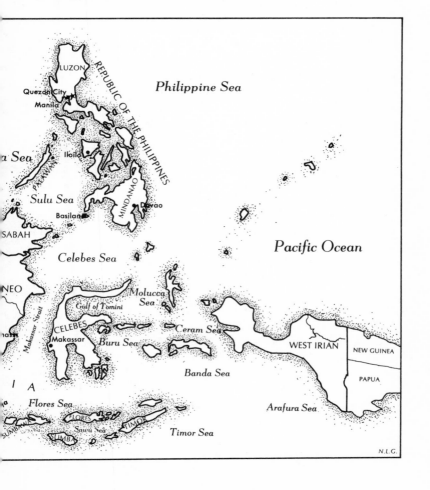

## MALAYSIA:

## DON'T SPIT ON YOUR NOSE

THE FEDERATION OF Malaysia is roughly the size of Montana, but like Pakistan is divided into two parts which are divided by about 600 miles of the China Sea. The western portion, Malaya, is part of the Asian mainland; the eastern half is part of the island of Borneo. Malaya is about the size of Alabama; some 50,000 square miles. Most of the people live here. Malaysia as a whole has about 10 million people, but only about half of them are Malays. Some three and a half million are Chinese, there are a million Indians, and the rest are Dyaks and other indigenous Borneo people.

Malaysia is the world's largest producer of rubber and tin. A fifth of the rubber went, in 1968, to the Soviet Union for its fast-growing automobile industry. The United States was the second biggest buyer. As well as producing some 40 percent of the world's rubber, Malaysia produces 42 percent of the world's tin. Consequently, Malaysia has one of the highest incomes per head in all of southeast Asia.

But there are economic troubles nevertheless. The chief headaches are sagging prices for Malaysia's two chief exports, and a high birthrate—population growth is about 3.8 percent. These factors have held down the growth of real income per head to a very modest 1 percent per annum. However, things would have been worse if the government hadn't been astonishingly successful—its success astonished President Marcos of the Philippines when he recently visited Kuala Lumpur, the capital of Malaysia—in holding the cost of living at a modest 7 percent increase since 1958. The Malaysian government also hopes to get the peasants to grow more food by double-cropping of rice, through irrigation. But industry has lagged, with manufacturing accounting for well under 10 percent of employment (brickmaking, biscuits, soap, rubber goods, canned pineapples). Malaysia also has the inevitable steel mill, and a fertilizer plant. And Malaysians may buy locally assembled Fiats, Volkswagens, and Toyotas; but only about 6,000 Malaysians do. Meanwhile, dollar-rich tourists fly right over Malaysia, between Bangkok and Singapore, by-passing Kuala Lumpur's modernistic airport, one of the only strips in southeast Asia able to take jumbo jets. Perhaps the flying tourists know that although the roads of Malaysia are excellent, the few hotels are poor.

The Federation of Malaysia was proclaimed on September 16, 1963. In addition to Malaya it comprises Sabah and Sarawak, both in north Borneo.

Also in north Borneo, and perhaps its most exciting part, is the tiny strip of coast called Brunei. Brunei is only 2,226 square miles in area, and has a population of only 110,000, but it is one of these oil-rich little bits of real estate, like Kuwait in the Persian Gulf. For that reason, Brunei is probably doomed to trouble. Its per capita income is almost as large as that of Britain. The sultans of Brunei were famous pirates who dominated all of Borneo's northern coast until the British stepped into the picture in 1840. Oil was discovered in the 1920s and the wells are worked by Shell, which shares the profits with the government of the sultan. The sultan, Hassana Bolkiah Muizzadin Waddaulah, had his coronation in 1968. It was an occasion of traditional oriental pomp and splendor that cost several million dollars. The sultan has declined to join Brunei in the Federation of Malaysia, fearing to lose both his power and his oil royalties, but in 1968 he went to London for serious talks with the British government, to try to persuade them not to withdraw their forces from the area by 1971, as the British government has announced it intends to do. The sultan is reported to have been told that this British decision is irrevocable. Brunei is very strongly Muslim, but the sultan is all for modernization, and has set up a Language Institute, and a Broadcasting and Information Department. Bruneians, being rich, are not much addicted to work, and the oil and building industries rely upon labor brought in from Malaysia, Hong Kong, and Taiwan.

The Republic of the Philippines has laid claim to Sabah. The Philippines' southern Muslims especially believe that as Sabah was once the property of the now defunct sultanate of Sulu, therefore it should be now part of the Philippines, not part of Malaysia. The Malaysian government accused the Philippines of training guerrillas to penetrate Sabah. Manila's disingenuous answer to the charge was that the guerrillas were being trained to put down rebels in the southern Philippines. Philippines President Ferdinand Marcos nevertheless signed a bill defining his country's territorial waters to include Sabah.

In spite of their intention to withdraw their military forces from the area by 1971, the British have said that they will come to the aid of Malaysia if the Philippines tries to seize Malaysian territory. The Philippines called this "saber rattling." The view of the United States Department of State, announced in 1968, is that back in 1963 the Philippines recognized that Sabah belonged to Malaysia, and did so "without qualification." The Philippines government called this American statement "a double cross."

Malaysia has other political troubles. In 1968, on the 20th anniversary of the Malayan "emergency"—that is Malaya's long guerrilla war with communists led by Chin Peng—the Malayan communist party demonstrated that it was still a force. In Saglar, Penang, and other places, dozens of red flags appeared and, following a bloody ambush of a police patrol on the Thai border, the Malayan government declared that the Malayan communist party was getting ready for renewed armed struggle. The authorities rounded up some scores of alleged communists, including university graduates, but mainly persons who were active supporters of the Malayan labor party, which gained 16 percent of the votes in the 1964 elections. Students at the University of Malaya complained that the works of Marx, Lenin, and Stalin were kept locked up in a special room, and that anyone who wished to read them had to sign his name. The students strongly suspected that the names went straight to the ministry of home affairs for investigation. Perhaps more significant, in view of subsequent race riots, were the racist graffitti that were scribbled by students in the library toilets.

Until May 1969, Malays, Chinese, and Indians seemed to have gotten over previous racial friction. But in the May elections the Malays and Chinese fought in the streets of Kuala Lumpur and elsewhere, and at least 200 people were killed.

The Chinese are the economic top dogs in Malaysia, but the Malays are the political top dogs through their control of the ruling Alliance Party which is a coalition of the United Malays National Organization, the Malayan Chinese Association, and the Malayan Indian Congress. All these came under the benign leadership of Tunku Abdul Rahman.

The apple cart was upset by the Pan Malayan Islamic Party, which is right wing and which demanded a more dominant role for Malays. The PMIP ran head on into the dynamic Chinese Democratic Action Party, which is linked with Lee Kuan Yew's People's Action Party in Singapore. In the aftermath of the riots, emergency powers were wielded by Deputy Prime Minister Tun Abdul Razak, with the gentler Tunku staying in the background. The Malays have a saying, "Spit in the air and it will land on your nose." By this they mean that one shouldn't cut off one's nose to spite one's face, and that one shouldn't, in one's own community, quarrel with one's own people. The Malaysians seemed, at least momentarily, to have forgotten this wise proverb.

## THE RED FLEET

MALAYSIA WANTS AUSTRALIA and New Zealand to keep military units in Malaysia as well as in Singapore. An American military presence does not seem to be desired by either Tunku Abdul Raman, or by Lee Kuan Yew the prime minister of Singapore. An intriguing question for both Malaysia and Singapore is what attitude they should adopt to a strong Soviet naval presence that is now manifesting itself in the Indian Ocean and in the Pacific. Is this good because it means a Soviet deterrent to Peking? Or is it bad because it brings the Russians that much closer?

Singapore was originally part of the Federation of Malaysia, but broke away in 1956. Singapore could not then have foreseen that its huge naval docks and other British bases, which provided 50,000 jobs and a quarter of Singapore's national income, would have to adjust to a British army, naval, and air force withdrawal by 1971. That decision seemed to leave the island republic of Singapore, which is not larger than New York City, at the mercy of either Malaysia or Indonesia. Lee Kuan Yew adopted the defense strategy of "the poisoned shrimp," which is too dangerous to eat in spite of seeming such a morsel. Lee Kuan Yew bought planes and antiaircraft missiles, and he hired Israelis, tactfully calling them "Mexicans," to train his Israeli-type army. He also persuaded New Zealand and Australia to station token military forces in Singapore. This provides him with an indirect link with the United States, as Australia and New Zealand are linked to the United States through the ANZAC pact. All this, however, still leaves Singapore with the problem of the soon-to-be abandoned bases. When and if Thailand and the Philippines come to face a similar problem, they may find that Singapore has pre-empted the solution of turning the bases into giant ship and aircraft maintenance and repair workshops for all Asia. Even Sattahip in Thailand or Subic Bay in the Philippines may not be able to compete, for instance, with Singapore's graving dock, 5 floating docks, and 35 naval workshops.

The Soviet Union has stationed in the Pacific Ocean 20 nuclear submarines, 80 conventional submarines, 60 missile firing vessels. China has about 30 submarines. Russian warships from Vladivostok touch at Singapore on their way through the Strait of Malacca into the Indian Ocean. Other Soviet warships will be able to enter the Indian Ocean from the Black Sea and Mediterranean when Suez is reopened, and can do so from the South Atlantic around the tip of South Africa. There is nothing but ocean between Singapore and Mauritius, and there is to be no British military force east of Suez after 1971. The Russians apparently mean to fill the gap. Admiral Sergei Gorshkov visited India in 1968, and Indian defense minister Swaran Singh said "We have only offered the Russians the port facilities that we have given the warships of Britain, the United States, and other countries." By this he meant fresh water and other such supplies, and emergency repairs. Similar facilities could be extended to the Russians by Singapore. Port Louis in Mauritius is also being eyed by the Soviet navy—the Mauritius area, incidentally, is where the Soviet Zond 5 space capsule that orbited the moon splashed down.

Peter the Great, who ruled Russia from 1682 to 1725, is the father of the Russian navy. He worked incognito in a Dutch shipyard to acquire the knack of maritime matters. His Baltic conquests and his building of St. Petersburg (now Leningrad) gave Russia a port on the world. His work was consolidated by Catherine the Great (who once employed John Paul Jones). Russia won control of the Black Sea, and fought the Ottoman Turks for the Caspian Sea. But in the 19th century, Russia had less luck in Asia; Russian fleets were destroyed at Port Arthur and at Tsushima by the Japanese in the war of 1904–1905. Stalin didn't have much use for a navy until after

World War II, when he found himself in posssession of the Baltic states. Since then, the Russians have pushed on with the expansion of their navy. This build-up was greatly accelerated by the 1962 Cuban crisis, which revealed grave weaknesses in Soviet naval power. The Soviet navy now seems to be both bigger and newer than the United States navy. The United States has more aircraft carriers. On the other hand, the Soviet Union has more submarines and, overall, many more warships.

# THE MEN WHO RULE MALAYSIA

MALAYSIA HAS AN elective king. He is elected by the nine hereditary rulers of the Malay states of Johore, Kedah, Kelantan, Negri Sembilan, Pahang, Perrak, Pelis, Selangar, and Trangganu. These rulers pick one of themselves to be king and the king has a five year term. However, he is only the ceremonial head of state; political power is in the hands of the prime minister. Since 1955, political power has reposed in the able hands of Tunku (prince) Abdul Rahman. The tunku was born in 1903, one of 45 children of the Sultan of Kedah. The sultan was a big spender. When Abdul Rahman was six years old, his father threw a big wedding party for the tunku's older brother, the crown prince. The wedding cost more than a million dollars and included such things as 30 cases of champagne every day for three months, says James W. Gould in his informative and entertaining *The United States and Malaysia*, published in 1969 by the Harvard University Press. The tunku's mother was a daughter of a Thai official and the tunku's wife is the part-Thai daughter of a Chinese merchant—neat illustrations of the ethnic complexities of this part of the world. Abdul Rahman studied at Cambridge University in England, then joined the Kedah civil service. He was still in it when the Japanese occupied Malaya. After the end of the war and the defeat of the Japanese, the tunku led the movement for the independence of Malaya from Britain. Independence was gained in 1957. The tunku heads the Alliance Party and his probable successor is his very old friend and deputy prime minister Tun Razak Bin Hussein who also has held the defense, home affairs, and national and rural development ministries, sometimes simultaneously. When the tunku goes abroad, which is often, Tun Razak takes over and runs the country for him. He is almost 20 years younger than the tunku and is an extremely reserved man. The government radio has a song in his honor which runs, "Even though you seldom laugh, you are appreciated by all." Like the tunku, Razak studied in England. But whereas the tunku always found it difficult to pass examinations, Razak passed his law examination in 18 months instead of the usual three years, and then helped the tunku to pass *his* examination. Razak is a Fabian socialist who believes in democratic socialism and mild socialist planning. As a member of the tunku's government he has poured money into education in Malaysia, with emphasis on science and technology. He also directed operations against the communist guerrillas during the Malayan "emergency."

Another strong political figure in Malaysia is Tan Siew Sin. Tan looks after the economic interests of the Chinese, in his post of minister of finance. He is also national chairman of the Malayan Chinese Association, following in the footsteps of his father, Tan Cheng Lock, who founded the association.

Indian interests are represented politically by Samban Than, who is president of the Malayan Indian Congress, and who dreams of establishing rubber plantations that will be co-operatively owned and operated by the workers.

Finally, a promising politician is Senu Bin Abdul Rahman— no relation to the tunku. Senu Bin Abdul Rahman once worked as a waiter in Los Angeles to support himself while studying at the University of California, where he got a bachelor's degree in political science. He was ambassador to Indonesia, then ambassador to West Germany, before becoming Malaysian minister of information and culture.

Malaya and Singapore are connected by the Johore Causeway, which carries a railway and a road. Thousands of automobiles and buses cross every day. It's rather like the constant traffic between Detroit, and Windsor, Canada. Lee Kuan Yew has been the leader of the People's Action Party (PAP) since its founding in 1954, and has been chief minister of Singapore since 1959. He is the son of a Chinese immigrant who was employed by the Shell Oil Company. Like Tunku Abdul

Rahman, Lee Kuan Yew went to Cambridge, England, where he won a "double first." He read Karl Marx and was influenced by the British Labour Party. In 1950, he returned to Singapore to practice law. He worked with labor unions and also with the communist leaders in Singapore, for independence—and he broke with the communists in 1961.

PAP runs Singapore, and is run by Lee Kuan Yew. In 1963, five days after the formation of Malaysia, elections in Singapore gave the PAP a solid majority. Most of this was due to Lee's personal campaigning in the four languages in which he is fluent: Mandarin, Hokkien, Malay and of course English. Lee's socialist, communist, and other political opponents thereupon went into a prolonged sulk, with the result that in 1968 the PAP won *all* the seats in the general election and Lee Kuan Yew obtained another five years of power. He does not have to face another election until 1973.

But Lee Kuan Yew had no sooner achieved political supremacy in Singapore than his relations with Malaya began to worsen. It was all rather like the perennial feuding that goes on between the City of New York and the State of New York, between New York's City Hall and Albany. There were bitter quarrels between Singapore and Kuala Lumpur, the capital of Malaya, about such matters as the share of the Singapore revenues that should go to the Malaysian Federation, and the protection of industries on the mainland against the free trade industries of Singapore. These issues were fought out by the finance ministers of the two territories, Goh Keng Swee and Tan Siew Sin. Goh Keng Swee and Tan Siew Sin happen to be cousins. This kinship seemed to make their fight all the tougher.

Soon, not just the two finance ministers and the two governments were quarreling, but there was race trouble between Malays and Chinese in Singapore. Malay leaders from Kuala Lumpur descended on Singapore and appealed to the Malays there, denouncing Lee Kuan Yew's "Chinese dictatorship," and calling Malays who had voted for the PAP, traitors. Riots broke out in the summer of 1964, heralded by leaflets which declared, "before Malay blood flows, it is best that Chinese blood should flow." In four days of rioting, 22 people were killed and about 500 were injured.

In January 1965, Lee Kuan Yew began to talk about Singapore breaking up the federation and going it alone. Tunku Abdul Rahman at first denounced the talk of separation as dangerous. But friction between Singapore and Kuala Lumpur continued and worsened. Lee Kuan Yew's press secretary and close friend Alex Jose was expelled by the Malayan government. There were threats of more race riots. In August, the tunku and Lee Kuan Yew announced the break-up of the federation. Subsequently, each accused the other of being responsible for it. Lee Kuan Yew insisted that "geographically, historically, and economically we are one." He said the tunku had thrown Singapore out of the federation. The tunku said or implied that Lee Kuan Yew had insisted on walking out. Whoever was to blame, the break-up of the federation was a backward move that could benefit neither. Singapore is the world's fifth largest port and leads the area in banking, trading, and insurance. A report on the region by a special mission of the World Bank in July 1963 said that a common market would have many advantages for all concerned. Customs union would result in greater economic growth for the whole area. However, as soon as the political federation broke up, Singapore and Malaysia began talking about erecting tariff walls aimed at each other's trade, and the Malayans talked of building up other ports, like Swettenham and Penang, as rivals to Singapore.

In North Borneo, meanwhile, the waters were roiled by a communist political group that called itself the clandestine communist organization, or CCO. The CCO was a kind of red Ku Klux Klan, which before independence had hoped to get the backing of Indonesia to start guerrilla warfare and stage a revolt against the British. After the British quit Malaya, the CCO turned its guns against the new Malaysian government. But the promised Indonesian support was never forthcoming, and after the fall of the Sukarno government in Indonesia in 1965, the CCO was compelled to go underground.

Much of the political activity in North Borneo was centered in Brunei. It began in 1956 when a political party called Parti Ra'ayat was formed by Sheikh Azahari. The sheikh wanted a federation of Borneo under Brunei's leadership. In the first elections ever held in Brunei, at the end of August 1962, Azahari's party won a landslide victory. This victory entitled it to all 16 elective seats in the legislative council of Brunei, but then the sultan stepped in and blocked the party from controlling the legislature. In consequence, a revolt broke out in December 1962, led by Azahari at the head of 3,500 rebels who seized the Shell Oil Company installations as well as other buildings. The British flew in troops from western Malaysia, and they put down the revolt and jailed most of the rebels, including Azahari. Sixty-seven people were killed and several hundred were wounded. Azahari had been promised backing by Indonesia, but, as in the case of the CCO, the Indonesian support never materialized. However, Azahari subsequently managed to make his way to Indonesia, and lives today in Java under a sort of polite house arrest. His two wives are still in Brunei. In 1967, the sultan abdicated in favor of his son, the present ruler, who is only 24. The young man, though otherwise amiable, seems in no great haste to introduce popular representative government. But the Azahari party is still in existence, though its leader is in exile, and considerable troubles may still lie ahead of Brunei and the rest of north Borneo.

Problems created by the considerable distance that separates western from eastern Malaysia seem to have been aggravated by the apparent indifference of Kuala Lumpur to local feelings in eastern Malaysia. For example, the politicians of eastern Malaysia were not even consulted about the separation of Singapore from the federation. This could very well lead to the same sort of uneasy relationship that exists between west and east Pakistan. There has been talk of Borneo breaking away from the federation and setting up on its own, the way Singapore has done. A combination of Sabah, Sarawak, and Brunei would be many times larger than the tiny island republic of Singapore. But Sabah and Sarawak seem fearful of being dominated by Brunei, and also have little in common with each other. As James W. Gould points out in his book, *The United States and Malaysia,* "There are few overlaps of tribes between the two states (Sabah and Sarawak); Kadazans and Bajaus are more strange to land Dayaks than are Malays."

Brunei has been nicknamed the "shellfare state." Revenues from the Shell oil fields, at Seria, are large and are freely spent. Some of the money has gone into showy extravagances, like a $700,000 national mosque. But a good deal has also been spent on schools and health. Medical care and education are both free. One awkward result of improved medical care in Brunei was an astounding 11.8 percent population growth in 1965.

# SINGAPORE THE SPARK PLUG

A FAVORITE PARLOR game of westerners who like to talk about Asia is to assume that there are in the region only three places that really count: China, India, and Japan. The game consists of regarding these three as if they were horses in a race, and trying to guess in what order they are likely to be placed in the Seventies.

It can be an amusing game, but is not one that deserves to be taken seriously. Who would have guessed 20 years ago, when a new era opened in Asia, that by 1970 Japan would clearly appear to be leading in the race? And who can even attempt to predict how things will be in 1980? The favorite western parlor game, in short, has little relevance to what seem to be Asian realities, and that little may be diminishing. A similar game played with Europe instead of Asia, after the disappearance of the Roman Empire as an effective political and military force, would not have picked either Venice or England as a leading light of the future. Nevertheless, the lush Italian city-state and the cold northern maritime nation both lit up the Renaissance. In modern Asia, the maritime Japanese have become the world's third industrial power, even after having suffered catastrophic defeat in war; and two great entrepôts of the trade of the Far East are Chinese cities that are not politically part of China: the British colony of Hong Kong, and the young Republic of Singapore.

Singapore, an island of two million people, has as its prime minister the remarkable Mr. Lee Kuan Yew, one of the most notable men in world politics at the present time. As we have already recounted, he was born in Singapore, is a graduate of Cambridge University in England, and has been political top dog in Singapore for a decade—though he is not yet 50. He is a brilliant linguist who is fluent in Malayan and in several Chinese dialects as well as in English, and who also speaks Tamil. Three quarters of the people of Singapore are Chinese, but the remaining quarter, though mostly Malays, are also English- and Indian-speaking, so that Lee Kuan Yew's languages contributed to his political success. Its main ingredient, however, is a nimble Chinese brain that has the good fortune to be linked with a highly persuasive personality. The infant republic's prime minister, however, is no demagogue. His public appearances are relatively rare. He has managed to provide his constituents with more than any other Asian leader in any other country. Yet he has almost always demanded more from them than he has promised them. Lee Kuan Yew provides material rewards, but only in exchange for continuous effort.

When Singapore was still a colony, its British rulers feared Lee Kuan Yew as a bold agitator whom they thought was probably a communist. And he accepted the communists as his allies in the struggle against colonialism. But by the time he achieved political power the communists had become his sworn enemies, and he was counting on the British—perhaps wrongly, it now turns out—to be his allies.

Lee Kuan Yew's People's Action Party (PAP) claimed, on coming to power in Singapore, that they found the treasury empty; a common complaint of successor administrations, but Lee Kuan Yew promptly took rigorous and unpopular steps to close the deficit. He increased taxes and he cut government workers' "dearness allowance" (cost-of-living compensation for rising prices) so that the bureaucrats were reduced to trying to make ends meet on their basic pay. These and other measures of financial prudence, the kind that are more often undertaken by conservatives than by radicals, were successful in replenishing the treasury, and in a couple of years or so the screws could be slackened. But at the time when they were tightened, the communists in Singapore commanded more than 30 percent of the popular vote. By taking a big political gamble, and more important by bringing it off, Lee

Kuan Yew at once established himself as a daring and resourceful leader. Many people call him a political genius.

In 1965, fresh troubles developed. As we have seen, a quarrel grew up between the new Malay government in Kuala Lumpur, and the city-state government of Singapore. The quarrel was due in part to Lee Kuan Yew's successful economic policy. Singapore was getting steadily richer, but the Singaporeans complained that 40 cents of every dollar had to be transmitted to Kuala Lumpur, and was never recovered. Lee Kuan Yew again adopted a daring solution. Though the island is physically connected to the mainland, by a causeway, Singapore proposed to launch out politically on its own, as an independent republic, with Lee Kuan Yew as its prime minister. Though he later claimed that the Singaporeans had been "kicked out" of the Malaysian federation; it seems reasonable to assume that the initiative for the break came from him. Once more, his daring seems to have paid dividends. Singapore may go on getting richer, with no obligation to hand over part of its growing wealth each year to Malaysia. And the estrangement between the two new states has been overcome to the extent that their relations seem now cordial. The prime minister of Malaysia, Tunku Abdul Rahman, visited Singapore in 1969, and Lee Kuan Yew offered troops to help defend Sabah, the Malaysian portion of Borneo, if troops should ever be needed.

Sabah is not at the moment in very great danger from anyone. It lives comfortably off the sales of its excellent hardwood, mainly to Japan, and has the least crime and one of the highest per capita incomes in southeast Asia ($336 per annum). But President Ferdinand Marcos of the Philippines laid claim to it, as did his predecessor President Macapagal; the claim to Sabah tends to be revived every four years, when the Philippines are about to have presidential elections. The southern Philippines have a large population of impoverished Muslims, and they eagerly seek employment in relatively prosperous Sabah. So do Indonesian workers from the Indonesian portion of the island of Borneo. The people of Sabah enjoy their relatively high living standard, and some of them pointedly contrast the crime-free condition of Sandakan, their principal town, with the lawlessness that is prevalent in Manila. Sabah came under Malaysian rule by popular vote. But Tunku Abdul Rahman seems a little fearful that, one day, the Philippines or Indonesia may seriously press a territorial claim and back it by force. The Philippines possesses American Sabrejet warplanes. And the Indonesians have Russian MIGs. The government of Malaysia became interested in acquiring new fighter aircraft, from France, Holland, Britain, or Canada. Yet French Mirages, for instance, are very expensive; and defense is already costing Malaysia about 5 percent of its annual gross product.

Singapore is either wiser or more fortunate, for though its income per head is the highest in Asia, it spends only about 1 percent of its GNP on defense. Yet the Singaporeans until quite recently felt like the Israelis of their part of the world. They had serious quarrels with their nearest neighbors on their hands. Singapore is largely a Chinese city, and the Chinese are not loved by the Malays. The Malayans resented the loss of Singapore's wealth. The Indonesians dislike the Chinese because the Dutch, when they ruled Indonesia, brought in Chinese to act as tax collectors. Indonesia under Sukarno launched a "confrontation" with both Malaysia and Singapore. Indonesian marines acting as saboteurs secretly entered Singapore and partly destroyed an important building, killing three people. The Singapore authorities caught and hanged two of the Indonesians, and for a while it seemed touch and go whether or not the Indonesians would actually invade Singapore. The Indonesian island nearest to Singapore is almost within hailing distance, and there are 100 million Indonesians, to Singapore's 2 million. Though all this hubbub subsequently died away, Lee Kuan Yew was determined that Singapore would defend itself as ably as its small numbers permit, if ever called on to do so. He studied Israel's defense strategy, and engaged Israeli military experts to help him organize his island's forces. The upshot is that every Singapore boy, and girl too, undergoes rigorous military training, and the government intends that every citizen shall be able in a crisis to shoulder arms, through instant and universal mobilization.

But the actual armaments program is modest. Singapore seems uninterested in acquiring Mach 2.0 warplanes. A few British Harrier strike aircraft or similar planes are to suffice, along with helicopters and patrol boats. It did, however, come as a considerable shock to Singapore when the British government announced that instead of its forces pulling out by 1975, this would be done by the end of 1971. The $120 million aid that Britain offered its former colony as a consolation prize failed to console. So, the island's home guard was supplemented by a joint Singapore-Malaysia air defense system. In a crunch, the British say that they could be back in the area with military forces in 16 or 17 hours. Lee Kuan Yew is looking to Japan and Australia to help keep the Straits of Malacca open for international shipping. This is in Japan's interests because of Japan's heavy dependence on oil supplies from the Persian Gulf. The same applies to Australia, for different reasons.

It is not, however, only or even primarily for defense that Lee Kuan Yew looks to both Japan and Australia. He has said that he does not lack faith in a regional organization like ASEAN, the Association of Southeast Asian Nations, that now includes Malaysia, Singapore, the Philippines, Thailand, and Indonesia. "But I also believe that if you want to propel yourself forward, you have to have some power. It is the difference between rowing and having an outboard motor. I am in favor of getting somebody with an outboard motor, like Japan or Australia, to join in the partnership. Then we have a motor. Otherwise, five underdeveloped countries each rowing away and not rhythmically—well, we will make progress, but it will be slow."

These are modest words, and Lee Kuan Yew sometimes uses bolder ones. On the same occasion, he declared he would like to believe that Singapore "can be the sparking plug for a better quality of life for Southeast Asia." His preoccupying fear quite evidently is that in his part of the world, a "soft" climate may produce a "soft" society. He wants instead to pro-

duce in Singapore a kind of Israeli hardness, and it is probably no coincidence that he is especially keen on the sorts of
technical training and corresponding technical proficiencies
for which Israel has become noted. In the next few decades,
Singapore probably is going to produce more engineers than
paper-shufflers. The prime minister's admiration of the United
States is genuine, but qualified; he admires American know-
how, but not all aspects of the American way of life. "I have
a very high regard," he has carefully explained, "for American
technology, gadgetry, drive, marketing, management skills,
and so many other things connected with the industrial and
technological society in which we live." But Vietnam for instance "is a human problem, not just a technological problem."
Do Americans understand how the South Vietnamese people
feel in their hearts, and what they are thinking? Manifestly,
Lee Kuan Yew doubts it. It seems rather obvious that he
wants some American military presence in southeast Asia after
the Vietnam war is over—partly for security, partly for the
economic benefits such a presence would continue to bring to
the area. (It was estimated that about a third of Singapore's
exports were generated by procurement of steel plates, building materials, and so forth, for Vietnam). But Lee Kuan Yew
and other southeast Asian leaders want the postwar American
military presence to be modest: say, a maximum of 5,000 men
in Thailand, rather than 50,000.

And as far as the Vietnam war itself was concerned, Lee
Kuan Yew plainly doubted that the South Vietnamese were
ever going to find the kind of leadership that might see them
through. It would, he conceded, be nice to think that when
the foreign troops on both sides left, then the South Vietnamese, protected by some international or United Nations force,
could freely choose the kind of government they wanted. But
even if that happened, would they in fact find a government
that would be able, in peace, to carry them on to the sort of
constructive society that Lee Kuan Yew himself is building
in Singapore? His conclusion was: "If it decides to go noncommunist, then good luck to South Vietnam and I think the
rest of southeast Asia will cheer and be greatly relieved. If

it decides to go communist and to rejoin the north, then . . . the South Vietnamese just didn't believe that the noncommunist South Vietnamese leadership was good enough for them."

Singapore's own communists declined any longer to run against Lee Kuan Yew and be beaten each time by him. They boycotted the ballot box, so it was not possible to tell what their strength was. One probably reliable estimate was 10 percent of the popular vote, which meant it had fallen by two-thirds. In 1961, there were 116 strikes in Singapore, mostly politically motivated; in 1969, there were only two strikes and probably neither was political.

But the price of liberty is prosperity. Communist strength might recover quite fast, if Singapore's economy hit a really bad patch. At the moment it is riding pretty high, all things considered. The rate of growth is a fantastic 11.9 percent. Manufacturing output has been going up almost 25 percent each year. Exports of manufactures, excluding refined petroleum, are worth $580 million, a 270 percent increase since 1960. Each month, about 350 Asians from nearby countries attempt to smuggle themselves into Singapore to share its prosperity; each is prepared to pay about $100 for the chance, a huge sum to an Asian peasant or unskilled worker.

The more orthodox visitor to Singapore who travels there by air has attached to his luggage a destination label that disconcertingly announces, in large letters, SIN. It couldn't be a more misleading description. This island of immigrants that would like to be thought of as the spark plug of southeast Asia is tropically green but suburbanly sedate. Its businessmen are all businesslike and think only about trade. The city itself is fanatical about cleanliness—there are heavy fines for litterbugs and even fewer flies than in China. Everyone is polite, but brisk. The large but tame traffic is efficiently directed by khaki-clad policemen and policewomen. Nearly all the street signs are still in English, the language everyone in Singapore speaks, and none of the names, or monuments, commemorating British rule have been removed. When the former British prime minister Harold Macmillan visited Singapore, the then mayor sulked in city hall and refused to go to meet him. Macmillan, unabashed, drove to city hall and politely requested tea and a chat. Since then, relations between the republic and the former colonial power have been more than cordial.

The taxes that Lee Kuan Yew collects from his hardworking people are fairly distributed and spent on roads, hospitals, and workers' apartment houses. There is no corruption; even the government's political opponents say as much. The workers' apartment houses, clean as picked bones by day and a blaze of light after dark, are creating a new skyline. They rent at $70 an apartment per month—but these are Singapore dollars, worth about 35 U.S. cents each. The rent in U.S. money is about $25 a month. And the apartment houses are carefully and deliberately integrated, though this is as difficult to accomplish in Singapore, which is 75 percent Chinese and 25 percent Malay, and et cetera, as it would be in Washington, D.C. Lee Kuan Yew is also encouraging families to buy their apartments, for the same reason the government now charges $1 (Singapore) a day for medical services that formerly were entirely free. He is anxious to teach people to be self-reliant. But the government itself continues to build new apartments, to replace slums; they are going up at the rate— the government proudly announces—of one apartment unit every 38 minutes. Formerly, it took 45 minutes.

Lee Kuan Yew long ago proclaimed that his ideal for Singapore was a socialist democratic republic. In fact, the island is too dependent on outside capital to practise socialism, and it's doubtful, in spite of Lee Kuan Yew's proven popularity, that it's a full democracy yet. Some $100 million of U.S. capital was invested in Singapore in a recent year, mostly in oil refining but also in hotels and factories. Singapore with its high skills can serve a wide Asian market. It is now a central point for supplying spare parts for American tractors all over Asia. A Japanese company is about to build, as well as to repair, ships in Singapore, in cooperation with the Singapore government. There are now 1,400 factories (Hong Kong has 12,000) and the number is going up by leaps and bounds.

Singapore and Indonesia are cooperating to exploit the fabled belles of Bali. The idea is to entice tourists traveling by the Taiwan–Hong Kong–Bangkok–Singapore route, or by the Taiwan–Manila–Singapore route. This, largely, means not Americans, but Japanese; already, Japanese tourists to Taiwan outnumber Americans, and the reckoning is that by 1985, many of the Japanese people will be in the state of affluence that most Americans enjoy now.

Lee Kuan Yew has been in power in Singapore continuously for over 10 years. He said in 1968 he wanted time off for a little thinking and "research." He then went abroad for nearly ten weeks, to talk and listen to American intellectuals at Harvard and Yale. This was believed to be the longest time that any active prime minister had ever spent away from his office, let alone 10,000 miles away from his country. But Lee Kuan Yew says that he regards himself as primarily an intellectual, not a politician, and seems to mean it. He also calls himself a "constructive optimist." There can be little doubt that the vast majority of Singaporeans are perfectly content to let him rule. The question is whether this will prove to be good for them in the long run, and not just politically. The republic has several political parties besides the PAP, despite the communist abstention. But the PAP has never lost a seat in parliament, so it holds all 58 of them. Government measures are debated in the British parliamentary style, and members get up and ask honourable ministers questions, in the British tradition. Nevertheless, the whole parliamentary set-up seems unreal. Lee Kuan Yew's critics claim that it is. They also say that he is turning Singapore into an efficient but inhuman ant hill, and that his workers' apartment houses are the equivalent of worker-bees' hives. There is an obvious danger that ten more years of such excellent government will turn Singaporeans into dull, or anyway bland, conformists. When the student editor of *Undergrad,* the University of Singapore paper, wrote a series of brilliant but biting articles, he was quietly summoned to the office of the president, and there gently reminded that he was attending the university on a free scholarship. The articles ceased.

But there is another side to the coin. Lee Kuan Yew has done everything in his power to make his island of immigrants an island of skilled workers, with the highest living standards in Asia. People with skills need to have brains, and people with brains ask questions and won't be easily satisfied with bland answers. Lee Kuan Yew is himself the living proof of this. When the serious questioning starts, the chances are he will have the right answers.

# INDONESIAN GIANT

INDONESIA IS BY far the largest country in southeast Asia; 3,000 miles of islands that stretch along the equator from Singapore to near Australia, with a total population of about 117 million, most of whom—staggering thought!—are under the age of 16.

The land and sea area covered by the Indonesian archipelago makes it as large as the continental United States. Unfortunately there are only bad roads, few railroad tracks, and the ports and harbors are highly congested—not so much because there is so great a volume of trade, as because the management of them is so inefficient. Probably more than half of the 117 million population live in a nonmoney, self-subsistence agricultural economy. That is to say, they grow the food that they themselves eat, but they do not eat well. In 1968, for example, the nutritive value of the people's diet was 1700 calories and 35 grams of protein per head—against a minimum need of 2100 calories and 55 grams of protein. Nevertheless, the Indonesian birth rate is so high that by the year 2000 the population will be about 280 million. The public service is vastly swollen by people who otherwise would be unemployed. They receive pay plus allowances, which however cover only a quarter to a half of the bare cost of food and other absolute necessities. The consequence of course is a vast amount of graft and smuggling. On the island of Java, the density of population approaches 1,000 persons per square kilometer. "And not a single customer among them!" observed one dour visiting American businessman.

Inflation, formerly rampant, was reduced in 1968 to a mere 85 percent, and to perhaps half of that in 1969. This may seem very high indeed even to Americans who complain they are suffering bitterly from inflation at 6 percent. But in fact the 85 percent inflation rate in Indonesia was rightly considered to be very good, because the previous year it had been 120 percent and in 1966 it was 635 percent. Indonesia is rich in rubber, coffee, pepper, tea, palm oil, tin, and perhaps oil and copper as well. But the country is financially bankrupt. The $700 million that it owes to the Soviet Union is only part of Indonesia's overseas debt. Indonesia owes other countries, in total about $2.3 billion. All the creditors are prepared to give Indonesia time in which to pay—with a thoughtful eye on the possible exploitation of the country's vast natural resources. The western consortium of which the United States is a principal member has taken the lead in this financial moratorium. But, in August 1969 Russia sent a new economic mission to Djakarta to discuss Indonesia's $700 million debt to the Soviet Union, and also to talk about completing Soviet construction projects which had been abandoned four years before, after the fall of Sukarno and the takeover by Suharto. These unfinished Soviet projects include a steel mill. It was believed that the United States would "look the other way" if Suharto sought new military aid from the Soviet Union to ease the strain on a tight budget. Meanwhile, the United States is contributing one-third of the economic aid which Indonesia is receiving from abroad. This aid seems to imply a large (and perhaps mistaken) American confidence that communism is unlikely to revive in Indonesia after the great 1965–1966 massacres of an estimated 250,000 to 300,000 people who were judged to be communist supporters and sympathizers.

The Dutch ruled Indonesia from the 17th century until 1949. The islands were under Japanese rule during World War II. In 1959, President Sukarno transformed the new, independent Indonesia republic into a "guided democracy." In 1963, Sukarno staged a confrontation with Malaysia. He apparently dreamed of establishing an empire which would include all Malays. In 1965, Indonesia walked out of the United Nations—which nobody else had done—in much the same way as Italy quit the League of Nations before World War II. In 1966, Sukarno was replaced as president by Suharto. Indonesia then returned to the United Nations. Suharto's term of office as president expires in 1973.

On the night of September 30, 1965, some Indonesian military leaders staged an attempted coup which apparently had been planned by the communist party of Indonesia. The military leaders of the coup were General Mustafa Sjarif Supardjo; Lieutenant-Colonel Untung, a member of Sukarno's presidential palace guard; and Omar Dhani, the former chief of the Indonesian air force. The plan was to murder the country's leading generals and then to take over the country, presumably proclaiming a new "people's republic." But the senior general Abdul Haris Nasution and General Suharto both escaped. Indeed, Suharto's name was not even on the list of those who were to be murdered that night. Six leading generals were murdered, but Suharto moved in quickly and put down the rebellion. President Sukarno was alleged to be a silent partner of the rebels. The story of the coup and its aftermath is, so far as it is known, well told by John Hughes, of the *Christian Science Monitor*, in his book *Indonesian Upheaval*, published by McKay. After the coup had failed, all hell broke loose. Mass executions followed mass arrests. Hughes says executions were usually by knife or by the broad-bladed sickles that many Javanese use for working in the fields. Many communists were beheaded as they kneeled with their thumbs tied behind their backs on the edge of their freshly dug graves. Hughes adds that in cases where informers pinpointed a village as being communist, everyone in it died. This included women and children over the age of six.

Today, the Indonesian communist party is still in eclipse. But it had at one time three million card carrying members. Its estimated six million followers are still around somewhere despite the 1965 killings. The party has quite deep roots in Indonesia's history. Although Sukarno has fallen, his Indonesia Nationalist Party (PNI) is beginning to reemerge, in spite of serious internal divisions. The 1965 killings of communists were mainly the work of Muslims. Indonesia has two Muslim parties, the PMI, Indonesian Muslim Party, which rebelled against the government in the 1950's, and the NU, Nahdatal Ulama, which is filled with religious zealots. The KAMI, the Indonesian University Student Organization that played a leading role in overthrowing Sukarno, has since been on the decline. However, corruption in top government echelons could revive the students' party.

To add to President Suharto's headaches, there is a little paratroop war in West Irian, the New Guinea territory that was also formerly ruled by the Dutch. In West Irian, some of the 800,000 Papuans are in revolt against the Indonesian government, in the central mountain range. The overwhelming majority of Papuans are supposed to have voted for West Irian to become part of Indonesia, but the Papuan rebels deny heatedly that there was any so-called "act of free choice."

Having come to power by putting down a communist coup, the present Indonesian leaders are naturally bitterly anti-communist, and specifically anti-Chinese. Peking was said to be behind the 1965 revolt. Nevertheless, Indonesia recognizes both North Vietnam and South Vietnam, North Korea as well as South Korea. It does not recognize Nationalist China, although it seeks trade with Taiwan. Indonesia's astute foreign minister Adam Malik expects increased "subversion" in southeast Asia after the Vietnam war is over. But he has advised President Suharto against military pacts, since both SEATO and the Vietnam war have, in his opinion, been flops. In place of military pacts and counterinsurgency, Malik prefers economic cooperation and development as a means of checking communism. Indonesia is a member of ASEAN, the Association of South East Asian Nations, along with Singapore, Malaysia, the Philippines, and Taiwan. "Economic cooperation and development" is difficult to define, but probably means a request, and certainly a need, for more foreign aid. In Indonesia's case the aid could conceivably pay off in economic as well as in political terms.

# AFTER THE MASSACRE

THE 117 MILLION Indonesians have set them-
selves a severe challenge, by trying to turn their capital city
of Djakarta into a new Rome. The visitor is duly impressed
by the number of huge monuments, broad roads and immense
traffic circles, plinths and columns, fountains and palaces. He
probably would be even more impressed if the vast majority
of the ordinary dwellings he sees did not seem to be hovels,
and if the traffic did not mostly consist of worn-out diesel
trucks belching thick black smoke, and battered passenger cars
that are always breaking down. But the monuments that
President Sukarno caused to be built remain under President
Suharto, and inevitably beckon the Indonesians on to a
splendid vision of their future. As Indonesia is so large that
its chain of islands would stretch from the east to the west
coast of the United States, and as its natural resources are
believed to be enormous, there appears no reason why the
vision of a prosperous future should not be realized. But this
is only superficial. Japan, with almost no natural resources,
has succeeded in emulating the British islands on the other
side of the world from Japan, and has become a rich industrial country. But the Japanese were arduously trained for
this task for two and a half centuries, by the iron-willed
national schoolmasters of the Tokugawa era. The Indonesians,
though they gained their independence from the Dutch over
20 years ago, by fighting for it, have still to demonstrate that
they can produce an effective leadership capable of meeting
the challenges of the modern world. President Sukarno built
national monuments, and can also be credited with building
a united nation. The other islands are no longer likely to

break away from Java, where 70 percent of the people live, though this was threatened at one time and is still a possibility. But Sukarno almost totally neglected the country's pressing economic problems, and even added to them with his princely extravagances, and the bill has fallen due in the period of President Suharto. It remains to be seen if the Suharto regime can succeed in revitalizing the economy as well as maintaining its still precarious political balance, or if it, too, will finish in a bog of failure, rebellion, and corruption.

Meanwhile, numbers of obvious carpetbaggers as well as honest businessmen have descended on Djakarta, attracted by tales of oil and mineral wealth still untapped, and by the prospect of making big quick profits in a backward country that is at the moment in no position to lay down strict conditions in return for permitting foreigners to exploit its natural riches. The way the American Embassy describes this phenomenon is that the businessmen and bankers who crowd the glittering Indonesia Hotel in Djakarta are "savoring the spirit of confidence engendered by" the Suharto regime's "relatively liberal investment policies." Only 10 percent of the capital of a joint venture need be Indonesian, and the state is prepared to concede half the ownership of its enterprises to foreigners. With the country's infrastructure of roads and other facilities far gone in decay, no cash in the treasury, and millions of unemployed, Indonesia is poorly placed for hard bargaining. Nevertheless, even the foreign visitor, far less the indigenous Indonesian, winces at some carpetbagger behavior. "Let's go, boy!" cries the huge American in the colored sports shirt, snapping his fingers at a diminutive Indonesian who is loaded down with the American's baggage. The Indonesian follows meekly at the heels of the buoyant white giant. But his thoughts may be less meek. The Indonesian authorities' hope is that, once serious exploitation of the oil and minerals has begun, exuberant Americans and other foreigners engaged in the business will be out of sight of the Indonesian public most of the time, in their camps and compounds in the interior jungles, or on their oil rigs offshore. Meanwhile, unfortunately, they are both visible and overpowering.

The Dutch ran Indonesia on a two-economy theory. There was the export economy, which mainly benefitted Holland, not Indonesia; and there was the subsistence economy, which was for the natives, who were expected to be content with rice and medicine and not to crave for either political power or higher education. The Indonesian government will try to prevent this sort of thing occurring again. But it does want the Americans to develop oil, the Japanese to cut timber and to fish, and the Canadians and others to dig for nickel, copper, and bauxite. As many as 20 American companies are after the oil, and there is excited talk of new offshore finds transforming Indonesia into another Middle East. In order to prevent the foreigners getting all the benefits, Major-General Ibnu Suwoto, the president-director of Pertamina, the state oil and mining company, proposed taxing the foreign oil companies at a fairly high rate (65 percent) and also arranging for gradual transfer of the oil-rich territories into the hands of the Indonesian working people. But for a country that for the past four and a half years has been run by the army, Indonesians are remarkably outspoken, and critics of General Suwoto say plainly that a good deal of money is already finding its way into his own treasury. His daughter's costly wedding was the talk of Djakarta. The wedding festivities continued for days, there were thousands of guests, and the General had closed-circuit television installed in his home so that he could watch the entire proceedings. The daughter of that master of extravaganzas, former president Sukarno, was also married in Djakarta, about the same time; but there was no comparison between the two events, the Suwoto wedding carrying off all the prizes for splendor.

The invasion by western and Japanese businessmen presents Indonesia with temptations and perils as well as with opportunities. The attitude of western governments and of the western press to Indonesian politics seems similarly two-edged. It is right that the west has decided to come to Indonesia's economic aid, and to try to keep President Suharto on his feet. In October 1967, in *Foreign Affairs,* President Nixon wrote that "With its 100 million people and its 3,000 mile arc of islands containing the region's richest hoard of natural resources, Indonesia constitutes by far the greatest prize in the South-east Asian area."

But it was downright wicked of the western press, and some western politicians, to appear to be gratified by the slaughter in 1965 and 1966 of over 250,000 people in Indonesia, simply because the victims were said to be communists. President Suharto might have put a firmer curb on his more fanatical anticommunist supporters, had the west made clearer that in its view cruel massacres of scores of thousands of men, women, and children can never be condoned. The victims were first and foremost human beings, and their slaughterers merely subtracted from their own humanity by such deeds—as did applauding onlookers. Some people in the west did condone the killings, and one result appears to have been a slackening of President Suharto's grip on the situation, and an ominous spread of abuses committed by the Indonesian army against ordinary Indonesian peasants, not only against suspected or proved communists. There are still thousands of political prisoners in camps all over the country. The government has sent some 60,000 of them to forced labor on rubber plantations in Borneo, where they are said to die like flies. The prisoners in the camps were slowly dying of starvation, and this may have been deliberate policy. Americans in Djakarta tried to persuade President Suharto to allow the prisoners to share American food shipments. The prisoners were compelled to exist on a handful of rice a day, and their relatives were forbidden to bring them more food. Though they were charged with having been members of the Indonesian Communist Party, in many cases their only real crime had been to shout slogans, like "60 percent of the crop to the tenant, 40 percent to the landlord!"—a distribution as between sharecropper and landowner that in some countries would be regarded as barely equitable to the sharecroppers.

Detention in starvation conditions or being packed off to

Borneo as slave labor was not all of those persons' punishment. Their wives, children, and other relatives were made to suffer, too. All Indonesians have to carry an identification card that contains information about their race, religion, and occupation. The cards of the relatives of political detainees bear, in addition, a warning that they are suspected of having communist sympathies. This usually means that they are refused jobs, or that they soon lose the jobs they have. That applies to the adults. The punishment of the children is to be refused admission to schools on the ground that they may contaminate other children. And most of the social welfare agencies in Indonesia, private as well as public and including those in the capital city of Djakarta, had refused to lift a finger to assist those children. Meanwhile, new suspects continued to be arrested and put in prison, or otherwise disposed of, although the attempted communist coup attempt occurred on September 30, 1965.

Four years after, the country was in the throes of an ever-widening witch-hunt, with fresh reports of new "plots" almost daily. It was alleged that the communists were plotting to bring deposed President Sukarno back to power. The authorities pounced on a poverty-stricken area in central Java, encircled it with troops, and then carted off some hundreds or thousands of persons, who were charged with planning another armed uprising. There were persistent reports that the army first tortured the suspects to extract information from them that would enable further arrests to be made, then handed some of the tortured persons over to civil guards, who slaughtered them. The civil guards are fanatical Muslims, and some of the detainees before being captured had found temporary sanctuary in Christian churches. These reports apparently caused the Netherlands government to withdraw an invitation to President Suharto to visit Holland. This rebuke took the regime by surprise, but did not cause the political witch-hunt to be called off. It could go on almost indefinitely, for the Indonesian communist party claimed to have 12 million supporters, and most people credit it with at least 3 million. The political witch-hunt far exceeds McCarthyism.

It resembles the treatment of Roman Catholics in England, following Titus Oates's Popish Plot.

The Indonesian Communist Party has suffered the fate that it once inflicted on others, and was apparently eager to inflict again, when it was vanquished by General Suharto. In 1948, the communists staged an uprising and systematically murdered as many of the Indonesian middle-class as they were able to lay hands on. In 1965, the communists staged another rebellion, and this time appeared to have President Sukarno with them—though appearances can be deceptive. Indonesians say that Sukarno was a sick man from 1963 onward, and that the events of September 30, 1965, were touched off by his Peking doctors confiding to the Indonesian communists that he might not have long to live—a forecast that proved to have been somewhat premature. But the communists took it seriously; they feared that if Sukarno died, the military would take over the country, instead of the communists who believed they were Sukarno's political heirs. The military abetted those fears by promising that a powerful anticommunist demonstration would be held on October 5. The communists decided to strike first, and to kill the leading generals, then call on the people to support a new communist regime. Sukarno himself had long sought to play off the military and the communists against each other, but now he appeared to throw his weight to the communist side. So did a group of the military. General Suharto escaped the fate of other generals, who were murdered, and at once moved against the communists and military rebels. But Suharto cannily did so in the name of President Sukarno, who, when the communist coup was crushed, remained for a time as nominally the head of state. But public opinion ran strongly against Sukarno as well as against the communists, and the army chose General Suharto to be its—and Indonesia's—new leader.

Suharto is regarded as personally modest, cautious, and unimaginative. The consensus opinion is that he may manage to remain in the saddle, especially by putting off his uniform and openly soliciting public support as a politician. However, should he allow events to get on top of him, the chances are that he will be compelled to retire in favor of a more vigorous candidate. One name that is sometimes mentioned in this connection is Major-General Ali Sadikin, the energetic governor of Djakarta, a new broom that is busy sweeping and cleaning up this untidy city of four million people.

## SUHARTO'S HARD CHOICES

THE INDONESIAN MINISTER of Foreign Affairs Adam Malik is an urbane Asian statesman who in his youth belonged to a revolutionary communist group. Fortunately, this awkward fact about his past is not widely known or remembered. It could prove awkward, when Indonesia is still passing through a phase of intense suspicion toward all persons thought to hold left-wing opinions, and "communists" are still being arrested wholesale.

Mr. Malik's opinions do not strike a foreign visitor to Djakarta as being revolutionary. He appears to have made up his mind, back in 1967, that the United States was not going to win in Vietnam, in the sense of achieving a military victory. There is no reason to suppose that he has since changed this view. As foreign minister, he is perfectly willing for Indonesia to agree to send a large military contingent to Vietnam—*after* the fighting stops, and in order to help to keep the peace, as part of a United Nations operation. The real Indonesian motive however would probably be to get at least a part of the country's 275,000-man army off the Indonesian budget and on to the budget of the United Nations, or the United States.

Like so many leading Asians, and in spite of Indonesia's current obsession with communist plots, Mr. Malik gives no sign of believing that a Chinese, Vietnamese, Soviet, or other external communist threat looms menacingly over his country. He and President Suharto both appear to think that, whilst there may be a danger of internal communism in several countries of southeast Asia, the best way for noncommunists to meet it is through internal political cohesion and strength, not by taking up arms. When Malik met his Thai counterpart,

Thanat Khoman the foreign minister of Thailand, he told that prominent anti-communist politician that the way to fight communism in northeast Thailand was to take land from big landlords and give it to poor peasants, the way the communists promise to do; and that the best method of dealing with current troubles in southern Thailand, where there are 700,000 discontented Muslims, is to discuss their grievances with them.

Mr. Malik suspects that one day Vietnam will be reunited under Hanoi's rule; and that no doubt this will encourage communists elsewhere in Asia. But he also suspects that even a communist Vietnam is going to be anti-Chinese, and that therefore Vietnam's own ambitions to expand at the expense of its neighbors, Laos and Cambodia, are likely to be circumscribed by the Chinese, who have thoughtfully extended a road from Yunnan into Laos, possibly with just such a contingency in mind. The Chinese themselves conceivably could be tempted to launch a southward drive, as the Japanese military did in 1941. But such a Chinese move would at once create powerful allies for the threatened countries in the path of a hypothesized Chinese steamroller. These allies might include Soviet Russia as well as the United States. In the circumstances, a Chinese military advance southward seems unlikely. And similar arguments apply to any attempt that the Chinese might make to blackmail their Asian neighbors by brandishing their nuclear weapons. Such a threat would not go unmarked by some reaction from the other nuclear powers, the Soviet Union and the U.S.

The Indonesian foreign minister, in short, appears to envisage no external military threat to his country or to southeast Asia in the near future. Perhaps for that reason, more likely because of its current strong distaste for communism in any shape or form, Indonesia has turned away from Soviet Russia and toward the United States. This leaves the Russians somewhat bewildered, for they severely condemned the Chinese for apparently encouraging the Indonesian Communist Party's abortive coup in September, 1965, and they supplied Indonesia with the arms, the submarines and destroyers, bombers and interceptor aircraft, which General Suharto fell heir to after President Sukarno's downfall. The Russians also supplied the light tanks, armored cars, and other weapons which Suharto's army used to quell the communists after the latter had killed some of the leading Indonesian generals. Nevertheless, in Djakarta today, the Russians who were formerly applauded are cold-shouldered, and the Americans who used to be excluded are made to feel warmly welcome.

The reason for all this is quite simple. Indonesia at the moment fears no external foe, therefore has little use for the Soviet arms except to mothball them or even try to sell them off to the Egyptians. But Indonesia does have urgent need of economic assistance, and feels that the United States and other noncommunist countries are much likelier to furnish reasonable amounts of aid than is the Soviet Union, which would probably demand some political price for any aid it gave. The United States also may expect a reward; American oil companies are known to be most anxious to lay their hands on what is now suspected to be the greatest source of oil that exists between California and the Persian Gulf. But the Indonesian government is gambling on its ability to persuade or compel the Americans to return a fair share of the revenues from oil and minerals to the Indonesian authorities, for the benefit of the Indonesian people.

Indonesia no longer has any quarrel with any of its neighbors. Its feud with Singapore is regarded by both countries as best forgotten, and there is no threat of a confrontation with Malaysia. "Confrontation" was former President Sukarno's last desperate gimmick for attempting to rally his people and to refurbish his fading popularity. Nor is Foreign Minister Malik inclined to give much credence to the Philippines' claim to Sabah, the portion of Borneo that is now part of Malaysia. His view appears to be that Sabah was given a free choice in the matter and that it chose to join Malaysia and is perfectly content with its choice. If all this means that there are very few foreign policy matters for the foreign minister to brood over, Mr. Malik seems content with that too. The policy he has long advocated is, after all, one of peaceful nonalignment, with Indonesia being involved in others' affairs only to the extent of its willingness to act as a mediator, if it is asked to do so. This is probably the path of wisdom, for if Indonesia is fortunate enough not to need a foreign policy, it more than makes up for this by the number and complexity of its domestic problems.

The west, including the United States, may succeed in retrieving past blunders and in salving its conscience by holding out a helping hand that will enable Indonesia to climb back on its feet without becoming a western dependent. The last western blunder was to applaud or to look the other way in 1965 and 1966 when more than a quarter of a million human beings were exterminated in Indonesia for the alleged crime of being communists or communist sympathizers. In 1969, the west was still making political blunders; for it would have helped President Suharto, not hindered him, if the western press and western governments had expressed concern over the harsh treatment of many thousands of political prisoners in Indonesia, and also over rough army handling of helpless Indonesian peasants as well as of the even more helpless Chinese minority. The west preferred to stay silent, apparently in the nervous belief that it is better for such things to be swept under the rug so as not to imperil the new found cordial relations with Indonesia.

But the western nations are fortunately doing something positive as well. Eleven countries besides the United States have formed themselves into an Inter-Governmental Group (IGG) to salvage the ruined Indonesian economy. In addition, the recently established Asian Development Bank is active, as is the World Bank, thanks mainly to the dynamic leadership of World Bank president Robert S. McNamara, who visited Indonesia to see for himself how things were, then dispatched an unprecedented resident mission of World Bank officials to Djakarta, to work there for at least two years, which are more likely to turn out to be ten years. The actual amount of foreign aid that Indonesia is receiving from all those sources is modest, and, in proportion to the size of the problem, is minuscule. But the country in its present state probably cannot absorb any more aid than is being received. The United States has wisely adopted what the Japanese call "a low posture," and has announced that it will not contribute more than one-third of the total of multilateral aid to Indonesia.

From 1967 to the end of 1969, U.S. aid to Djakarta amounted altogether to about $400 million. The aid, and the Indonesian government's own measures, have produced some results. Inflation is being brought gradually under control, and the value of the Indonesian rupiah has risen. The price that has been paid is a large credit squeeze, that has brought a great deal of Indonesian business to a standstill. The literally concrete evidences of this, in Djakarta, are a number of impressive but only partly finished buildings on which work has had to be temporarily suspended. But inflation is now said to be "only" 4 percent a month, though the improvement may be due as much to a good rice crop as to draconian economic curbs on businesses. Watching the inflation is like watching an express train begin to slow down; it is still going fast, but no longer is just flashing past.

The Indonesian government has launched a five year plan. In the course of the plan, Indonesia hopes to be able to borrow from abroad about $3 billion, or one-tenth the annual cost of the Vietnam war. This means that by the end of the plan period, in 1974, Indonesia will owe $6 billion instead of $3 billion, which is the sum of its foreign debt now. But there is no prospect of the $3 billion that was borrowed earlier being repaid, unless Indonesia can be put back on its feet. By the end of the plan, it is hoped to have raised farm output by 50 percent, as well as having repaired the country's worn-out roads and neglected irrigation works. A peasantry that is earning more—and fully 75 percent of Indonesians are still peasants—will buy more consumer goods, which will furnish a base for expanding light industries. Eventually, Indonesia may be able to afford steel mills. The planners' first target is more food; and in order to produce more food, it is proposed to initially double the amount of fertilizer produced locally, and then if possible to double it again. The natural gas which is a by-product of oil production will come in very handy for producing nitrogen fertilizer. Indonesian peasants already have a tradition of helping one another in the fields, and it is hoped to apply this to marketing. The planners are also thinking in terms of enlarged trade in the "Pacific basin," between Indonesia, and the fast-growing economies of Taiwan, Hong Kong, South Korea, and Australia.

The Indonesian economic planners have no difficulty working harmoniously with the Harvard Group of American economists who are in Djakarta, with the Ford Foundation and the World Bank, and with ADB and IGG; for the simple reason that ·the Indonesian economists got their training mostly in the United States, either at Berkeley, Harvard, or MIT.

But the planners and their foreign allies are under no illusions about the difficulty of the tasks they have set themselves. Indonesia has a high population growth rate (about 2.7 percent) but it is also a fruitful land, so that it is said even the beggars are fat. The main problems are political ones. It will be possible to start utilizing Indonesia's large natural resources for the economic benefit of the Indonesian people, if a period of about five years of reasonable political stability can be guaranteed. If however that proves impossible, all its natural riches may not save Indonesia from either civil war, or communism, or more likely a combination of the two.

There are between three and four million Chinese in Indonesia, and they are regarded with almost universal distrust. The present Indonesian phobia about communism has aggravated an ethnic problem that already existed. The Chinese are often accused of secretly working on behalf of Peking; but just as frequently they are charged with being agents of Taiwan. The real charge against them is that they are richer, and work harder, than the average Indonesian. In Djakarta it is explained quite frankly, by government officials, that "when a volcano erupts, or a river overflows, the people go out and kill some Chinese." The Chinese are regarded as the cause of any and every misfortune. Wise Indonesians feel that the solution of this problem is to strive to raise up Indonesian peasants until they no longer feel inferior to Chinese. Then it will be easier for the two races to intermarry, as they now do in Thailand, and the Chinese will cease to stand aloof from Indonesian culture and will become true Indonesians, instead of strongly feeling and being felt to be foreigners. But in the meantime, the Chinese are the obvious target of attack by the discontented, especially the 3.5 million Indonesians who are unemployed, and the other 14 million who are under-employed.

The hapless Chinese suffer most of all from the Indonesian soldiers, who since General Suharto replaced Sukarno as president regard themselves, with considerable truth, as the real rulers of the country. There are in Indonesia about 400,000 men in uniform, including the police and the paramilitary forces as well as the army. The soldiers and the police are paid only about $10 a month. In consequence, the soldiers and the civil guards and other units supplement their incomes by the simple process of collecting money from Chinese storekeepers and other Chinese at the point of the bayonet. They also get as much as possible out of accused communists, before making political prisoners of them. And these uniformed bandits also prey on ordinary Indonesian farmers, peasants who are little better off than themselves. The soldiers go to the farms collecting "taxes." They collect ten times more than the farmer actually owes in taxes, and often they give him a receipt for the money. But in any event they are back, in a week or so, demanding the same sum all over again. The melancholy result is that a revolutionary army that was initially acclaimed by most people as the saviours of the country has become an army of occupation.

President Suharto has promised that there will be elections in Indonesia in about a couple of years. But, in the meantime, the parliament that meets is a packed parliament, with three-fifths of its members appointed by the army. The parliament contains some members of the former political parties, but these are not allowed to function as parties. A postponement of elections is understandable, and may be desirable. The politicians who fawned on Sukarno were, with some honorable exceptions, a miserable crew who, without Sukarno or someone else to tell them what to do, were incapable of any action. But the question that thoughtful Indonesians ask is how there are to be elections if there are no politicians, or political parties, and whether the army will really retire into the background in order for a democratic structure to be built and to function.

While the economic planners are busy with their blueprints, and Djakarta is filled with foreign concession-hunters, the plain people are being pillaged by the ragged soldiers, and some of the top generals in the army are living in the capital like pashas, surrounded by every luxury. If this spectacle filled President Suharto with anxiety, he showed little outward evidence of it. The president is a plain soldier himself, and no one suggests that he shares in any degree in the army decadence and corruption. Nor would it be correct to say that the army has turned itself into a junta and that Indonesia is now a police state. On the contrary, the press is, in the circumstances, remarkably outspoken; the regime's shortcomings are freely discussed.

Suharto is in a difficult position. The other generals are powerful. Suharto may have to temporize. However, there is growing recognition that the nation may not long endure the corruption, and the conditions of semi-banditry. Indonesians have a reputation for being almost too docile at one moment, only to flame into action and run amok the next. The Suharto regime may be seated on a powder-keg that is steadily getting hotter. The tension will be eased if President Suharto manages to take a firmer grasp of the situation, which means winning a showdown with the corrupt generals in Djakarta as well as with regional commanders who more and more seem inclined to go their own way without regard to the central government's wishes. If Suharto fails to do so, he could conceivably share the political fate of General Naguib who overthrew an Egyptian dynasty that had outlived its usefulness, only to be pushed aside, in turn, by Nasser.

## THE FILIPINO VOLCANO

THERE ARE 36 million Filipinos, and about three quarters of them are under the age of 25. The population is growing at a faster rate than that of India. This makes the rate of human growth 3.5 percent, one of the highest in the world.

Like Indonesia, the Philippines are a vast sprawl of islands. There are 11 main islands, and more than 6,000 small ones. The islands were conquered by Spain—the Spanish conqueror was Magellan—in 1521, and were ceded by Spain to the United States in 1898. In 1935, the Philippines became a self-governing commonwealth, but were occupied by Japan between the years 1942 and 1945. After the end of World War II, the Philippines became an independent republic, in 1946.

The form of government in the Philippines is modeled closely on that of the United States. The Filipino independence day is July 4th. I once knew a Filipino sugar millionaire who had six sons. The sons were extremely disgruntled young men in spite of their wealth. The reason was that their father had insisted that each of them choose July 4th as his wedding day. It was plain they felt not so much wrapped as stifled in the Stars and Stripes.

As in the United States, there are two main parties in the Philippines; they call themselves the Nationalists and the Liberals. The communist party of the Philippines has been banned since 1957. Nevertheless, the country is, to employ the phrase of President Ferdinand Marcos, a "social volcano." Many people have to make do on an income of less than $100 per year. Because of the burgeoning population, 800,000 new jobs are needed each year. But only 600,000 become available, and many of them are for only a half-day's work, for half a day's pay. As in Indonesia, the clamor for jobs has been partly met by simply creating government posts and grossly over-stocking government offices. As these government jobs carry very small pay, corruption is rife. There is more smuggling than even in Indonesia, and customs officials are among the leading smugglers. Additionally, the underemployed Filipinos feel their deprivation all the more keenly because most of them are well educated. But their education does not fill their stomachs. Lawyers drive taxis as a moonlighting occupation. It is said that every single Filipino employed at the Manila Hilton has a degree. More than 30,000 Filipinos leave their own country each year to go to the United States alone. There is of course immigration to other countries, although America is first and foremost the favorite. Life might be more bearable were it not that a vast gulf yawns between the handful of very rich and the mass of very poor Filipinos, and that the well-to-do manage to pay no taxes.

In 1950, these manifest social evils produced the inevitable communist movement. The communist organization called "Huks" had in central Luzon about 15,000 armed men, sup-ported by some half-million friendly peasants. The Philippines probably were saved from a communist takeover by Ramon Magsaysay. This energetic and imaginative man not only fought the Huks by military means; more important, by means of farm credits, resettlement of the landless, and other reforms, he won over the peasants and even some of the Huk leaders.

In 1953, the universally popular Magsaysay was elected president of the Philippines, and by 1955 the Huk movement seemed to be broken. But after the death of Magsaysay in an airplane crash in 1957, the old gap between the rich and the poor, the government and the peasant, reopened. The Huks crept through the gap and came back, dedicated to a long period of "protracted conflict." Today, they have in effect a shadow government in central Luzon. There they deal out rough justice, shooting oppressive landlords and in other ways attempting to win the peasants back to their side. They also run brisk gambling and other profitable rackets in Angeles

City, at the gates of Clark, the great American base, and are said to make $6 million a year from these activities. Moreover, in 1969 the Huks seemed to be preparing themselves to re-form as regular guerrilla fighters, bent upon attempting a communist revolution once again.

Clark is the second biggest United States military base, coming after Eglin, in Florida, and is the biggest American air base in all Asia. From Clark, supplies go out to Vietnam, and wounded Americans come in from there. Clark is the headquarters of the 13th Air Force. Thirty-three thousand American service men and their families live on the base, in the usual kind of military PX economy and environment; they own 20,000 automobiles. Just around the corner from Clark, as it were, is Subic Bay, 60 miles from Clark, and a major naval base for the 7th Fleet. It is regularly used by aircraft carriers and other warships. There is nothing the navy could conceivably want that Subic cannot supply, including spare gun barrels for the battleship New Jersey. The American bases in the Philippines employ some 50,000 Filipinos, and throughout the Vietnam war had brought an estimated $150 million a year revenue in one way or another to the Philippines— which nevertheless managed to have a trade deficit of $300 million a year.

The Filipino press, which is large, voluble, and vitriolic, happily engages in verbal warfare against the American bases and against "ugly Americans" in general. Many Filipinos say they would like the bases to be removed. Other Filipinos figure hopefully that Clark and Subic will become more necessary to the United States when the U.S. returns the island of Okinawa to Japan in 1972. If so, the Filipinos are extremely likely to let the bases stay only on their terms. The Philippines already receive concessions from the United States. For example, they get special tariff rates and quotas on their exports to the United States, including a sugar price that is three times the world price. These special rates are embodied in an agreement, the Laurel-Langley Agreement, that expires in 1974. The Filipinos will probably try to get this agreement extended, and improved from their point of view. At the same time, American business in the Philippines, under the agreement, received special privileges, which the Filipinos will attempt to have reduced.

In the history books, the Philippines in the 1960s may receive mention less for those tumults and frictions, but because at Los Banos the new "miracle" rice strains were perfected. They were made possible partly as a result of generous financial support from the Rockefeller Foundation. The new strains created a "green revolution" that promised to transform the economic life of Asia by greatly stepping up production of food. The history books might decide from hindsight that the green revolution was more important and more lasting in its effects than a whole series of political revolutions could have been.

## TOMORROW'S CUBA?

THE CATHOLIC CITY of Manila, largest in the Philippines, is a cheerful but fearfully disorderly place. Manila teems with people (1.3 million, back in 1965) and always seems to be tottering on the brink of breakdown. From the twentieth floor of a Hilton hotel, the view is one of broad boulevards, green parks, and sparkling fountains. But at street level, the prospect is one of broken sidewalks, hovels, and heaps of garbage. The traffic, wild and raucous, only mirrors the lawlessness that has now become the keynote of what may be Asia's most turbulent town. It is not surprising that there is considerable crime in Manila and throughout the Philippines. The yawning chasm between rich and abysmally poor Filipinos invites crime. Many homes are mere sheds open to the noisome street, and would scarcely be used for sties in more fortunate parts of the world. Meanwhile, a few wealthy Filipinos indulge in such extravaganzas as flying a complete orchestra from Europe, in order to entertain their guests for one evening.

Each year, thousands of Filipinos apply for visas to go to the United States where they hope to find work and a better life than is possible for them in their own country. Recently the number of would-be American citizens so markedly increased that the most pathetic sight in Manila was the long daily queue of Filipinos at the American Embassy. The consular staff was overwhelmed with work, and the sharp-tongued Manila press eagerly seized on an incident involving two American women in the consul's office who were accused of displaying "anti-Filipino feeling." The newspapers whipped up a campaign to have the two women deported, and com-

pelled the government of the Philippines to demand expla-
nations and an investigation of his staff by the American
ambassador. The ambassador refused to be ruffled and managed to cool the incident, which however was a good illustra-
tion of how onion-thin Manila skins are, and how Filipinos
feel toward the United States.

The southern Philippines population includes Muslims who,
like the Indonesians and the Malays, were converts of the
Arab merchants from Yemen who brought Islam along with
the spice trade. But the vast majority of Filipinos are Roman
Catholics. The islands are named for a Spanish prince, and a
common saying is that Filipinos spent 300 years in a Spanish
colonial convent, then 50 years under American tutelage,
when they learned to behave more like Hollywood Americans
than like real ones. This seems a cruel saying, but in fact
history has been even crueler to the Filipinos than the sharp
quip suggests. Their indigenous culture scarcely survived the
three centuries of Spanish rule; and those centuries under
Spain endowed them not only with Roman Catholicism but
also with torrential Spanish feelings, which have made it very
difficult for them to become like Americans. Yet that is what
many of them would most like to be. At one and the same
time, the Filipinos cherish their political independence, and
model themselves as closely as possible on the United States.

Manila's English-language newspapers are filled daily with
such headlines as "Solons Slate Veep Probe." In Manila,
the spirit of Randolph Hearst still lives. But so also does a
touchy Filipino nationalism, that is understandably oversensi-
tive because at the heart of it there burns a flame which is
fed by Spanish pride, that resents the copy-catting of American *mores,* as well as resenting the Philippines' painful dependence on the United States. This dependence is increased
by a perennial lack of suitable jobs for skilled Filipinos, which
causes a brain drain toward the U.S. But it is increased also
by an overproduction of unskilled Filipinos. Poor Filipino
families depend on the $100 million that emigrés annually
remit back home. That sum is said to be earned by the 16,000
Filipinos who work on U.S. military bases in South Vietnam,

on Guam, and on Wake Island. In addition, of course, the U.S. naval and air bases in the Philippines, Subic Bay, and Clark Field employ many thousands of Filipinos, and without the bases the country's unemployment problem would be even graver than it is. Filipinos being very human, their dependence on the United States in those ways irks them— as much as the American way of life, at least in its superficial aspects, obviously attracts them.

It is not too much to say that these ambiguities have lately turned the Philippines into what can only be called, even at the risk of hurt feelings and misunderstanding, a smiling cesspool of hate, as far as Americans are concerned. "They want to be loved by Americans," an observer in Manila explains, "that is why they smile. But they strongly suspect they aren't loved, that's why they hate." The Manila newspapers, which are politically powerful and are controlled by rich men, hardly ever let pass an opportunity to lambaste the United States by daily sneer and innuendo as well as by open attack. Many Filipino politicians, most of whom are also rich men, similarly attempt to build or consolidate their political fortunes by attacking the United States, when it does not better suit their book to be sickeningly sycophantic. Hitherto, the United States has complacently accepted the flattery, and has shrugged off the abuse, on the old adage that sticks and stones may break bones but words can't really hurt us. And, so far, the boldness and harshness of Filipino words toward the United States are in laughable contrast with Filipino timidity when it comes to deeds. In 1969, some Filipino politicians who had never been behindhand in slinging mud at America were wringing their hands in public at the thought of the government of the Philippines belatedly following countries like Spain and encouraging trade with eastern Europe. And permission that was given a Bolshoi Ballet troupe to perform in Manila was carefully balanced by a concurrent visit from the Vienna Boys' Choir.

The man in the middle of those ambiguities, though he was assuredly neither their architect nor their benefactor, was President Ferdinand Marcos, a World War II hero who was seeking and who won an unprecedented presidential second term. The president of the Philippines always has had two functions to perform, vis-à-vis the United States. He is judged by his own people according to the number of benefits and concessions he succeeds in wheedling from Washington; but also by the extent to which he dares to defy what may appear from time to time to be Washington's wishes. On the first count, President Marcos had got some favors from President Lyndon Johnson, by posing as Johnson's "right hand in Asia." Johnson and Marcos both signed the Manila communique about Vietnam; and Marcos uncovered an alleged plot that involved an unnamed Chinese general who was supposed to have secretly landed in the Philippines to mastermind Johnson's and Marcos's assassinations. On the second count, defying Washington, President Marcos earned applause from having sternly warned the United States that if it reduced its forces in Asia (meaning, if Washington cut its military spending there) Marcos would feel compelled in prudence to seek a *modus vivendi* with Communist China. The warning could scarcely have frightened Washington. In any event it was mainly intended for domestic consumption.

The favors that Marcos received from Washington were discouragingly few, in a period when the U.S. seemed intent on cutting aid. Perhaps for that reason, they did President Marcos little good at home. For instance, the brave bid by his pretty first lady Imelda to be a Ladybird, by creating for Manila a culture center to which President Johnson was said to have contributed $30,000, met with a harsh response among Filipinos. The critics declared that instead of building culture centers, she and her husband ought to be waging a war on poverty. Imelda, as Ladybird did on a similar occasion, is reported to have burst into tears. The disclosure that the 2,000 troops whom Marcos had sent to South Vietnam for guard duty, were paid by the United States, caused Marcos' critics to denounce him for being an American stooge.

As his first term drew toward its close, President Marcos was accused of all sorts of things. He was charged with having secretly transferred millions of pesos, obtained no one cared to specify how, to safe deposits in the United States. One of his opponents in the presidential election campaign, Senator Jovito Salanga, declared that the president had a "material interest" in a stock-swap deal which involved the government of the Bahamas, and a Filipino mining company called Benquet Consolidated Incorporated, and which was supposed to have gained Marcos a fortune. The weeping Imelda was accused of buying a lot of jewelry in New York, though the accusers left unclear why that was considered a criminal act. Finally, President Marcos suffered a stomach upset, which led to the revelation that several attempts had been made to poison him and that in consequence he employed a food taster.

During his four-year term, President Marcos had succeeded in carrying out at least some of the promises he had made when he was elected. The Philippines formerly did not grow nearly enough food for its 36 million population, though it has under cultivation almost exactly the same amount of land as Japan, which has almost three times as many people (100 million). Under Marcos, Filipino rice production increased, so that instead of importing food, the Philippines was able to export some. Marcos also had more roads built, and perhaps more schools, than had any of his predecessors. He promised to raise the rate of economic growth from three to five percent, and it actually went over six percent; while the rate at which the population of the Philippines is increasing may under Marcos have fallen from almost four to nearer three percent.

When Marcos was first elected President, a good many people remarked that he was probably the Philippines' last chance, and that if he failed, the deluge would come after him. President Marcos had not exactly failed. But what he had apparently succeeded in doing—raising the rate of economic growth, increasing rice production, building roads—still fell far short of what has to be done to make his country viable, either politically or economically. The government is not collecting from the rich the taxes they owe under the law; and the poor meanwhile are ground down by the weight of regressive import and sales duties. What is worse, the insufficient revenues the government does manage to collect are often either misspent, or stolen. Corruption is rife among government officials at all levels. That is why the air is constantly filled with noisy allegations and counterallegations. Even though many of those miss their mark, there is a considerable fire burning somewhere behind the volume of smoke. The net result is an accelerating cynicism among all Filipinos about the whole political process; the kind of cynicism that is the deadliest eroder of a democratic system, which the Philippines certainly have. People vote; but they evade paying their taxes if they can, when they see (still more, when they don't see) what is being done with their money. When revenues falter, corruption among officials increases, because the pie they have all been nibbling at has shrunk. One reason why some of his former political supporters vainly wished Marcos to lose in November 1969 was their feeling that he had had four years in which to amass a personal fortune from the public funds, and therefore he ought to quit, to give someone else a chance to feed at the trough.

The thickening aura of corruption and self-seeking disgusted all honorable Filipinos. Senator Manglapus, for example, quit main-party politics, in disgust, and sought to form a new third party. Other hats still in the political ring belonged to Senator Sergio Osmena Junior, who has a powerful political base in Cebu, the country's second largest city; ex-president Diosdado Macapagal, who hoped to make a comeback; and Senator Genaro Magsaysay, who had little going for him save his late older brother's fame, and who suffered the grievous handicap of being accused, no doubt unjustly, of enjoying the financial backing of the United States Central Intelligence Agency.

A man who might have successfully opposed Marcos in 1969, except that at 36 he was still too young to become president under the Philippines constitution, was Senator Benigno Aquino, who therefore would have to wait until 1973 for his chance. All Filipinos without exception have immense personal charm, and Senator Aquino has more than most. He graduated from college when he was 17, and became a war correspondent in Korea. Then he returned home to help President Magsaysay fight the Huk Communist guerrillas (the Huks) and he actually talked the Huk leader Luis Taruc into surrendering on Magsaysay's reasonable terms. There has been no stopping Aquino since then. His career reads like an American dream: mayor of his home town when he was 22, governor of a province at 28, elected a senator before he was 35.

Aquino's American hero, if he had one, would be Herman Kahn the think-tank man, whom he somewhat resembles both physically and mentally. Like Kahn, Aquino is fond of making people's flesh creep with scenarios of doom. Aquino's most notorious scenario for the Philippines involves the free use of plastic bombs as a means of exploding his country out of its current vicious circle of economic sluggishness and political corruption. This recipe seems to owe more to the Great Proletarian Cultural Revolution of Mao Tse-tung, than it does to Herman Kahn, and it need not be taken too seriously. But what Senator Aquino was plainly hinting has to be taken quite seriously. He was saying in effect that if the rich men and the politicians (often the same people) did not soon reform, a new Luis Taruc would appear, leading a new Huk movement which this time might succeed. Ironically, Aquino is a rich man himself, thanks to sugar and real estate interests; and his wife is richer still. Words come easily in the Philippines. More than one past presidential aspirant has promised radical reform with apparent sincerity, then failed dismally to keep his promises. Only if and when the youthful Senator Aquino enters the president's palace will it be known how much he means of what he says. He sounds as if he meant a good deal.

The Republic of the Philippines was long an American colony; and it is a colony still, but not an American one. It is colonized by 50 rich Filipino families who flaunt their wealth and exploit their factory workers and farm hands more than any foreigner or foreign firm would dare to do. Some of these rich Filipinos are trying very hard to squeeze American interests out. If they succeed, it seems probable that the lot of the poor Filipinos would be harder than before. About $900 million of American private capital is invested in the Philippines. It is a sobering thought that this is almost the same amount as was invested by Americans in another Roman Catholic country that was once under American rule, and where there was recently a successful revolution—Cuba. But the Philippines may not go the same road as Cuba. The Filipinos hold frequent elections, and vastly enjoy them, even though quite a few people get killed in shooting affrays during a campaign. Most Filipinos, rich and poor alike, plantation owner or sharecropper, are cousins in some degree. Blood generally proves stronger than class consciousness. There are also regional and clan ties; rich or politically powerful Pampangos see that poor Pampangos get jobs, and Leytenos and Ilokanos likewise stand by their own folk. There is a good deal of evidence that many of the poor actually enjoy the spectacular extravaganzas that the rich put on, if they can only boast that the free spender is a kinsman of theirs.

On the other hand, the current despair among the few honest politicians, many intellectuals, and growing numbers of middle-class professional people, is genuine and it is deepening. These people are becoming desperate. They see little future for themselves or for their children in a lawless, corrupt society that neglects or misuses the country's natural wealth. More scientific farming, and modern factory methods and bigger corporations may eat away the unique, feudal family ties that are really all that prevent the Philippines blowing up politically, and which at the same time hinder the country from developing faster economically.

President Marcos seemed aware of this. He said in 1969 that it ought to become easier for the Philippines to get on to better terms with China eventually because the "external" communist threat was "minimal." But he went on to say that there was a "growth of internal communism, arising from urgent economic problems." And President Marcos declared: "We have lost confidence in ourselves because we fail so often, and we fail so often because we have lost confidence in ourselves." Marcos might or might not have been aware of Lenin's three preconditions for a successful revolution. But his words echoed Lenin's, consciously or otherwise. For Lenin's preconditions for revolution were: a government that has lost faith in its capacity to solve problems; a people that has lost faith in the government's capacity; and the ripeness and readiness of a hard-core communist leadership to seize the opportunity that these present to it. All that now seems to be lacking in the Philippines is the third condition. This may be why increasing numbers of Filipinos, especially educated, middle-class ones, are anxious to get out, before the storm bursts. Experience elsewhere suggests that the American military bases in the Philippines are likelier to provoke such trouble than to avert it.

# AMERICA AND THE MALAYS

IN THE COURSE of his 1969 election campaign, President Marcos of the Philippines found it expedient—and the adverb is more than usually precise—to insist that the real threat to the future of the Philippines was an internal one of social disruption, not an external one of military aggression. He talked with unusual warmth about the possibility of the Philippines trading with the Soviet Union, Eastern Europe, and Communist China; and he was correspondingly harsh in his scornful references to the United States military bases in the Philippines. In short, the United States was fulfilling its traditional function in Philippines politics, as a whipping boy. Yet what Marcos was saying was essentially true. The real problems of the Philippines are internal; and the American military bases cannot solve them and may aggravate them. If a wealthy conservative like Marcos believed that he could make political capital out of attacking America and by hinting at "imperialist" abuses, there is no need to imagine what effective use the Huks can make of the same sort of charges against the United States.

Confronted by this rising tumult, the United States could of course just cut and run. It could pull out of the Philippines without waiting to be thrown out. But this would be to run away from responsibility. Some Filipinos contend that the United States is at least in part to blame for some of the bad conditions now in evidence in the Philippines. For instance, the quid pro quo for favorable treatment of American business in the Philippines is a generous United States sugar quota, a subsidy in all but name for Philippines sugar producers. But the sugar barons are a cause of much of the grave social injustices that have turned the Philippines into a volcano. And so long as they can confidently count on receiving continuing American economic support, they can continue to turn a deaf ear to the cries of outrage and anger that rise up against them from their own countrymen. Insofar as the sugar quota gives the United States leverage with the Philippines sugar barons, it ought to be used to pressure them into standing aside and allowing reforms, instead of, as they now mostly do, employing all their strength to block reforms. And this would be in the true interests of the sugar plantation owners themselves, for if they go on blocking reform, a blow-up that will destroy them seems inevitable.

The issue of the bases is likely to solve itself, in time. If public opinion in the Philippines is beginning to turn decisively against the bases, as seems probable, the United States will have no choice but to leave. The timing is of course important. But it might be wise to set a reasonable date for withdrawal and announce it at once, as the British did in the "east of Suez" declaration (out by 1975, which they then advanced to 1971). Not only would such a declaration of American intent calm the anti-base agitation in the Philippines, it might lead not to total United States withdrawal but to a new defense arrangement that would better suit both countries.

Turn now to Indonesia. The United States has always looked on Indonesia as a country of major strategic as well as of economic significance. Even while he was expressing America's sympathy with Malaysia, when that country was enduring President Sukarno's "confrontation," Adlai Stevenson in the United Nations Security Council debates also emphasized America's hope for an Indonesian change of heart that would make cordial U.S.-Indonesia relations possible once again. Malaysians frowned on this at the time as being two-faced; but after the fall of Sukarno in 1965, and his replacement in 1966 by Suharto who went out of his way to express friendship for Malaysia, the Malaysian prime minister Tunku Abdul Rahman warmly applauded United States economic assistance to Indonesia, and declared at the 1966 commonwealth conference that Indonesia "needs assistance quickly from all countries, to recover her bearings." But, as in the case of the Philippines, the really tough problems of Indonesia are internal, and social. Should Suharto fail to solve them—and by something a good deal more positive than mere anticommunism—either Indonesia will experience another communist rising which may gain popular support, or Indonesia will fall into the hands of another military-backed demagogue like Sukarno, who will once again seek a way out of his difficulties by turning his militant glare on Malaysia and Singapore. American policy toward Indonesia should take this possibility into account; for the United States has historically been concerned (since 1800) with the security of the Straits of Malacca, and of Singapore, which is now the world's fifth largest port and the "lynch-pin of southeast Asia," as Lee Kuan Yew calls his island-city-state.

The relations of the United States and Malaysia have had disconcerting ups and downs. Thus, Malaysia was one of the first countries in the world to respond to the offer of President John F. Kennedy to send Peace Corps volunteers. Soon after the Peace Corps was founded, in 1961, Malaysia asked the United States to send teachers, nurses, doctors, and technicians. The first batch of these volunteers arrived in January 1962, and they quickly spread throughout Malaya and Borneo. After the assassination of President Kennedy, President Johnson attempted to continue these cordial relations with Malaysia. He sent Attorney General Robert Kennedy to Malaysia to attempt to stop the war between Malaysia and Indonesia. After Malaysia's formation, on September 14, 1963, President Sukarno had begun a campaign which he called "*ganjang Malaysia.*" This meant literally, devour Malaysia. In its attempt to halt Sukarno, the United States supported Malaysia in the United Nations and suspended a large part of its economic assistance to Indonesia. Robert Kennedy managed to get an agreement to a cease fire on January 25, 1964. Sukarno unfortunately paid little heed to the cease fire and American threats which followed to stop all aid to Indonesia provoked Sukarno's famous cry, "To hell with your aid!"

This at least should have led to good American relations with Malaysia, whatever it did to America's relations with Indonesia. But an American offer of arms assistance to Malaysia had quite the opposite result. Department of Defense officials who went out to Malaysia to negotiate the terms of assistance insisted that Malaysia should pay 5 percent interest on the loan. The Malaysians felt that this was ungenerous, especially when compared to American assistance that had been given to Asian nations like Vietnam, Korea, India, and Pakistan on easy terms. Indonesia, too, had received better terms, the Malaysians alleged. Anti-American riots broke out in Kuala Lumpur, the capital of Malaysia. The rioters attacked and partly destroyed the United States Information Service Library. When the Malaysian government apologized, the United States immediately granted Malaysia a loan of $11 million at 3 percent, not 5 percent, through the export-import bank, for the purchase of arms, and also made Malaysia a direct loan of another $5 million. That healed the breach with Malaysia.

But the next year, 1965, America was in trouble with Singapore. The prime minister of Singapore Lee Kuan Yew revealed that an agent of the Central Intelligence Agency had attempted to bribe a Singapore official. Matters were not improved by Secretary of State Dean Rusk at first hotly denying and then admitting Lee Kuan Yew's allegation. These incidents rather threw into the shade the offer that President Johnson made in his speech at Johns Hopkins University, in the spring of 1965, of a loan of $1 billion to support regional cooperation in Asia.

The following year, 1966, things picked up again when the United States made an initial contribution of $200 million to the new Asian Development Bank. However, in the same year, there were renewed anti-American demonstrations in Malaysia, this time against America's part in the Vietnam war. In Kuala Lumpur the USIS Library was again wrecked. The First National City Bank of New York building was damaged. In March 1966, the Assistant Secretary of State for the

Far East, William P. Bundy, arrived in Kuala Lumpur and was greeted by angry demonstrators. There were further riots in July of that year, this time occasioned by the arrival of American troops in Kuala Lumpur on rest and recreation from Vietnam. Finally, there were more riots in October 1966, on the occasion of President Johnson's visit to Malaysia. There was serious anti-American rioting in Penang, Malacca, and Ipoh. In Kuala Lumpur, a Chinese youth was killed in front of the USIS Library. This boy's funeral drew a crowd of 3,500 people.

In spite of those ups and downs, however, the first American gesture toward the Malaysians has continued to be a success. By the end of 1966, more than 1,000 Peace Corps volunteers had served in Malaysia, including doctors, dentists, nurses, and laboratory workers, as well as radio technicians and agricultural workers, teachers and development workers, librarians and others. As a result of this experience, one American in 200,000 now speaks fluent Malay; formerly, almost no Americans did. The Malaysians themselves have now taken up the Peace Corps idea, and plan to send Malaysian volunteers to help other less developed countries which are their neighbors. Malaysia is one of the strongest supporters of the United Nations. One prominent enthusiast for the UN is Tun Razak, Tunku Abdul Rahman's righthand man. The Malaysian ambassador to the United Nations holds cabinet rank. He has advocated giving the United Nations muscle—"a supra-national authority with physical as well as moral power." Malaysia sent troops to the Congo from 1960 to 1963. And it has been suggested that the military complex in Singapore might make an excellent base for a United Nations regional force, if one were ever to be established. Should it be, the United States would certainly be asked for at least a financial contribution.

Although Malaysia suffered from a long-drawn communist rebellion which appeared to be mainly Chinese inspired, the Malaysian government has always argued that mainland China should be admitted to the United Nations, though it has also insisted that Taiwan should not on that account lose its present United Nations seat. Singapore's attitude to Red China and the United Nations is that China should be admitted to the international organization without conditions.

By its policy of "containing" China, the United States has shown that it believes in the so-called domino theory—that is, that China's smaller neighbors are threatened by Chinese expansion and are in danger of falling one by one. More recently, Secretary of State William P. Rogers and other official spokesmen of the Nixon administration have had a change of mind on this subject; that China after all is not quite the military menace it was formerly held to be by, for example, former Secretary of State Dean Rusk.

The dominos themselves do not seem to believe much in the domino theory. Tunku Abdul Rahman once affirmed that although the Chinese had encouraged the guerrilla movement in Malaysia verbally, they had given it no material support. Tunku Abdul Rahman also called the South East Asia Treaty Organization (SEATO) "ineffective, negative, outmoded, and under the stigma of western domination." All the countries discussed in this chapter are reluctant to be members of any anticommunist military alliance and they are also allergic to foreign military bases. They believe that pacts should be for the purposes of trade and cultural exchange. Modest military support from Australia and New Zealand apparently would not be unwelcome to Singapore and Malaysia. This it seems would not be regarded as western domination, presumably because of the low military posture of both these countries. Under the Anzus pact, the United States has pledged itself to go to the defense of Australia and New Zealand should they be attacked. That kind of indirect American military presence is the one that seems least unpalatable to the southeast Asian countries. It is probably the only way in which a powerful country like the United States can have a "low posture."

In his Johns Hopkins University speech of 1965, President Lyndon Johnson called upon "the countries of southeast Asia to associate themselves in greatly expanded cooperative effort for development." For this purpose, he promised to find $1 billion of assistance money. Years earlier, President Eisenhower had offered a more modest $200 million for regional economic cooperation in Asia. The countries of the region have not hitherto been very good at economic cooperation; witness the failure of Malaysia and Singapore to establish a common market. This broke down even though all the experts agreed that a customs union would produce greater economic growth. However, the Malaysians, the people of Singapore, and other peoples of the region feel that in spite of American offers of aid, the United States itself is not all that interested in economic cooperation. For instance, relations between the United States, Malaysia, and Singapore have been plagued by a ridiculous quarrel over shop towels, which are the simple cotton textiles that are woven into long sheets and then cut into shorter lengths and used to wipe the grease off machinery. In 1962, the United States joined an international agreement, called the Long Term Agreement regarding international trade in cotton textiles, or LTA for short. This was done in order to protect American textiles, and what it did was to put volume-restraining quotas on foreign exports of cloth. One favorite way for new nations to industrialize is by manufacturing cotton cloth for export. But LTA permits developed nations like the United States to cut off imports of cotton cloth which threaten their own producers. What usually happens is that the newer, developing country is compelled to promise, by a "gentlemen's agreement," not to try to export more than a certain amount of cotton cloth.

Singapore began to make shop towels in 1965, and Malaysia in 1967. The United States promptly pressured Lee Kuan Yew's Singapore government in August 1966 to accept a limitation of 35 million square yards of textile exports to the United States each year, for the next three years. Singapore was in effect told that if it didn't agree to this condition—and the quota did after all guarantee work for about 3,000 people—worse would befall. However, the limitation placed by the United States on Singapore immediately tempted the

Malaysian manufacturers to get into the business. Soon, cotton goods were being shipped to the United States from Malaysia.

Then the sequence was played over again. The United States threatened reprisals unless Malaysia, too, agreed to limit its exports—which in effect meant limiting the expansion of industry in Malaysia. Many United States officials argued in private, and some even in public, that the United States was being both bull-headed and short-sighted. The manufacture of simple cotton textiles more properly belongs to the modest resources and skills of the developing nations than to the highly paid skills of American workers. It would be better to retrain and to relocate American textile workers than to do everything possible to hang onto the business and thus retard the industrialization of poorer nations. Hitherto, instead of accepting or even examining this argument, administrations in Washington have gone on imposing quotas, at the same time as they make grandiloquent gestures like offering $1 billion of assistance to countries which will cooperate economically. It is perhaps not surprising that the Asians take these periodic offers with a grain of salt.

Malaysia is the world's largest producer of both natural rubber and of tin. The United States stockpiles both those commodities in prodigious quantities. Result: when the United States government decides from time to time to reduce its stockpiles by selling off large amounts, these sales depress the price Malaysia receives for its primary exports, and scores of thousands of Malaysians suffer unemployment. The price of rubber began sinking after the Korean War ended, and fell every year of the 1960s. A decline of 1.5 cents per pound means a 7 percent fall in the incomes of Malaysians. Malaysia has been luckier with its tin. There is a world shortage, so the price of tin has been climbing. Unfortunately, however, tin mining employs only about 50,000 Malaysians, whereas the rubber plantations employ 600,000.

What is the remedy for these drastic ups and downs in the prices of Malaysia's chief exports? International commodity control schemes have been tried and have not worked well, besides being probably against the general economic interest. A better plan would no doubt be for international financial organizations like the World Bank to lend needed funds to a primary producing country like Malaysia in hard times, against the promise of repayment and, perhaps, a pledge not to charge more for its tin or rubber than an agreed maximum, in times of large world demand for them. Such an arrangement, in which the United States would inevitably have to play a large part as a major industrial consumer, has yet to be worked out, but if it were, it would of course be an arrangement quite different from the United States' subsidization of Filipino sugar plantation owners which enables them to oppress their countrymen at the cost of keeping the price of sugar to American consumers artifically high.

**8**

# TWO CHINESE ISLANDS

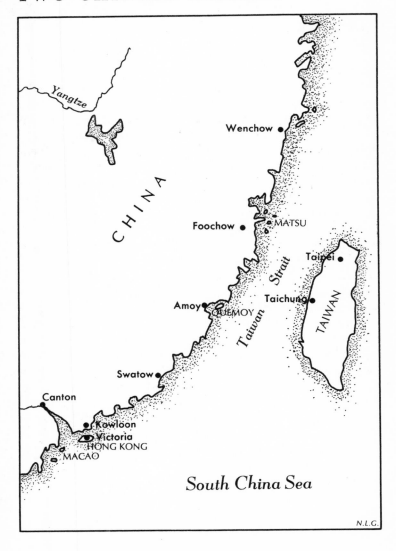

*Yangtze*

C H I N A

Wenchow ●

Foochow ● ● MATSU

Taipei ●

Amoy ● QUEMOY

Taichung ●

*Taiwan Strait*

TAIWAN

Swatow ●

Canton

● Kowloon
● Victoria
HONG KONG
MACAO

*South China Sea*

N.L.G.

## HONG KONG

THE ISLAND OF Hong Kong, only 32 square miles, was acquired by Britain in 1842, after the first opium war. For reasons of trade and military strategy, Britain was anxious to impose its will on China, and so it forced war on the Chinese with a very odd pretext. The Chinese government of the day was endeavoring to prevent the importation of opium, and the British claimed this was a grievous restraint of trade. This and similar acts, said Bertrand Russell, ironically, "did much to persuade the Chinese of the superiority of our civilization." The British appetite for Chinese territory grew. In 1860, after a second "opium war," the British acquired, in addition to Hong Kong, Stonecutter's Island and Kowloon, a total area of 3.75 square miles.

Meanwhile, in addition to seizing these bits of Chinese territory, the British had forcibly opened up five Chinese ports to British trade and, with the French, had bombarded and destroyed the Summer Palace near Peking. This building, Bertrand Russell noted, contained treasures which must have been the equal of Saint Mark's in Venice, and greater than the artistic value of Rheims Cathedral. Then, in 1870, the Chinese were rash enough to murder a British diplomat— so the British went to war again and got five more ports. In 1898, Britain got from China a 99-year lease on the New Territories—365 square miles of mainland area adjoining Kowloon, plus 335 adjacent islands.

What the New Territories lease means is that most of the land area of the Crown Colony of Hong Kong, which today contains about four million people, and represents most of what remains of Britain's colonial empire, is due to revert to China in 1997. Most people would not bet on Hong Kong remaining a British Crown colony that long. However, in spite of the British decision to withdraw militarily from "east of Suez" by 1971, Hong Kong's garrison was slightly increased in 1968—although the British frankly indicated that no effort would be made to retain Hong Kong in the face of a serious Chinese armed push.

But the Chinese may not push. Hong Kong is valuable to them in various ways. And a curious symbiotic relationship has come to exist between Hong Kong and Peking. Thus, the British authorities put down Hong Kong communists when they riot, breaking communist Chinese heads and handing out stiff jail sentences; yet in 1968 the colony was amicably permitting the existence in Hong Kong of 20 Chinese communist schools. It may very well be that Peking tolerates Hong Kong partly *because* it is a colony and not a democracy. However, this isn't entirely the fault of the British who, in 1968, tried to increase the number of registered voters in Hong Kong for the 1969 urban council elections, by sending out 146,000 blanks; fewer than 7 percent of these were returned by the hoped-for electors. Polling stations are also provided, but very few people bother to use them.

Hong Kong has its own stock exchange, and it has something like $400 million of its financial reserves safely banked in London. Hong Kong is also a member of the Asian Development Bank. But the biggest bank in Hong Kong, occupying the tallest building on the waterfront, is the communist Bank of China that is owned and staffed by Peking.

Both Singapore and Hong Kong are merely specks on the map of Asia. But they are Chinese cities, and this as well as the fact that they possess fine natural harbors gives them far more importance than their size might suggest. Singapore is now an island republic, whereas Hong Kong is still a British Crown colony administered in archaic eighteenth-century fashion. But in each case what really counts is the dynamism of the Chinese. By sheer energy, combined with considerable brains, the Chinese have transformed both these places into throbbing workshops of the Far East that are successfully doing business with the entire world.

Hong Kong (which means fragrant harbor) has a population of four million; but another four million people visit it each year, by ship and by plane. And a truly revealing statistic about Hong Kong's population is that it has attained the highest density on earth, a density which is 20 times that of London. The foreground of the daily Hong Kong scene is occupied by sailing junks, and sampans at anchor that are the floating homes of the Hoklo tribe of sea gypsies. But the background to all this is an astonishing little Manhattan. Straight up from the foreshore, and literally scraping the low clouds, stand huddled together row upon row of 16-story and 25-story buildings. These buildings climb up into the hills; but they also thrust out into the sea; for in order to provide themselves with more *lebensraum*, the people of Hong Kong are constantly shaving off hills to make flat spaces for putting up buildings, then depositing the rubble in the sea, thus creating more land on which to erect still more buildings. The foreshore therefore is always changing, and it advances ever outward.

Singapore has as we saw a socialist prime minister who is determined to turn his island-city into a model welfare state. But Hong Kong practices capitalism in its most undiluted, laissez faire form. The employers of the colony's 185,000 textile workers claim that their employees are guaranteed a minimum wage, an eight-hour day, and other benefits; and this may be true, as far as it goes. The fact remains that Hong Kong's 12,000 registered factories enjoy the advantage of what must be almost the cheapest labor force in all Asia. The factories have made full use of this cheap labor to attain a value of exports that now greatly exceeds $1 billion a year, compared with $40 million 20 years ago. Many of the owners of those factories are refugees from mainland China who arrived in Hong Kong penniless, and have since become very wealthy. Most of the factory workers are also refugees from mainland China who hope that with hard work and a bit of luck they too may one day be rich. They are certainly prepared to work; and, though they now constitute a mass of low-paid labor, many of them have the souls of capitalists, or at least of entrepreneurs.

The factory workers of Hong Kong who used to live in refugee huts or on sampans now occupy miles of tall tenements whose grimy greyness is brightened by balcony after balcony of gaily colored washing hung out to dry. But these tenements are also the secret sanctuaries of the colony's innumerable unregistered, illegally operated workshops. No one knows how many such workshops there are. From time to time, fire sweeps through a tenement, caused by faulty electric wiring or by a cigarette dropped in one of the secret workshops. Then the police and other authorities swoop down and close the place. But no one doubts that it will soon reappear phoenix-like elsewhere. The families who own those workshops (and who do most of the work in them) are probably destined to be tomorrow's Hong Kong capitalists. It is the dream of every factory worker to be able to scrape together a little money so as to launch out with a workshop of his own which will employ himself and his family. In that sense, Hong Kong is still at least one step ahead of Singapore; for in the workers flats of Prime Minister Lee Kuan Yew, the occupants have not yet discovered how to set up illegal workshops, but do have to be restrained from keeping pigs and other livestock on the premises.

In spite of its unbridled capitalism, and its huge heroin traffic, Hong Kong is on the whole well run. Law and order are maintained by 11,000 smart Chinese policemen—and Chinese policewomen—who manage to keep order with very little display of force, though recently they felt compelled to apply to the government for bullet-proof vests, because of the ructions created by communist demonstrators. Hong Kong has at least an outward appearance of British calm, as befits a British colony. It is so British in fact that its colonial administrators manage to turn China tea into a stewed brew that is too strong for any but British palates. The best hotel in Hong Kong gravely serves this brew to surprised travelers who have been unwary enough not to order coffee. The stewed tea is poured from silver teapots into delicate eggshell-thin cups.

Hong Kong's affairs, and the lives of its 4 million Chinese inhabitants, are managed on behalf of Her Britannic Majesty by two British knights; Sir David, and Sir John. The governor is the personal representative of the Queen; but the financial secretary does all the real work. In 1969, the financial secretary triumphantly budgeted for a surplus. Hong Kong was one of the very few governments in the world able to do this. Yet there is a 15 percent ceiling on income tax. In administering the colony's affairs, the governor is assisted by an Executive Council and a Legislative Council. Neither body contains any *elected* representatives. The Exco has six "official" members, and eight "unofficial" ones; but the latter are all picked and appointed by the governor. Legco similarly has 12 "official" and 13 "unofficial" members, and only nine of the 13 are what the British call "local people." Below Exco and Legco there are 40 departments of government, all of them staffed exclusively by career civil servants. The only electoral element that is allowed to intrude upon this set-up is in the Hong Kong Urban Council, which has 26 members of whom 10 are elected. The Urban Council is permitted to frame by-laws, on matters like public health; but all its decisions require Legislative Council approval.

The Chinese, including the million or more who are refugees from the mainland, display little resentment of this eighteenth-century administrative framework that duplicates the one that made eighteenth-century Americans' blood boil. The reason may simply be that they are Chinese. More likely, the reason is that, whatever their feelings, they know they are between the devil and the deep blue sea. An assault on British colonial rule probably would only throw them into the embrace of mainland China. A full quarter of them are in Hong Kong precisely because they fled from communist rule. Here, at least they have a chance to prosper, if not to have full political freedom. When the demon of discontent gnaws them, all they need to do in order for life under British rule to seem quite bearable is to contact a recent refugee and listen to his tale of how people are faring in China, just a few miles away.

When the British from time to time use force to quell demonstrations by communists in Hong Kong, that comes under the head of maintaining law and order, not of confronting China. In the last serious riots, the British jailed a number of Hong Kong communists, and Peking in retaliation seized a British journalist, Anthony Gray, and imprisoned him in his own house in Peking until the Hong Kong communists were released after serving most of their jail sentences. In spite of this tit-for-tat policy of Peking, however, the British in Hong Kong believe that communist demonstrators who have planted bombs and committed other acts of sabotage were not acting on Peking's instructions, but were anxiously trying to prove to Peking, at the height of the Chinese "Cultural Revolution," that they could be relied upon to act as violently as Mao's Red Guards. They may have misinterpreted Mao's intentions toward Hong Kong. Not only has Peking recently ceased to shake a threatening fist at the British colony; Peking also abandoned its tirade of abuse directed at the nearby Portuguese colony of Macao and, instead, loaned the startled Macao authorities a labor supply for building a causeway that will enhance Macao's attraction for foreign tourists. This *volte face* by Peking bewildered China Watchers in Hong Kong, but it encouraged investors to pluck up heart, and to put more money than ever into the British colony. For 20 years, Hong Kong has been under the Chinese communist gun, and has lain there quite helplessly without ever a shot being fired. The British, and also the vast majority of the four million Chinese, sometimes have dared to hope that the lease of the New Territories might actually run its full term; and a great deal can happen in 28 years.

Meantime, Hong Kong necessarily is a place of confusing paradoxes. Not the least is that the most imposing building by far, among the tall buildings that constitute Hong Kong's Manhattan-like silhouette, is the one that is owned and occupied by the communist Bank of China. It stands cheek by jowl with the Hong Kong Hilton, and American tourists often wander, in innocent error, into the communist bank to try to cash a traveler's check.

Another feature of Hong Kong is that the colony serves as a home and convenient observation post for those westerners who are professionally employed to study, and if possible to make sense of, Mao Tse-tung's mysterious Chinese opera. In Hong Kong, the China Watchers can read a great many Chinese communist newspapers, and study other Peking documents, as well as listening to the Chinese communist broadcasts, and interviewing refugees and others who come out of mainland China into the British territory. The China Watchers, who comprise American and British diplomats and other experts, have been at their Hong Kong post for two decades, but it cannot be truthfully said that they have had much success in translating what happens in communist China into intelligible western terms. Each new development has taken most of them by surprise, just as it has caught everyone else by surprise. This seems to have applied with still greater force than usual to the Great Proletarian Cultural Revolution. One China Watcher has confessed that it is now probably a waste of time to read anything that was written about communist China before the Cultural Revolution, which may have completely altered the Chinese political landscape, and which no one anticipated. This pardonable failure does not however prevent some China Watchers assuming an air of infallibility. The traveler to Hong Kong who is jaded by normal sightseeing may find refreshment in visiting a Chinese restaurant that is a favorite haunt of the China Watchers. There, he is likely to see those professional western observers expertly twirling their chopsticks, or slurping their Chinese soup, while they bark in Chinese dialect at the waiters, and portentously discuss the latest tid-bit of information about Mao Tse-tung's communist wonderland. But however avidly he eavesdrops, the traveler is not really likely to glean anything that he could not have guessed for himself, or that he could not read in one of Hong Kong's English-language daily newspapers.

The Hong Kong China Watchers do not include any known

Soviet experts on China. But the Russians and their navy will probably bulk larger in China's immediate future than will the American and British warships at anchor in Hong Kong harbor. Russia is busy forging trade links and trying to create goodwill in southeast Asia, from Singapore to Taiwan. It seems a reasonable assumption that this is being done with a Soviet eye on China. There are border clashes as well as severe ideological strains and stresses between the two huge communist countries. Russia may be tempted by China's apparent military weakness and internal political turmoil. A *serious* Russian military move against China probably would not take place in the inhospitable barren regions of the Amur River, near the disputed island of Chenpao. But one might be launched against Sinkiang, which is believed to be rich in oil and uranium, as well as being the site of China's nuclear installations. Sinkiang, besides, has large non-Chinese minorities, and several times in recent years Russia has accused China of oppressing the minorities, by "driving them from their ancient lands into lifeless deserts."

The ethnic minorities are apparently not the only people in Sinkiang who are having a hard time. A group of senior Chinese nuclear and ballistic scientists in Sinkiang were recently arrested, accused of being Soviet agents and saboteurs. These charges may have been made in order to cover up embarrassing failures of Chinese nuclear weapons that were being tested; but there have also been some signs of significant struggle among various Chinese factions for control of the nuclear installations in Sinkiang. The Russians, meanwhile, have themselves installed missile sites in Outer Mongolia at Buir Nor and Noirobiansan, from where they could destroy China's nuclear plants in Sinkiang; but they might prefer to try to capture them, on the pretext of liberating both them and Sinkiang from the ideological heretics in Peking.

In the course of China's stormy Cultural Revolution, Mao Tse-tung finally toppled his chief rival, Liu Shao-chi, for opposing Mao's policies. But this may only have opened the door to a power struggle by the factions of Lin Piao, Chou

En-lai, and Mao's wife Chiang Ching. The Great Proletarian
Cultural Revolution seems to have raised up a whole host
of provincial and local, age-group and occupational, rivalries
throughout China. Angry students, roused peasants, and
finally factory workers have been behaving like successive
waves of Boxers, the militant religious fanatics who indulged
in frenetic xenophobia in China 70 years ago. This time, however, there are few foreigners left to attack and so the con-
tending groups have been attacking one another. Almost every
part of China has shown evidence of turmoil, but few parts
have shown it in so marked a degree as Sinkiang.

One outcome of the confusion has apparently been to put
the Chinese People's Liberation Army, under Lin Piao, in a
more commanding position than either the Chinese Communist Party, or the Chinese governmental structure that
seems to be headed by Chou En-lai. But though the army
may be in command of the situation, at least for the moment,
it will have its work cut out for it to restore order to all of
China. So long as the army is engaged in this task, China will
be in no position to take on external foes; and China's in-
capacity to do so may prove too strong a temptation for those
Soviet leaders who did not hesitate to risk war in Europe by
occupying Czechoslovakia.

This state of affairs poses many questions for the China
Watchers of Hong Kong. They do their best to try to find
answers that will appear to make sense; but the best of them
do not profess to be prophets or fortune tellers. Their crystal
balls are usually as cloudy as Hong Kong's weather. And the
American China Watchers who work for the Department of
State appeared until recently to suffer an additional handicap.
They had been advising for a long time that whatever else
might be said about China, it was not a strong military power,
and the strategy that its armed forces had adopted was one
of defense in depth, rather than one based on attack. China's
military weakness, not Chinese strength, may be about to
become an ominous factor in world affairs. Yet the Department of State, and the Pentagon, seemed always to be en-

visaging a militarily powerful, bellicose China. "We cranked it in white," one American China Watcher in Hong Kong said recently; "but somehow in Washington it always seemed to come out black."

## TAIWAN

THE CHEAP PLASTICS and other goods which are nowadays pouring out of Taiwan are made by girls from farms. They work eight hours a day and six days a week in factories, instead of bending over rice paddies in the hot sun all day every day. The girls in the plastics factory make $25 American a month, and they enjoy the companionship of other girls, and such factory amenities as cafeteria meals, movies four times a week, a free library and beauty shop, and night classes in cooking and sewing that should lead one day to happy marriages. That beats life down on the farm for most girls.

The consequence of such industrial employment, and for young men as well as for girls, is that though the farmers in Taiwan mostly own land and have television sets and motorcycles, and therefore are better off than most Asian farmers, there is a rapid exodus from farming to factories. Some 90 percent of the young people of Taiwan are leaving farming for jobs in towns. In an attempt to prevent this exodus, or at least to prevent it harming the output of the farms, the Taiwan government has proposed to step up the mechanization of farms, and to make long-term loans to farmers to enable them to purchase things like $1500 power tillers; $1500 being more than a Taiwanese farmer earns in four years from his rice and banana crop.

Politically speaking, Taiwan is much more of an anomaly in the eyes of mainland China than Cuba is in the eyes of the United States. "Imagine," says Donald S. Zagoria, "an American government-in-exile in Havana, supported by the Russians and Chinese, periodically raiding the Florida coast and proclaiming its intention to conquer the entire country." Not perhaps a very exact analogy; but that, no doubt, is about how Peking sees it.

Taiwan, an island 13,885 square miles in area, is about twice the size of Hawaii. The population is about 14 million, and about 1.5 million people live in the capital, Taipei. Mainland Chinese, from Fukien province, began settling in Taiwan about the end of the 15th century. They got to Taiwan only just ahead of the Spaniards and the Dutch. The Dutch fought and beat the Spaniards, but then the Dutch were thrown out of Taiwan by emigrating Chinese who had supported the Ming dynasty, which the Manchus had defeated. From Taiwan, the former Ming supporters harried the Manchus, until the Manchus captured Taiwan in 1682.

After the war of 1894 between China and Japan, Peking ceded Taiwan to Japan. But the Chinese inhabitants of Taiwan declared a republic, the first in Asia, and the Japanese had to subdue them by force. Between 1894 and 1945, the Japanese did a good deal to build up and develop the island (the Americans were simultaneously developing the Philippines). For instance, schooling in Taiwan under the Japanese was much in advance of the education available on the Chinese mainland. A former Japanese governor-general of Taiwan has written piously in his memoirs, "we found the Taiwanese savages, and when we left them they had become civilized and respectable ancestor worshippers."

After Japan's defeat that ended World War II in 1945, Taiwan was returned by the allies to China, but then Taiwan became a refuge for the armies of Generalissimo Chiang Kai-shek that the Chinese communists had defeated. The Taiwanese evidently felt about this much the way the Ming dynasty supporters had felt about the Manchus. The Taiwanese were very roughly treated by Chiang Kai-shek's regiments. A Taiwanese revolt broke out on February 28, 1947, and was suppressed with great severity. In December 1949, when Chiang Kai-shek was finally defeated, he and about one million mainland Chinese arrived in Taiwan, where they have remained ever since.

After the Korean war broke out in the summer of 1950, President Truman ordered the United States navy to prevent a communist attack on Taiwan. Twenty years later it is still the proclaimed intention of the Chiang Kai-shek regime on Taiwan to use the island as a base of operations against the Chinese mainland to which they propose one day to return in victory. However, although they make armed raids on the mainland from time to time, the hope of a Chiang Kai-shek restoration has nearly faded. The generalissimo is now well over the age of 80. Madame Chiang is almost 70.

Taiwan is a member of the United Nations and occupies one of the five permanent seats on the Security Council. Nobody knows how long this will continue. Most countries, probably including the United States, would favor a solution of the "China problem" whereby both Peking and Taiwan were members of the United Nations. However, both Peking and Chiang Kai-shek resolutely spurn such a proposal for "two Chinas." Nor does there seem to be much chance of either of them permitting the Taiwanese to govern themselves as an independent, non-Chinese republic. Yet the Taiwanese, who of course outnumber the mainlanders now resident in the island, have been separated from the mainland for about 400 years and no longer regard themselves as being truly Chinese. They even seem to have a rather strong if sneaking regard for their former conquerors, the Japanese, who have greatly influenced their way of life. Meanwhile, the rivalry between the Chiang Kai-shek regime and mainland China takes some odd forms. Thus, Africa is regarded by both as an important diplomatic target; no doubt in recognition of the growing influence of the Africans in the United Nations. Both mainland China and the Chinese on Taiwan have offered to help the African nations with technical and other forms of assistance. Twenty-one African countries have diplomatic relations with Taiwan, eleven recognize Peking. Taiwan has made special effort to procure the friendship of India, no doubt in hope of catching the Indians in their violent rebound from mainland China.

Taiwan's population of 14 million includes 600,000 men and

women in uniform; one of the world's largest armies. On Taiwan there are said to be almost 1500 people to a square kilometer of cultivated land, one of the highest population densities in the world. Population growth is 2.3 percent, which is high, but a family planning research institute hopes to reduce the rate of natural increase to 1.9 percent by 1972. Although Chinese mainlanders control the government of Taiwan, and also command the armed forces, about 80 percent of the rank and file of the army are Taiwanese, an inevitable consequence of the aging of Chiang Kai-shek's army.

Political control, like military security, couldn't be tighter. Local elections are held for offices ranging from village chief to provincial assemblymen, but national elections, it is explained, cannot be held until the Chinese mainland has been regained. In the 1968 local elections, out of 71 provincial assembly seats, 61 went to Chiang Kai-shek's Nationalist Party, the Kuomintang. There are two minority parties on Taiwan, the Young China Party and the Democratic Socialist Party; each of these parties won one seat. The provincial assembly's powers are consultative and recommendatory. It and the local government are subordinate to the national government whose members, except for fresh appointments by Chiang Kai-shek, have remained virtually unchanged since 1947 and 1948. However, the Kuomintang has tried to shake itself up and put the accent on youth. Everything is relative. A recent party secretary general got the job because he was "only" 56. Another young hopeful who became chief of the policy committee was "only" 58.

About the same time as the Chinese Communist Party held its 9th congress in Peking to choose a successor to Mao Tse-tung—though of course nobody who attended admitted that this was the reason—the Kuomintang held its 10th congress in Taipei, the capital of Taiwan, to rubber stamp the succession to Chiang Kai-shek—though nobody admitted that either.

Chiang Kai-shek is in his eighties and his son, Chiang Ching-kuo, in his mid-50s. Chiang Kai-shek has vowed not to leave Taiwan until he can once again set foot on the Chinese mainland. But Chiang Ching-kuo travels frequently, and he recently visited Seoul, where he was cordially received by South Korean president Park Chung Hee.

Chiang Kai-shek makes few appearances even on Taiwan. He is invariably surrounded by scores of bodyguards. When he flies, all other aircraft are grounded. The area where he lives has been cleared of all buildings that could overlook his residence.

Chiang Ching-kuo has no such emperor complex. He travels with guards, but they stay well in the background. His manners are simple. He strikes most people as being a quiet, shy fellow; rather dull, perhaps. But this is quite deceptive, at any rate in terms of power. Chiang Ching-kuo is a formidable political boss, and everyone in Taiwan knows it, and fears him.

In 1947, the Taiwanese rebelled against the harsh military rule that hád been imposed on them by poorly led Chinese regiments who were fleeing from the Chinese mainland and the Chinese communists who were plainly winning the civil war. The Taiwan rebellion was suppressed ruthlessly, and to this day the Taiwanese put most of the blame for the massacre of 10,000 or 20,000 people on Chiang Ching-kuo. In the ensuing twenty-two years, Chiang Ching-kuo has attempted to blur this bad image through considerable self-effacement. In true oriental style, he has adopted a low public posture. The fact remains that the political machine, which the 10th congress of the Kuomintang assembled in Taipei for the purpose of oiling and cleaning for the use of Chiang Ching-kuo, is in large degree an apparatus of dictatorial terror. The terror is low-keyed, like Chiang Ching-kuo's public posture. Its implements are blackmail and intimidation, rather than executions and physical brutality. It is political terror nonetheless, the same that is found in Greece, in Spain, and in some other countries.

Army units are stationed in every Taiwanese village, and they act as the government's eyes and ears. There are also civilian spies and informers everywhere, even in the high schools. Informers turned in two high school kids, who, in ill-timed jest, had raised three cheers for Mao Tse-tung. The kids got three years in jail. This sort of thing helps to explain why fully 97 percent of the 2,000 college graduates of Taiwan who are allowed to leave the island each year for advanced study .abroad fail to return. Other Taiwanese who get abroad probably would not return either, except that the government makes clear, to businessmen and the like, that their relatives still on Taiwan are hostages for their good behavior abroad, and for their safe homecoming. Politically, everything is run by the Kuomintang. The two other parties, the Young China Party and the Democratic Socialist Party are extraordinarily difficult to find.

This hidebound system may now be beginning to prove counterproductive. The effect on the students of unremitting and unintelligent anticommunist propaganda has been to convince some of them that Mao Tse-tung can do no wrong, precisely because the Kuomintang says he has never done anything good.

People on Taiwan say that Chiang Ching-kuo has not only adopted a low posture himself, but that he is really trying to ease things and to slacken the reins a little bit. Informers no longer can brazenly swear away someone's freedom with impunity; if an accused person proves that the accusations are lies, the informer may go to jail instead of the accused, possibly for life.

The biggest thing Chiang Ching-kuo has going for him is Taiwan's impressive rate of economic growth, averaging an annual 9 percent. Taiwan's economy was given a huge shove by American economic aid that totaled $1.4 billion from 1951 until 1965 when it ceased. The island's economy is built on pineapples, bananas, textiles, cement, and petrochemicals. American aid also financed a successful land reform program that created more independent farmers, and thus reduced the number of tenants.

Not everyone however shares equally in this prosperity. Strikes are forbidden; factory workers earn very small wages. Foreign capital is admitted on generous terms—unlimited repatriation of profits, no income tax during the first five years. After that, the corporate tax has a low, 18 percent ceiling.

Taiwanese businessmen as well as foreigners have done well

out of the island's boom. There are 10 million native Taiwanese; they outnumber the mainlanders 5 to 2. Taiwanese businessmen are smart and have become rich in some cases. Some also occupy important political posts—but most often by appointment, not by election, and so they can be summarily dismissed. These appointees are kept on a very short string, and for this reason self-respecting Taiwanese generally refuse to accept public posts; doing so as politely as possible, of course. But in any case, a mainlander is nearly always preferred over a Taiwanese. Old mainland habits die hard. Businessmen who are mainlanders have the ear of the government, and they have a strong competitive advantage because they receive government favors of credit and patronage.

As time goes by, it becomes increasingly evident that the mainlanders on Taiwan are not going to reconquer China, so they have to make their regime more acceptable to the native Taiwanese. The Taiwanese would prefer that the taxes they pay were put to better uses than the upkeep of a huge army that no longer has any real purpose. The Taiwanese themselves have no wish to "return to the mainland." They know that time is on their side. The mainlanders have to rely on them increasingly; the mainlanders' children intermarry with them. What the Taiwanese would like would be for Taiwan to have political independence. The island's population of 14 million is bigger than the population of Australia, and more than that of many members of the United Nations.

The American military aid to Taiwan is now below $40 million, and, save for gifts of surplus arms, it is steadily shrinking. The 7th Fleet is busier in the Bay of Tonkin than in the Taiwan Straits. Taiwan during the Vietnam war is a refueling base for B-52s on the Guam-Vietnam run, and consequently Taiwan's main airbase Ching Chuan Kang, in Central Taiwan, bustled with 6,000 U.S. airmen. Additionally, there were almost 22,000 U.S. military people in Taiwan. Normally, however, the U.S. military in Taiwan consists only of 600 men in the Military Assistance Advisory Group. Military aid to Taiwan takes the form mainly of salvaged military equipment that comes from Vietnam, and for which the Chinese Nationalists pay only the transport costs.

The Chinese nationalist government on Taiwan was reported in the summer of 1969 to be planning a major reorganization of its 600,000-man armed forces, for the first time since the Chinese Nationalists retreated from the mainland to Taiwan. The idea is to turn the large and unwieldy—and aging—army into a somewhat smaller, better armed, and more mobile force. The Nationalists insisted that this military reorganization did not really mean that they were giving up their idea of reconquering the mainland one day. But it was perfectly clear that doubts were growing and would continue to grow about this goal. The man behind the military reorganization was Chiang Ching-kuo. Before becoming deputy prime minister, Chiang Ching-kuo had been minister of defense. The chief of the United States Military Assistance Advisory Group, Major General Richard C. Ciccolella, said that the Chinese were now going to build their own helicopters in Taiwan, and that they already had factories that could produce M-14 rifles, machine guns, trucks, and field radios. And then, General Ciccolella, as reported by *The New York Times,* added very significantly, "It has reached the point where the Chinese really do not need us any more."

What Chiang Kai-shek and his son Chiang Ching-kuo would like would be to have those United States nuclear weapons that are to be removed from the island of Okinawa by 1972 to be brought to Taiwan. But this is most unlikely to happen, if only because the nuclear experts think that "close in" nuclear weapons are of steadily diminishing utility in the age of nuclear submarines and intercontinental missiles. After the Vietnam war ends, Taiwan's military significance for the United States is likely to diminish also—if indeed the island is not already a military as well as a political liability. Chiang Kai-shek and Chiang Ching-kuo must feel that they are in imminent danger of being quietly put on the shelf by the United States. What, then, should they do?

In a remarkable speech that he made at a Chinese New

Year function, Chiang Kai-shek, in one of his rare public appearances, startlingly accused Mao Tse-tung of "destroying" Marxism. Simultaneously, while everyone was dazedly muttering "how's that again?" Taipei wall slogans denouncing Soviet Russia were scrubbed. These strange happenings were preceded by two equally momentous events. A Soviet "journalist," Victor Louis, a smooth, Kremlin-directed operator well-known in Paris and in London as well as in Moscow, visited Taipei for talks with leading Kuomintang officials including, of course, Chiang Ching-kuo. And Chiang Kai-shek directed a good friend of his, Ku Yu Shiu of the University of Pennsylvania, to visit Moscow.

Victor Louis is a Soviet citizen of French descent. He is also believed to be connected with the intelligence unit of the State Security Services of the Soviet Union.

After his visit to Taiwan, Victor Louis wrote an article in the *Montreal Star*. In this, he praised the Chinese Nationalist regime on Taiwan, and the economic progress of Taiwan. Describing his meeting with Chiang Ching-kuo, Victor Louis wrote, "when I was being introduced to him, he presented himself in very passable Russian as a former worker of a dynamo factory. Although I knew that he had spent 14 years in Russia, and that his wife is Russian, I was still taken by surprise. Chiang showered me with questions about Moscow, which he had last visited in 1946 on a mission to Stalin to complain about the activities of Mao Tse-tung."

Chiang Ching-kuo is a man whom the United States has supported as an anticommunist ally. Yet he reminded Victor Louis, without any reticence, that he was a former worker in a Soviet factory. According to Japanese sources, Chiang Ching-kuo was involved in an unsuccessful anti-Stalin plot and was exiled to Siberia, where he later secured a position as director of a factory there. The Japanese say that he then denounced his father as a traitor to the Chinese people. He did of course make it up to his father, and returned to China, and thence to Taiwan. But he has always managed to keep a footing in Moscow, just as he is reported to have a secret footing in Peking. He is widely believed to have continuous secret contacts with both those communist capitals that are now at verbal war with each other.

The object of these exercises seems evident. The Kuomintang's tenth congress agreed to "step up psychological warfare against the Mao Tse-tung regime" which, the congress claimed, "has been pushed by its own violent internal struggle for power to the brink of destruction." An apparent rapprochement between Moscow and Taipei would be bad news for Peking. Moscow nowadays appears to be anxious to be on good terms with as many Asian countries as possible, from Singapore to Japan—why not also Taiwan, therefore? Russia is offering the Asian countries trade. Taiwan, now no longer in receipt of American economic aid, is anxious for all the trade it can get. Export and imports account for a full fifth of Taiwan's total trade.

And Taiwan, furthermore, has suddenly become of military significance to Moscow. Chiang Kai-shek's 600,000 soldiers, though they are getting old, still pin down, in Canton, almost half (56 divisions) of the Chinese People's Liberation Army. This, too, when the Sino-Soviet fight has got to the stage of serious military clashes between the two giants in at least two places along their enormous borders: Ussuri and Sinkiang. The two Chiangs might even be hoping to get weapons from Soviet Russia to supplement dwindling American military assistance. The Taiwan government is in constant need of money to maintain its large armed forces, which cost $275 million a year. The U.S. stipend of under $50 million doesn't go very far, even when it has been supplemented by the $68 million a year that the temporarily swollen United States military presence on Taiwan costs the United States because of the Vietnam war. Defense accounts for about 60 percent of the Taiwan budget.

Nobody can foretell what all this will lead to. But it is at least possible to argue that, in the end, a Taiwan that had achieved home rule might suit the Kuomintang remnant on the island better than getting into the toils of the Soviet Union. And such an arrangement might even suit Peking as well in the long run.

Chiang Ching-kuo will not simply hand over Taiwan to the Taiwanese, if he can help it; that would leave him with nothing and with nowhere to go. But a deal with Peking that left him in effective political control of the island could be a different matter, and in due course he might manage to broaden his political base among the Taiwanese. This could be the dividend of his current "low posture."

Why should Peking countenance making such a deal with Chiang Ching-kuo? A Taiwan that was virtually autonomous, but was officially Chinese, could give Peking two voices and two votes in the United Nations, as Russia in a somewhat similar fashion now has three votes in the United Nations; its own and those of the Ukraine and Byelo-Russia. Such an outcome could be attractive to Peking, should China's gathering quarrel with Russia make membership in the United Nations not merely attractive but a matter of urgency for China.

And such an outcome probably would not be downright unattractive to the native Taiwanese, whose chief wish is for home rule. To continue for a time under the rule of Chiang Ching-kuo would not be too much of a price, as they are doing that now anyhow. To give vocal support to Peking's foreign policies would probably not be too much of a price either; at present, the Taiwanese are compelled to assent to Chiang Kai-shek's foreign policy, which is both risky and unrealistic.

One hundred miles from Taiwan, but only one and a quarter miles from mainland China, is the island of Quemoy. The Chinese Communists for a long time rained shells on Quemoy. But the last real shelling was 18 years ago. What happens now is rather ridiculous but is typically Chinese. Not every night, but every other night, shells do land on Quemoy, fired from the mainland. But they are loaded only with propaganda material. It is quite a while since the people of Quemoy paid attention to this peculiar shelling. They simply go about their business and till their fields, ignoring both the shells and the loudspeakers which blare back and forth continually between the mainland and the island.

There are about 60,000 civilians living on Quemoy, but

there are also about 40,000 Chinese Nationalist troops of Chiang Kai-shek. And there are plenty of fortifications, both above ground and underground. It also bristles with guns. What appear to the outward eye to be only bus stops and temples actually turn out on closer inspection to be also bunkers for machine guns. Many of the houses on the island are built of concrete as well as brick, and this is so that they can serve as gun emplacements as well as homes.

Major General Richard C. Ciccolella, the chief of the United States Military Advisory Group in Taiwan, told *The New York Times* correspondent Fox Butterfield, "The Chinese Nationalists are so well dug in on Quemoy, and they have so many supplies stored up that there is no way the Chinese can take the island. In fact," added General Ciccolella, "I doubt if *we* could take it."

Quemoy—and also Matsu, the other Chinese Nationalist held island offshore—are not included in the 1955 mutual defense treaty between the United States and Taiwan.

# AMERICA AND THE

# "OVERSEAS CHINESE"

TWO CHINESE ISLANDS—or three if the city-state republic of Singapore is included—are among the most thriving places in Asia, from the point of view of material progress. Although they are only specks on the map, they may be more significant as pointers to the future than other Asian countries that are larger and therefore seem more important. For most of Asia has yet to enter the 20th century. And in order to do so, it now seems clear that for the most part the Asians will have to achieve their own modernization, and will have to raise themselves by their own bootstraps. Singapore, Hong Kong, and Taiwan are places that have accepted this challenge and seem to be making a success of it. It is true in the case of Taiwan that the island did receive the considerable impetus of almost $1.5 billion of American economic assistance. But a good many other places have received considerable American aid and have made very indifferent use of it. Taiwan's success story does in truth owe much to American help, but it is nonetheless a success story, at least in terms of economic progress. And in those same terms, Hong Kong and Singapore are also successes.

It now has to be asked if this success may be due to the fact that the islands we are talking about are wholly or largely Chinese in their ethnic composition. Everyone knows that the Chinese are a hard-working and pragmatic people who generally make a success of whatever they put their hands and minds to. So for that matter are the Japanese; and, in the case of Taiwan, there is also a strong Japanese influence, as the

Japanese ruled this island for half a century, from 1895 to 1945. The Japanese are in many ways the Far East counterparts of the British, who are likewise islanders and similarly pragmatical; and Singapore and Hong Kong of course bear witness to British customs and institutions. This then may be one of the keys to their success as well as the fact that their populations are so largely of Chinese origin.

While these three islands are basically Chinese, they are not at present under the rule of Peking. There is, moreover, very little likelihood that Singapore ever will be; and it may very well be possible to work out some arrangement with Peking, whereby those thriving communities in spite of their Chinese identity shall continue as separate political entities. They do not wish to be ruled from Peking, and that alone should entitle them to continue their separate careers. Their very existence, in fact, raises up the whole issue of the overseas Chinese, who total some 20 million people. A breakdown of the overseas Chinese would be somewhat as follows:

| | |
|---|---|
| Burma | 500,000 |
| Thailand | 3,500,000 |
| Philippines | 500,000 |
| North Vietnam | 135,000 |
| Laos | 37,000 |
| South Vietnam | 1,500,000 |
| Cambodia | 500,000 |
| Malaysia | 3,500,000 |
| Singapore | 1,500,000 |
| Sarawak | 250,000 |
| Sabah | 115,000 |
| Indonesia | 3,500,000 |
| Hong Kong | 4,000,000 |

These 20 million overseas Chinese, or *Hua Chiao*, were to a large extent sucked out of south China into all those countries in the 19th century by the colonizing Europeans opening up the countries and demanding more labor. They have mainly become traders and money lenders and middle men, usually competing with Indians. They have been constantly reminded by the Chinese Nationalists, the Kuomintang, that they ought to attend Chinese schools, exercise a postal vote in Chinese elections on Taiwan, and regard themselves as members of a "single pure race," citizens of the Chung Hua Min Kuo, the middle flowery people's kingdom. The Chiang Kai-shek regime in Taiwan, in short, insists that the overseas Chinese are citizens of China. But Communist China has specifically renounced claims to double citizenship for the overseas Chinese, and has admitted that the overseas Chinese are indeed nationals of their countries of residence.

Peking, for reasons of its own, seems inclined to tolerate if not to encourage the continued separate identity of Hong Kong. While Hong Kong remains separate from China, it is a source of considerable income and foreign exchange for the Chinese communists. What should American policy be toward Taiwan? The Chiang Kai-shek regime has no realistic hope of returning to the mainland to rule over China. The native Taiwanese have no wish to remain indefinitely under the harsh undemocratic rule of the Kuomintang.

Senator Edward M. Kennedy has several times addressed himself to the problem of America-China relations and what American policy toward China and Taiwan should be. He has several times pointed out that, to Peking, the question of diplomatic recognition seems wholly linked to the question of whether the United States will withdraw recognition from Nationalist China and concede that Taiwan is part of the territory of Communist China. Senator Kennedy says that both the communists and the nationalists claim Taiwan as part of China, "but our own government regards the status of the island as undefined, even though we maintain diplomatic relations with the nationalists."

This is correct, though not often understood. Since World War II, political uncertainties have kept Taiwan's status an open question, while the inhabitants of the island have been deprived of the right to decide their own destiny. Though both the Chinese nationalists and the Chinese communists are united in their claim that Taiwan is an integral part of China, the United States in 1954 stated the legal position as follows: "Technical sovereignty over Taiwan and the Pescadores has never been settled. That is because the Japanese peace treaty merely involved a renunciation by Japan of its right and title to these islands. But the future title was not determined by the Japanese peace treaty, nor was it determined by the peace treaty which was concluded between the Nationalist Republic of China and Japan. Therefore, the juridical status of the island is different from the juridical status of the offshore islands, Quemoy and Matsu, which have always been Chinese territory."

Senator Kennedy has raised what he calls three critical questions. Will the minority regime of the Chinese nationalists continue to control the island's Taiwanese population? Will the Taiwanese majority eventually transform the island's government through the exercise of self-determination? And will an accommodation be worked out between a future Taiwan government and the Peking regime?

To help to elicit Peking's interest in negotiations, Kennedy said, the United States should withdraw its token American military presence from Taiwan. This demilitarization of Taiwan could take place at no cost to United States treaty commitments, or to the security of the island. Yet, it would help to make clear to Peking the United States desire for the communists, the nationalists, and the Taiwanese to reach a negotiated solution to the status of Taiwan. The senator further suggested the possibility that the people of Taiwan might be represented in the United Nations as an autonomous unit of China, by analogy to the present status of Byelo-Russia and the Ukraine in the United Nations as autonomous provinces of the Soviet Union. Some other people interested in the problem have suggested that the United States ought to invoke the United Nations to get a plebiscite held on Taiwan, to find out what the majority of the people want. This would be difficult to achieve as long as the Kuomintang rules the island through its agents rather than through elections.

It was probably unfortunate at this juncture that in the fall of 1969 the Nixon administration should have picked an old

CIA man as director of the State Department Bureau of Intelligence and Research. Mr. Ray S. Cline was given the rank of assistant secretary but not that title, so that he was not subject to confirmation by the Senate. According to the usually well-informed *I. F. Stone's Weekly,* Cline had left the Central Intelligence Agency in or about 1949. But he had close ties with the Chiang Kai-shek regime. He served for a time in Taiwan, and was said to have been in charge of flights of U-2 spy planes over China. He was also called "a hard-line cold warrior," and it was reported that the influential Anna Chennault had played a part in his latest appointment in the State Department. The appointment came at a time when Secretary of State William P. Rogers and Mr. Elliott Richardson, the number two man in the State Department, had been talking about a new China policy. Whether a new China policy was to be expected from a man who had been a close friend of Chiang Ching-kuo, the son of Chiang Kai-shek, remained to be seen. I. F. Stone pointed out that, in his new capacity, Cline would sit on the powerful Board of National Estimates, the U.S. government's highest intelligence body. The State Department itself said Mr. Cline would be the Department's "principal source of long-range forecasts and analysis of political, economic and sociological trends throughout the world." I. F. Stone doubted that "cloak-and-dagger" was "the right training for a sane view of world politics."

Meanwhile, there was considerable evidence that most native Taiwanese regarded the United States government as being chiefly responsible for the present political backwardness of Taiwan. They pointed to the massive military, economic and political support given by the United States to Chiang Kai-shek's regime. Few of them denied that Taiwan had made striking economic advances. Nevertheless, they regarded the continuous American support of Chiang Kai-shek as the decisive factor in perpetuating a backward and tyrannical political system that has no roots in the island. What the Taiwanese people plainly would have liked to see was for the United States to withdraw its support and also to withdraw diplomatic recognition from the Chiang Kai-shek regime, but at the same time to guarantee the autonomy of Taiwan by keeping the United States 7th Fleet in the Taiwan Strait. Such a policy would get rid of the Chiang Kai-shek regime but at the same time would prevent Taiwan being swallowed up by Communist China.

This Taiwanese advice to the United States might be dismissed as a counsel of perfection, put forward for obvious reasons of self-interest. But no American policy toward this part of the world will be truly realistic that does not take into account the existence, the importance, and the peculiar problems of the overseas Chinese. In places like Malaysia, Thailand, and the Philippines, the large Chinese minorities—almost 50 percent of the population in Malaysia, over 10 percent in Thailand and the Philippines—must of course merge themselves among their fellow citizens and become loyal communities of the states where they have chosen to live. And fortunately Peking, if not Taipei, has acknowledged this. But the overseas Chinese nevertheless can serve as a valuable cultural bridge between their countries and mainland China, which is the huge and sometimes frightening neighbor of all those countries. None of the countries wish to be swallowed up by China; and their citizens of Chinese origin can help to make this clear to Peking. But in order to do so, they must not be forbidden to have any contacts with Peking, on pain of being accused of being Chinese communist agents. Nor should they be prevented from having contacts with Taiwan, though probably they would be foolish to continue for much longer to pay lip service to the Kuomintang regime, or to help finance its operations, or to take part in its carefully stage-managed elections; if only because this will suggest that they feel their loyalty is to "China" rather than to their own governments. It will be a delicate, complex, and probably lengthy task to persuade Peking that nationalism, not communism, is the political wave of the future in Asia, and that therefore no amount of reminiscing about ancient Chinese history, the good old days when everyone paid their humble tribute to the emperor of China, will ever bring all that back again. The emperor has been dead a long time, and China will be lucky to avoid political fragmentation of its heartland, let alone hope to extend its suzerainty far and wide. But in Peking's own interest there should be a large interchange going on in all this region, so that it gradually will come to be understood that nobody loses and everyone including Peking gains from considerable political autonomy.

The policy that the United States ought to pursue used to be called the "open door." Free and frank contacts between the United States and all the countries of the region, including mainland China, can best take the place of the unreal containment of China that United States support of the Kuomintang remnant on Taiwan has too long symbolized.

In attempting to carry out this up-to-date—and much improved—version of the traditional American policy of the open door, the United States ought to seek the sympathetic understanding of the 20 million overseas Chinese in southeast Asia. It is surprising that this has not been done. Both the Chinese communists and the Chiang Kai-shek regime on Taiwan are stuck fast in outmoded and untenable ideological positions. Mao Tse-tung has quarreled with the Kremlin, and Chiang Ching-kuo received the Soviet Russian agent Victor Louis. The latter move was sheer opportunism. The former was a gesture of ideological fanaticism. The United States is a practical and pragmatic minded country that puts little credence in political ideologies. All the more strange, therefore, that it should choose for a staunch ally a regime like that of Chiang Kai-shek. But the overseas Chinese (including in this definition the native Taiwanese) are much more the United States cup of coffee. They too are practical and pragmatical. The overseas Chinese are the merchants, the traders, the skilled artisans, the bankers of southeast Asia. Like Americans, they are people who want to get on. It is now pretty clear that the salvation of Asia is not going to be found in ideologies, but in pragmatic and hard-headed political and economic arrangements for bettering the conditions of ordinary people's lives. The future of Asia will not be either "socialist" or "capitalist", but some kind of rule-of-thumb eclectic mixture—like Lee Kuan Yew's Singapore, or British governed but Chinese run Hong Kong.

In short, the overseas Chinese are the natural allies of the descendants of those practical Yankees who not long ago were successful traders in these parts. Between them, there seems no reason why they should not manage to speed up material progress, and at the same time to gradually lure the mainland Chinese into a more reasonable frame of mind.

# 9

# CHINA: RED CLAY?

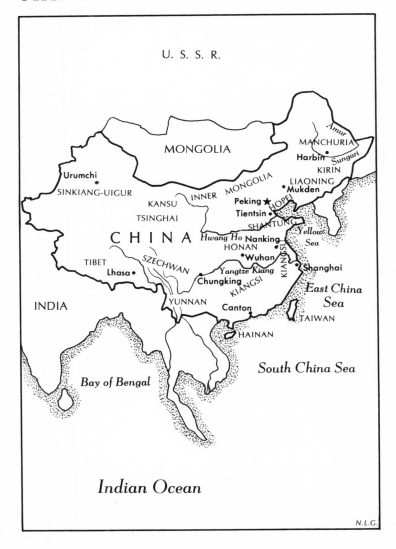

U. S. S. R.

MONGOLIA

MANCHURIA

*Amur*

Harbin *Sungari*

Urumchi

KIRIN

SINKIANG-UIGUR

INNER MONGOLIA

LIAONING

Mukden

KANSU

Peking ★

HOPEI

TSINGHAI

Tientsin

SHANTUNG

C H I N A

*Hwang Ho* Nanking

*Yellow Sea*

HONAN

TIBET

SZECHWAN

Wuhan

KIANGSU

Lhasa

*Yangtze Kiang*

Shanghai

Chungking

KIANGSI

INDIA

YUNNAN

*East China Sea*

Canton

TAIWAN

HAINAN

*South China Sea*

*Bay of Bengal*

*Indian Ocean*

N.L.G.

## THE BAROMETER WIFE

CHINA IS THE biggest country in the world, sprawling over more than 3.5 million square miles, with a population of about 700 million. Of these some 658 million are Chinese; 42 million are Tibetans, Mongols, Uighurs, and so forth. Most Chinese are peasants, but there are vast crowded cities. In order to demonstrate that he isn't afraid of nuclear war, Mao Tse-tung hinted sometimes that he might even be prepared to sacrifice large urban centers, but that China in the main would still survive a nuclear war. The cities that Mao might conceivably sacrifice in a nuclear holocaust include Shanghai, population 7 million; Peking, population 4 million; Tientsin, population 3 million; Shenyang, population 2.5 million; and Wuhan and Chungking each with a population of about 2 million.

China is very ancient and does not really change its ways. The Han dynasty lasted from about 200 B.C. until after A.D. 200. During this period, China's official ideology became the teachings of Confucius. Today, China's official ideology is the "thought of Mao Tse-tung." Mao like Confucius was a philosopher and poet as well as a politician and soldier. The greatest period in Chinese history was that of the Tung dynasty, in the 7th to the 10th century of our era. The Sung dynasty lasted from the 10th to the 13th century. It was overthrown by the Mongols, in the age of Genghis Khan and of Kubla Khan who in the poem by Coleridge built a stately pleasure dome in Xanadu. After the Mongols came the Ming dynasty, in 1368, which restored Chinese rule. The Mings, as we earlier noted, were ousted by the Manchus, in 1644. The Manchus lasted a long time, but their Ching dynasty was overthrown in 1911 by the revolution of Sun Yat Sen. That brings us to modern times; in 1931 Japan seized Manchuria, and in 1949 Mao Tse-tung overthrew Chiang Kai-shek. The communist People's Republic of China was proclaimed in Peking on the 1st of October, 1949.

At the end of the 1960s, it looked as if Mao Tse-tung's Great Proletarian Cultural Revolution had left the Red Army in fairly effective command of most of China; "Maoism" was theoretically triumphant, but in practice was in full retreat. Directives from Peking to the rest of the country had called for an abolition of the national network of Red Guard organizations, an end to the wanderings of students and their return to school, and the compulsory dispatch of intellectuals to the countryside, there to labor alongside the very peasants whom the intellectuals—on Mao's orders—had been dutifully attacking for backsliding and for attempted reversion to "capitalism." In fact, however, the Chinese students in large numbers continued to wander about "free and unrestrained," to use their own delightful phrase. The students said they had discovered as a result of the cultural revolution that this sort of life was the kind they preferred. All this of course was made possible only by virtual paralysis in Peking, where the moderates had momentarily vanquished the leftists but could not be sure that the next unpredictable turn of fortune's wheel would not once again put Maoism back into full fashion. The west's professional China Watchers used the ups and downs of Mao's wife Chiang Ching as a kind of barometer of the political weather inside China. The China Watchers kept track of her name as it rose and fell in the official listing of the Chinese communist hierarchy. When she was up, the fanatics were riding high, and when she was down, the moderates were on the upswing. The semantics of this struggle inside China took the form of long-drawn verbal battles between "factionalism" (the bad guys) and "genuine proletarian factionalism" (the good guys).

The chances were that all that had been achieved by the vast upheaval was the defeat of what the Japanese would call the "antimainstream faction", led by Liu Shao-chi. But the defeat of the antimainstream faction only brought out in the open an intense struggle that went on between power-seekers like Lin Piao, and Chiang Ching, for the succession to the aged Mao Tse-tung. Meanwhile the cost appeared to be immense. Schools were closed for years at a time; there was a grave decline in public health and cleanliness. The bugs and fleas that the Chinese revolutionaries had claimed to have exterminated were back again. According to the invaluable *Far Eastern Economic Review,* published in Hong Kong, almost nothing except the works of Mao Tse-tung was being published in China. "There was no indication," said the review, "that even textbooks and dictionaries were being printed." Whatever else the Great Proletarian Cultural Revolution produced, it was obviously not culture.

# THE GREAT SCHISM

A FASCINATING SPECULATION is how the United States would have reacted if Mao Tse-tung had revealed his independence of the Soviet Union in 1949, instead of 15 years later. For even in those earlier years the official American aim was declared to be a China that was friendly to America, therefore independent of the Soviet Union. China today is of course not friendly to the United States, but it is independent of the Soviet Union. The rulers in Peking call the men in the Kremlin social imperialists. The men in the Kremlin call the men in Peking fascists.

President Nixon's secretary of state, Mr. William P. Rogers, said in Canberra, Australia, in the summer of 1969, that China was neither the political threat nor as yet the military power that it had once been thought to be. Mr. Rogers also said that the United States would not be restrained from seeking better relations with Communist China by fears that Russia might suspect American intentions. Rogers further said, in Canberra, that Peking would soon be asked to reopen the Warsaw talks that the Chinese had suspended. In November 1968, someone in Peking had invited the United States to another round of Warsaw talks, and that someone presumably was still around in Peking, even though Peking had withdrawn the invitation at the last moment. The State Department indicated that it was no longer going to try to stop Americans going to China if Peking would let them in; and American tourists were permitted to purchase up to $100 worth of Communist Chinese goods and bring them back to this country. Previously they had been forbidden to do so, and Communist Chinese items were confiscated. Observers pointed out what the new relaxation meant in principle. There was no real difference between U.S. tourists and U.S. businesses trading with China.

In Hong Kong, Secretary of State Rogers said that the United States wanted to see China back in the world community. That could only mean China's eventual entry to the United Nations. However, Rogers tried to assure Chiang Kai-shek that the United States commitment to the Nationalist Chinese regime on Taiwan remained "constant and firm," and that the United States 7th Fleet was not about to leave the Pacific Ocean.

The statements by Mr. Rogers hinted at important changes in American foreign policy in Asia and toward China. And these changes almost certainly were connected with the rapidly deteriorating relations between China and Russia.

The Great Proletarian Cultural Revolution in China was closely linked with the friction between China and Russia. To all appearances, Mao Tse-tung and Lin Piao were unbending in their opposition to the Soviet Union. But there were powerful elements in the Red Army, the Chinese communist party, and the Chinese government bureaucracy which secretly opposed the quarrel with Russia. The opponents of Mao and Lin Piao did not dare go so far as to appear publicly pro-Soviet. But many of them obviously felt that if China were to cease to be backward, it simply had to get external military and economic assistance—and the only possible source of this was the Soviet Union. By contrast, Mao Tse-tung spurned the very thought of renewed Soviet friendship, and turned to his Cultural Revolution Red Guards in order deliberately to create conflict and insure a "permanent revolution" inside China. It was apparently Mao's notion that only a constant ferment could succeed in smashing the molds in which new classes and "revisionism" constantly threatened to form inside China, as he believed had already happened to a disastrous degree inside Russia, which as a result had turned revisionist and was reverting to capitalism. Mao saw his internal task as no less than the forcible creation, through severe struggle, of a new sort of *homo* beyond *sapiens,* able to survive and to conquer in the coming world environment, instead of always failing and falling back into bad old ways. To this theory the critics of Mao Tse-tung were sometimes apt to make rude replies. For instance, one Teng To declared: "If a man with a swelled head thinks he can learn a subject with ease and kicks his teacher (the Soviet Union) out, he will never learn anything." Chinese who thought like Teng To felt, not without reason, that Mao and Lin Piao were simply proposing to throw over the "socialist camp" led by the Soviet Union, and go it alone, thus taking a grave risk of being attacked by America. At the same time, Mao and Lin Piao appeared prepared to try a new Great Leap inside China, despite the awful consequences of the previous Great Failure, which was still very fresh in every Chinese mind. The critics of Mao were perhaps especially horrified by their intuitive feeling that, in pursuit of his possibly high ideals, Mao quite likely *hoped* for China's involvement in a war in which invaders would fight on Chinese soil, and the Chinese would sacrifice the cities and the urban populations and then would once again retire to the mountains and the caves for another long bout of soul-purifying guerrilla war, as in the years from 1931 to 1947.

The Chinese government did repeatedly propose what it called an overall settlement of the Sino-Soviet boundary question through peaceful negotiations. Peking suggested that boundary negotiations be held in Peking between the Chinese and Soviet sides. But this was mere sugar on a very bitter pill. For even after the Kremlin agreed to this, Peking went on savagely attacking the Russian rulers, whom it accused of "defending tsarist Russia's imperalist crimes of aggression against China."

The Chinese took great pleasure in pointing out that Lenin himself had said in April 1917: "Both Nicholas II and Wilhelm II represented the reactionary and capitalist classes of Russia and Germany. Both had pursued a policy of plundering foreign countries, plundering China, subjugating Persia, carving up and partitioning Turkey." Yet, Peking complained, the Soviet government had the nerve to assert that only the Hans were Chinese, neither the Manchus nor the other minorities of China could be regarded as Chinese, and therefore none of the

regions inhabited by these minorities were truly Chinese
territory.

So Peking thundered in its constant propaganda blast:

*China became a unified country as early as more than 2,000
years ago. China's territory was never confined to the regions
inhabited by the Hans. Over a century ago, Engels pointed out
that the "principle of nationalities was nothing but a Russian
invention concocted in order to destroy Poland." The aim of
the Soviet government is to split the Chinese nation and to
occupy China's frontier regions inhabited by her minority
nationalities. With regard to the eastern sector of the Sino-
Soviet boundary, the Soviet government has asserted that the
Heilung River Basin was first settled by Russian immigrants,
that it always belonged to Russia and the Hans and Manchus
were never there. Anyone with a slight knowledge of history
knows that it was not until the end of the 15th century and
the beginning of the 16th century that Russia became a unified
country. It was not until the latter years of the 16th century
that tsarist Russia crossed the Ural Mountains and expanded
into Siberia, and it was not until the middle of the 17th century that a handful of tsarist Russian colonists invaded the
Heilung River Basin, while China had exercised jurisdiction
over this area many centuries before. In the first half of the
17th century, when the Manchus became China's ruling nationality, China's Ching dynasty continued to exercise jurisdiction over this area, stationing officers and officials for defense and administration, and recruiting soldiers and collecting taxes.*

*The Soviet government has alleged that the "Willow Pale"
in the Ching dynasty formed the then northeastern boundary
line of China. Thus, the Soviet government vainly attempts to
prove that the Heilung and Wesuli River Basins were not
Chinese territory. What was the Willow Pale? It was a willow
fence built by the Ching dynasty authorities to mark the limits
of forbidden areas. Ordinary inhabitants were prohibited from
crossing the fence for hunting, grazing their flocks, or collecting ginseng. That the Soviet government should describe the*

*Willow Pale as forming China's state boundary is as absurd as describing the walls of the Kremlin as forming the state boundary of Russia.*

The Chinese further say that political, economical, and cultural ties between the Sinkiang region and the rest of China have existed for at least 2,000 years. Far back in the years before Christ, the Chinese say, the Chinese Han dynasty set up administrative organs in the vast area east and south of the Balkhash Lake. Yet the Russians have the impudence to claim that in the '40s of the 18th century, the Chinese minorities east and south of the Balkhash Lake had been naturalized as tsarist subjects, implying that the area had long belonged to Russia.

Peking also complained that the Soviet government had further asserted that the Chinese northern frontier was marked by the Great Wall.

*This is not the invention of the Soviet government, the inventor of this theory was Nicholas II, the last of the old Czars. The different sectors of the Great Wall were built in the 4th century B.C. while the linking up of this section by the Ching dynasty took place in the 3rd century. The Great Wall did not form China's boundary. While discussing the Sino-Soviet boundary question, the Soviet government referred to the Great Wall which was built more than 2,000 years ago and dwelt upon it with great relish. So we should ask: What was Russia's boundary at that time?*

The Soviet reply to these Chinese complaints is that the Chinese in the 19th century signed treaties—whether unequal or not—which now must be respected. This doctrine may strike some western readers as a bit comical; the raving Bolshevik revolutionaries have become positively bourgeois in their respect for legalities. Russian official spokesmen heatedly declare: "The Chinese leaders say that the treaties that were concluded between Russia and China in the past, which clearly establish the border between the two countries, were unequal. The Aigon, Tientsin, and Peking treaties, as well as the protocols, agreements, and maps that defined and finalized the border between China and the Soviet Union, are valid. They represent law, which both sides must respect." This, say the Soviet spokesmen, applies both to central Asia and to the Far East.

Russia grumbles constantly that the Chinese leadership has "done everything it can to wreck relations established between the countries from the first years of the victory of the revolution and the formation of People's China. Trade valued at nearly 2 billion rubles in 1959 was cut to 86 million rubles in 1968. Scientific, technological, and cultural exchanges have been completely broken off. The Chinese side has been responsible for annulling or freezing treaties on economic cooperation, one after the other. Even our most rabid enemies have never resorted to such unworthy methods and on such a scale as the Chinese leaders are now doing to discredit the activities of the Soviet Union and the other countries of the Socialist community, and our peace loving foreign policy." The Russians further alleged that the Chinese leaders were turning everything upside down, for they kept on saying that far from fighting the imperialist aggressors, the Soviet Union was striving for a deal with the imperialists.

The Russian version of Far East history is strikingly different from the Chinese version. The Russians say that early in the 18th century, the Manchu rulers of China conquered Mongolia, and in the process slaughtered over one million people. In this way, the Ching emperors established their rule over vast areas . . . that are to this day called Sinkiang, which means the new frontier, peopled by Uighurs, Kazakhs, Kirghizes, Dungans, and other nationalities. The Manchu-Chinese expansion was also directed southwest and to the south.

*By accepting the principle that the nationality of territories is determined by reminiscences about old invasions, one could arrive at absurd conclusions. For example, Latin America would obviously have to return to Spanish rule and the United States would have to return to the British crown. Greece, as the successor of Alexander of Macedon, could in fact claim possession to contemporary Turkey, Syria, India, Pakistan, Egypt, and so forth. The fact is that the Chinese leaders are making territorial demands against the Soviet Union. They are openly demanding land which historically belongs to Russia. Nevertheless, all treaties on Sino-Soviet boundaries were signed by plenipotentiary representatives of both sides and were fixed with state seals. These treaties therefore are effective permanently. For this reason, from a legal point of view, they are absolutely effective today.*

But the Chinese bounce the ball right back. They then counterattack by declaring that the "Soviet revisionist renegade clique" has taken over the mantle of the old tsars and is frantically engaged in military adventures, aggression and expansion.

*It is dreaming the fond dream of old tsars to conquer the world. The only difference between this revisionist clique and the tsars is that the clique in the Kremlin is even more voracious than tsarist Russia was, and it stretches out its claws further than tsarist Russia did. It is a horde of new tsars through and through.*

Peking radio has described a rally and demonstration that was held in Urumchi, in Sinkiang. "At the rally, U Chin-lin, husband of Sun Lung-chen, the herdswoman killed by the Soviet frontier troops, in bitter terms denounced the murder thus committed by the revisionist clique. He said: 'In the vicious old society my father was tortured to death by a hard-hearted landlord and I still have the scars on my body from bayonet wounds while fighting against the American Chiang Kai-shek gang. Now, wolfish Soviet-revisionist new tsars have killed my wife who was six months pregnant. The Soviet clique and U.S. imperialists are jackals from one lair. I must turn my hatred into strength and respond to our great leader, Chairman Mao's call to grasp revolution and to promote production and to act to give severe counterblows to the Soviet revisionists.'" Peking radio concluded: "Over and over at the rally cries broke out of 'anti-China scoundrels will come to no good end.'

'Down with U.S. imperialism.' 'Down with Soviet revisionism.'"

Peking says it regards both the Soviet Union and the U.S. as "overlords" and "nuclear jackals from the same lair" and as "the two scoundrels of the world" who are "conspiring to encircle China." Soviet propaganda meanwhile alleges that ever since 1953, Peking has been making unwarranted territorial claims and demands on "almost all neighboring nations"; listing Russia itself, as well as India, Nepal, Sikkim, Bhutan, Cambodia, and Burma and Thailand and Korea—and Vietnam as well.

The fact seems to be that what is now going on in the 7,000 miles of boundaries between the Russians and the Chinese is only a repetition of what went on before World War II between the Russians and the Japanese in Manchuria, along their 3,000 miles of borders. Both the Russians and Chinese now complain, as the Russians and Japanese used to complain, about unlawful firing, "unlawful surveying, kidnapping, detention of fishing boats, smuggling, air trespassing, sea violation, and plots to transgress the border." According to Russian files for the years 1932–1945, there were 2,000 such incidents, or two per week. And now it seems to be happening all over again, this time between the two communist giants.

Reporters like Harrison E. Salisbury of *The New York Times* have claimed that preparations for war were already far advanced in both countries. It was said that on the Russian side there were hundreds of thousands of troops who had been brought into Mongolia or were stationed in areas adjacent to the region of likely operations against China. Huge new air installations were said to have been built across Siberia. Mongolia was described as having been turned into an armed camp by the Russians. The Chinese were said to have maintained their main troop concentrations in north China and Manchuria, the regions that would be threatened by any thrust by Russia. The Chinese had also sent extra troops into inner Mongolia and into Sinkiang, to guard their nuclear production centers. Both the Russians and Chinese were said to have nuclear launchers now aimed against each other. Over one million soldiers are certainly now deployed by both sides. And the soldiers and civilians in both countries are being whipped to hatred of each other by constant torrents of virulent propaganda. Not that ordinary people in either nation want war. Probably their rulers do not want it either. But the tension is now terrific, and could become unbearable.

## THE SLEEPING GIANT

NAPOLEON SAID CHINA was a sleeping giant that should be let lay, for when it woke it would shake the world. John Hay, Abe Lincoln's private secretary who later became Secretary of State, said the peace of the world rested with China, and that whoever understood China held the key to world politics during the next five centuries. A more recent Secretary of State, Dean Rusk, talked fearfully about a billion Chinese armed with nuclear weapons.

Rusk, Napoleon, and Hay all exaggerate China's importance. China is the largest country in the world. People say that every second Asian is Chinese. But another way of putting this is that every other Asian *isn't* Chinese. The peace of the world may rest in the hands not of 700 million Chinese, but of 100 million Japanese. Asians, including most Chinese and Japanese, believe the key to world peace is held by 200 million Americans, whom they regard as powerful, inscrutable, and unpredictable.

China is a very poor country. About nine out of ten Chinese are crowded in an area the size of the Congo, or of the United States east of the Mississippi. The supply of arable land per head in China is only about one-fifth of what it is in this country. China has few natural resources of any kind—certainly fewer than in either the United States or the Soviet Union. The Chinese national product is only a small fraction of this country's, and the Chinese literacy rate is only 10 or 15 percent. The Japanese rate of literacy is almost 100 percent.

Nor is China a militarily strong country. Because of its population, it has quite a large army—about 2,500,000 men. But—only six artillery divisions. Only six airborne divisions—and with obsolete aircraft. A small air force, also with obsolete air-craft. A small navy—four destroyers, to Russia's 130, and America's 200. The Chinese probably have submarines capable of firing missiles with nuclear warheads. In three or four years from now, they may have some intermediate range ballistic missiles, able to fly about 1,500 miles. Before 1980, they may have some intercontinental missiles. The fact remains that China, militarily speaking, is extremely badly equipped, es-pecially for wars of conquest.

China and India—and Russia—are vast countries with similar problems. All three struggle with the problem of cities versus countryside; industry versus farming. Do you concentrate on building factories, so as to be able to look the west in the face; or do you ensure that everyone gets a square meal, even if that puts you behind in the 20th century rat-race for steel mills? All three countries have moved uneasily back and forth between the two policies; China perhaps more than the other two. There was the Great Leap Forward that fell on its face—though China may have coped with bad weather and poor harvests better than did India, and perhaps even than did Russia. China made a lot of progress in agriculture from 1961 until 1967. India leaned too heavily on grain shipments from this country and wishes she had done more for her farmers. But the Chinese and the Indians have both failed to solve another problem; the problem of strong central government versus separatist tendencies. After half a century of Soviet republics, it isn't at all sure the Russians have solved that one either.

Instead of just doing a bit better, the Chinese might have done very much better than the Indians if they hadn't spent so much more of their income on armaments than India did. Now China spends about 10 percent of her national product on defense; India, about 3.8 percent.

The fact that China spends three times as much on defense as India, doesn't necessarily mean the Chinese are thrice as warlike; though the Indians think so. A case might be made that it's the U.S., as well as Russia, that compels China to spend so much on armaments. If so, then we are making the

Chinese even poorer than they otherwise would be; and they are so poor that, in spite of spending such a big chunk of their income on defense, they don't really end up with much military power.

The Chinese see this country as a very rich, very powerful enemy. What's more, they see their recent communist ally Russia as this country's evil accomplice, both of us hellbent on wrecking China and ruling the world.

How, you may ask, did they ever get this extraordinary notion? The answer seems to be more or less as follows.

When this country bombed North Vietnam, and sent a lot more American troops into South Vietnam, in the spring and summer of 1965, the Chinese began to think seriously of the possibility of an American invasion of China. They were really alarmed and their first natural thought was, What will Russia do, if it happens?

There isn't any reason to believe the Chinese have been able to find a reassuring answer. Russia stopped giving China military help long before President Kennedy was killed in November 1963, and before Khrushchev took his missiles out of Cuba in 1962, and signed the test-ban treaty with us. There have been frequent border clashes between Russia and China.

For years, American policy has been (with some semantic variations) the "containment" of China. From time to time, there are somewhat more conciliatory speeches; but in the very recent past, the makers of the conciliatory speeches have been apt to find themselves compelled to resign from the State Department or the White House, and having to find teaching jobs at Columbia or Harvard Universities. The picture that comes through, to the American public or to the Congress— and most of all of course to the suspicious Chinese—isn't at all conciliatory.

President Kennedy did think about trying to dilute suspicion, and there have been all those Chinese-American sessions in Warsaw. But Kennedy did not in fact get around to doing very much before he was killed; things like relaxing trade restrictions and reconsidering this country's United Nations policy. And a tougher American policy in Vietnam, after the death of Kennedy, who was dubious about Vietnam, and of Ngo Dinh Diem, who was losing it, coincided (in Chinese eyes) with new gropings toward each other by Russia and America, the two countries that China now regards as her bitterest enemies. Are they plotting China's destruction together? The Peking *People's Daily* seems to think so; it calls the Russians "shameless scabs acting as advisers to the American gangsters."

We, of course, know better. But if, nevertheless, American official policy does remain the "containment," by some means or other, of China, what is it we are seeking to contain?

Let me at this point quote a senior American correspondent in Asia, Frank McCullough of *Time* and *Life* magazines. He says: "Tell anyone you are 'containing' them, and you are pretty sure to enhance any paranoid tendency they have. Are we seeking to contain Chinese military might? Where is it? Are we containing land-grabbing by China? China has yet to grab a square foot of foreign ground in Asia. Are we seeking, then, to contain an idea? But you can't contain an idea by bombing it, only with a better idea. So far, nowhere in Asia have we offered a better idea."

One answer to Mr. McCullough is that, if this country had not adopted a policy of containing China, there *would* have been land-grabbing by China in Asia. The Indians presumably would say so, and possibly others as well. But the border dispute between China and India has two sides to the argument and it is by no means sure that all of the justice lies on India's side of the case. And it seems highly improbable that China lusts after the so-called southeast Asian rice bowl, since southeast Asia is barely capable of feeding itself, and would cease to be able to do even that much if the Chinese launched an armed invasion of the area.

The Chinese have historical claims on some parts of Asia, and they strongly wish to compensate for more than a century of humiliation by now asserting themselves as a major power— certainly in Asia, and probably in the world—and as the equal of both the U.S. and of Russia. But none of this attempted assertion has much to do with China being communist—and it is communism that American official spokesmen affirm that we are containing. If Chiang Kai-shek ruled in Peking, instead of Mao Tse-tung or some other communist, the chances are that China would still be pressing border claims, would insist that Tibet is Chinese, and would possess nuclear weapons. William Chapin, an American Foreign Service officer who has served in Laos and elsewhere in Asia, had this to say: "We can assume that China's basic national interests and objectives, as these affect foreign relations, would not differ very much from those of a strong and united Chinese state under a non-communist regime. They would include adequate protection for the nation's frontiers; the expulsion of American and other external military forces from the mainland of Asia and, somewhat less urgently, from the island periphery as well; world recognition of China as the peer of the United States and the Soviet Union; and the predominant voice in Asian affairs."

Turn back for a moment to the very confused state of affairs inside China. The present masters of China are communists; and what is happening in China seems, at least in part, to be a typical Marxist struggle. Lenin fought against the Mensheviks; Lenin's Bolsheviks after his death fought one another. Mao Tse-tung in his old age engaged in an ideological tussle with his opponents, who were also his life-long comrades. Had this happened to Lenin in his lifetime, we may be sure, so enormous was his reputation, that both his faction and the opposing factions would have insisted they were fighting to protect something called Leninism. This happened to Marx. He saw his followers fighting one another, all in the name of Marx, and the spectacle so embittered him that he is said to have remarked, "Thank God, I am not a Marxist." It happened to Mao Tse-tung. He was disgusted with the bureaucratic party edifice in China and he tried to tear it down. But the party fought back, and it did so in the name of Maoism. Everybody quoted the sayings of Mao in justification of their actions. When the Bolsheviks fought one another after Lenin's death, they managed to keep it an intraparty dispute, and to keep the army out of it. In China, the army has been compelled to take part in politics, and may now be running the

# AMERICA AND CHINA

THE WHOLE ASIA policy of the United States has
been focused on China. This would be understandable if it
were because there are in China over 700 million people, or
almost the equivalent of the combined populations of India,
Pakistan, and Indonesia. Unfortunately that is not the reason.
United States policy in Asia has been concentrated on the
containment of China because the United States policy-makers
long believed, and still often seem to proclaim, that the Chinese communists are immensely strong militarily, and that
they are constantly plotting and striving to fall upon all their
Asian neighbors and to devour them, as a necessary prelimi-
nary to attacking the United States itself. This is apparently
why the United States is in Vietnam. President Lyndon Johnson declared in Baltimore on April 7, 1965, "Over this war—
and all Asia—is another reality: the deepening shadow of Communist China . . . The contest in Vietnam is part of a wider
pattern of aggressive purposes." It may be added that the
Chinese communists appear to suffer from an identical misconception as regards the intentions of the United States toward them.

If the Chinese communists are wrong to fancy that the
United States constantly plans to attack them, they are at
least right in believing that the United States is an immensely
strong military power. The American policy-makers however
appear to be wrong on both their counts; China is probably
not intent on seizing and devouring China's neighbors, and
even if it were eager to do so, China is far from being a strong
military power. But the American policy-makers suffer in addition from an obsession with the mainland Chinese who used

to rule all China from Peking but who are now on Taiwan. The upshot is that American policy toward China, and so in a real sense toward all Asia, has pivoted for 20 years on a misconception and an obsession.

The fate and future of the fallen Chiang Kai-shek dynasty has been allowed to occupy much too large a share of the American policy-makers' attention. And this has continued stubbornly even after a fairly general realization has set in among thoughtful Americans that Generalissimo Chiang Kai-shek, like Humpty Dumpty, will never sit on his Great Wall again. In spite of a growing awareness to the contrary, American policy about China has for all practical purposes been conducted as if we did indeed expect Chiang Kai-shek or at least his son Chiang Ching-kuo to return some day to the mainland, to rule in Peking. That is to say, an apparent presumption of American policy has been that the communist regime that has been installed in Peking since 1949 is only a temporary aberration that will pass. American policy in the Far East has somehow managed to cherish this illusion, while simultaneously insisting that the communist regime that is confidently expected to collapse is immensely strong in military terms and is getting steadily stronger, so that it constitutes a great and growing danger to Asia and also, in the not too long run, to the United States as well.

The present communist regime in China very likely will pass away one day. Dynasties, even in China, do not last forever, and this one may turn out to be more precarious than many of its predecessors, some of which endured for centuries. In ageless China, the 20 years of communist rule are but the flutters of a butterfly's wing. But this possibility, or even likelihood, cannot excuse the fact that meanwhile, during those 20 years, American relations with China have been nonexistent, save for sporadic and apparently fruitless meetings between American and Chinese communist representatives in the city of Warsaw, in Poland. Instead of things becoming better, however slowly, they sometimes appear almost to have become worse. For, as American relations with Soviet Russia have very slowly thawed to something less icy than sub-zero, that slow thaw has seemed simply to confirm that it is really China that is "the enemy."

And the Chinese communists, staying true to their own set of misconceptions and obsessions, have meanwhile gone out of their way to aggravate the American errors. Intensely bellicose pronouncements from Peking, which were at first aimed at the United States alone but have more recently been directed against both the United States and China's late ally the Soviet Union, have helped to build up an American image of an enormously menacing China. This glowering image assumed its most sinister frown in the dire warning of the former American Secretary of State, Dean Rusk, about a billion Chinese armed with nuclear weapons.

That picture of China is still rather clear and threatening in most American minds. Yet it never was quite as clear cut as Rusk insisted, in the minds of most of his own State Department China Watchers: and since Secretary Rusk's departure, in 1969, the State Department has tended to concede that in fact China is a problem for the world because of Chinese weakness rather than from Chinese strength. Meanwhile, the Russians have taken an old leaf from the American book, and profess to fear Chinese "aggression" against Soviet territory at several places along the thousands of miles of Sino-Soviet border (much of it only vaguely defined or not demarcated at all). Yet a good many close observers of the scene suspect that Russia may in fact be tempted by China's present internal troubles and obvious military weaknesses to launch an invasion of China, if only in order to destroy the Chinese nuclear installations that are still in their infancy, before they can become truly formidable.

A war between Russia and China might grow into a considerable calamity for all mankind, especially if nuclear weapons were used, which both sides have strongly hinted would be the case. It is therefore in the American national interest to attempt whatever can be done to avert such a war. But the interesting point, meantime, is that it is a Sino-Soviet war that appears to be threatened, not as the American policy-makers have hitherto assumed a Sino-American war. The fact is that in spite of all the propaganda about the Chinese threat to American interests in Asia, there has been only one occasion during the past 20 years when a serious risk existed of war between the United States and Communist China. The sole exception to a rather peaceful record came of course in the Korean War, when the strategy adopted by General Mac-Arthur brought Chinese "volunteers" into the war against the United Nations forces that General MacArthur commanded. The final upshot of that affair however was not that President Truman declared war on China, but that he fired General MacArthur. In the Vietnam war also, as Henry Brandon has pointed out in his book *Anatomy of Error* (Gambit, 1969), "the State Department's China experts—overrated the risk of Chinese intervention." The Chinese never entered the war, even when American bombs were falling near them.

A further significant and rather cheering fact is that in spite of their bitter quarrel, Soviet Russia has never ceased to maintain that China ought to become a member of the United Nations. Chinese membership in the international organization would not preclude a war between China and Russia. But it could conceivably cool their fiery antagonism. It seems all the more odd, therefore, that while Russia continues to support China's entry into the UN, the United States at the end of 1969 continued to oppose such entry. Yet the UN is in New York City; and the presence of a Chinese communist delegation at the UN might well lead, in time, to fewer tirades by Peking and a more moderate expression of Chinese aims.

But even if the United States were to abandon its now increasingly pointless opposition to Communist China's entry to the UN, there would still be an obstacle in the way of China joining the international organization. Taiwan, calling itself the one and only true China, and claiming that it really represents the 700 million Chinese people (as well as the several millions of overseas Chinese) is a member of the United Nations with a seat on the Security Council as well as in the General Assembly. Peking insists for its part that there cannot be "two Chinas" and that Taiwan must be expelled from the UN before the Chinese Communists will even consider China becoming a member. But no one has tried to argue with Peking that one seat on the Security Council plus two seats in the General Assembly might be as advantageous to China as it is to the Soviet Union to have the Ukraine and Byelo-Russia represented on the international body, thus giving Russia not one but three votes. This device would imply the existence of an autonomous Taiwan; but it would also represent a Chinese gain. The United States cannot even consider such a proposal, far less espousing it, so long as the U.S. is officially committed to upholding the Chiang Kai-shek regime on Taiwan as the real government of China. Yet hardly anyone can any longer argue seriously that the continued existence of the Chiang Kai-shek regime in Taiwan ought to be a mainstay of American policy in Asia, and that it should be allowed to stand in the way of restoration of relations between the U.S. and the one-fourth of this generation of mankind who inhabit mainland China.

**10**

# THE TWO KOREAS

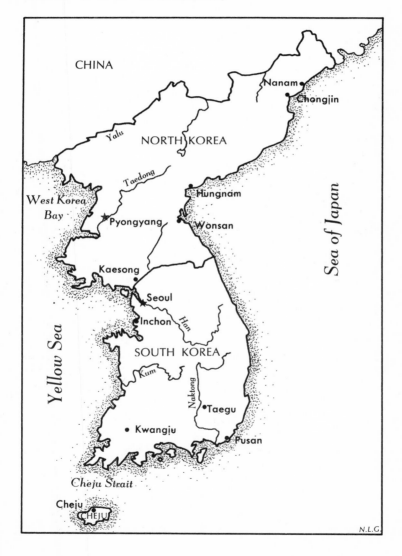

TWENTY YEARS AFTER

IN 1969 MY wife and I flew from Taipei in Taiwan, to Seoul in South Korea. Most of the way we flew close
to the coastline of mainland China. Our aircraft flaunted the
Nationalist Chinese insignia and so was liable to be shot down
by the Chinese communists who regard Chiang Kai-shek as
still at war with them. Nothing whatever happened; the voyage was pleasant, the skies blue and empty; the service could
not have been better.

South Korea is almost exactly the same size as Indiana—
36,000 square miles—and has a population of 33 million. But
10 percent of them live crowded in the capital, Seoul, which
incidentally has the world's largest women's university, Ewha.
The sturdy Koreans seem to live largely on very hot, thick,
green, spiced, and sweetened tea, and on two types of pickles,
one for the winter and one for the summer. The winter *kimchi*,
as it is called, consists of cabbage, turnips and radish, and is
very hot. The summer *kimchi* is mainly cucumber. Other items
of diet are rice (of course), kidney beans, and beef with lots
of soy sauce, green onion, sesame seeds, and pepper. The
Korean chopstick is rather like a thin steel needle, and correspondingly more difficult to manipulate than Chinese or Japanese chopsticks. The men wear a traditional hat which is made
of semi-transparent, stiff black net. *Chogari*, the Korean kimono, has long-flowing skirts, instead of being a tight wrapper
like the kimono in Japan.

In the dim and fitful light of early Korean history, three
separate kingdoms are discernible between the 1st and 7th
centuries. But Pijke, Koguryo, and Silla gave place in the 7th
century to the Silla dynasty; which formed an alliance with

the Chinese Tang dynasty that compelled Silla's eastern and northern rivals to capitulate. The Silla dynasty had its capital at Kyongju, just as Japan's old capital was Nara. In the 10th century, Silla gave way to the Koryo empire, from which the name Korea is derived. In terms of culture, the Koryo empire produced glazed celadon vases and, more significant perhaps, the world's first use of movable type, in 1234. The Yi dynasty (1392–1910) produced ornately decorated porcelains. Hangel, a phonetic alphabet of 28 symbols, developed by King Sejong in 1443, is still in use in Korea. The Japanese invasion of Korea in 1592 caused much devastation, but the Koreans claimed victory at sea through the use of iron-clad ships.

Korea extends from Manchuria, as everybody who fought in the Korean War of 1950 knows, but Korea enjoyed practical independence from China by formally paying tribute to the easily satisfied Chinese emperors. However, in 1873 Japan took advantage of China's 19th century weakness to penetrate Korea. By the end of the century Korea was virtually controlled by Japan, and, after the 1905 war between Russia and Japan, the Japanese in 1910 formally annexed Korea. Koreans became second-class citizens in their own country, the Japanese language took precedence over Korean and the Koreans were turned into hewers of wood and drawers of water for the Japanese conquerors. Higher education of Koreans was for the most part discouraged by the Japanese, yet the Koreans learned a great deal from their Japanese masters which they were to put to very good use on their own behalf later. At the end of World War II, after Japan's defeat, the Japanese withdrew from Korea. The Soviet Union occupied the northern half of the country, the United States occupied the southern half. In their portion of the country, the Americans put into power Dr. Syngman Rhee, who came from Hawaii where he had been living in exile, and who had been all his life a fighter for Korean independence from Japan. Rhee became president of the Republic of Korea in 1948. But Rhee had no notion of parliamentary democracy and no patience with a political opposition. He did once remark that if his political foes insisted on it, he would then give them a "little opposition party of their own." But that of course did not mean that he intended to yield an inch of his power.

Meanwhile, in the north there had been installed a communist regime under a man certainly not a bit less dictatorial than Rhee, the ambitious Kim Il Sung. The North Koreans under Kim Il Sung were condemned by the United Nations for invading the south in 1950, and the Korean War that ensued lasted until 1953. It ended in a military truce, and the uneasy acceptance of the division of Korea into two parts, one communist, one still dominated by the aging Syngman Rhee.

In April 1960, Rhee's government, which had become increasingly tyrannical and was very corrupt, was overthown mainly by student protesters and army sympathizers. It was succeeded by a democratically elected government, but the duly elected president proved either too civilized or too weak to rule this rough country. After only one year, his government in turn was overthrown, this time by the military led by General Park Chung Hee. Following his coup, Park did go on to hold and win a presidential election on October 15, 1963. He won by only a narrow margin, but a month later his Democratic Republican Party won 110 of the 175 seats in the National Assembly. President Park has governed South Korea ever since. In October 1969 he won a national referendum which was held to decide whether he could stand for a third term as president. The South Korean constitution plainly said no, but Park's party claimed that they needed his strong hand at the helm for at least one more term. Park indicated that if the referendum went against him he would resign, but in the upshot he was not put to that test. His second term ends in 1971. He will, of course, then have to win an election in order to serve a third term. But in 1969 he was expected to win a 1971 election rather easily.

Under Park, South Korea sent about 50,000 men to serve on the American side in the war in South Vietnam, and Park also signed in 1965 a treaty with Japan which restored friendly relations between the two countries for the first time in almost a century. The *Far Eastern Economic Review* said that President Park "has so strongly put his own imprint on the government during his years in power that effective government without him at the helm is becoming increasingly difficult to imagine." President Park had a narrow escape in January 1968, when a North Korean communist suicide squad secretly entered Seoul and got within yards of the president's palace intending, they subsequently confessed, to assassinate him. As part of a tightened up security program, the Korean Home Ministry enforced nationwide registration of all citizens. Some 95 percent of the population, or over 29 million persons of both sexes and all races, had to register.

South Korea was rendered uneasy and unhappy by the refusal of the United States to consult the South Korean government about America's negotiations with North Korea for the release of the American spy ship *Pueblo*. The United States did manage finally to get the *Pueblo's* crew released by North Korea, but the view of the South Korean government was that instead of negotiating with the communists, the United States ought to have attacked the North militarily. As a gesture to the South, the United States offered President Park increased military aid. What President Park wants however, is a more specific American pledge to go to war immediately should South Korea ever be attacked again.

Twenty years after the Korean War had begun, 17 years after it had ended, the Americans and North Koreans still were meeting regularly for mutual slanging matches, at Panmunjom. These truce talks had become so routine that they had been transformed in part into a tourist attraction; buses regularly took tourists to Panmunjom, to peer through the windows of the truce talks hut at the two sides negotiating with each other across a large table. Though these talks go on, scores and sometimes hundreds of North Korean saboteurs and spies are caught or killed in the South each year. Some of them sneak across the 150 mile long, closely guarded and fenced demilitarized zone between North and South; most land on the coast of South Korea, at night. The South no doubt similarly attempts to penetrate the North with its agents. The

South Korean government after all has its own highly organized, highly efficient, and usually ruthless Central Intelligence Agency.

In spite of all this tension, the South Korean economy after years of stagnation and setbacks was in a condition of almost continuous boom during the '60s. The Koreans have never lacked confidence in themselves, and of course they have allies. Their 50,000 fighting men in Vietnam are matched by the presence of 50,000 American soldiers in South Korea. The spending of the Americans benefits the Korean economy, and additionally, about $150 million a year flows back to South Korea from its troops in Vietnam, and from other South Koreans who have gone to work for construction and engineering companies in Vietnam. The American Secretary of State William P. Rogers, on a visit to Seoul in August 1969, assured the South Koreans that the U.S. "stands by its treaty obligations to our treaty allies," and added that one of the purposes of his own visit was "to assure you that you should have no apprehensions." Thus assured of American support, and having buried the hatchet with Japan, the Koreans have been encouraged to forge ahead economically. Nevertheless, they would like to have the further assurances that American support will continue to take the form of having American soldiers physically present continuously in South Korea, as they have been for so many years. They do not want the two American divisions withdrawn. Because they fear that some sort of American military cutback is in the cards, the Koreans were not wholly satisfied by Secretary Rogers's promises made in Seoul.

In the spring of 1969, the government of South Korea conducted a countrywide war exercise. Half a million soldiers, and two million Home Guards, were instructed to behave as if North Korea had once again launched an all-out attack on the South. However, this operation was not given a code name that referred to the Korean War 19 years before, when North Korea attacked the South in actuality and the United States and other members of the United Nations came to South Korea's rescue. The spring operation was called Ulchi, in honor of a commander who repulsed Chinese invaders in the 7th century. Koreans have long memories.

Before Ulchi, the United States had also launched an exercise, called Operation Focus Retina, which displeased President Park Chung Hee and other South Korean leaders. The operation was the longest airlift in history, and it involved 7,000 American and South Korean troops, and 77 aircraft. Combat-ready troops were flown from North Carolina to Seoul in twenty-two hours, using Okinawa as a stopover. Why were the South Koreans displeased with this U.S. operation? Because they saw it as paving the way for the eventual withdrawal of the 50,000 U.S. army troops and the 10,000 U.S. airmen who are at present stationed in South Korea. If it is possible to airlift American soldiers to Korea in a few hours, all the way from Carolina, then it seems unnecessary to station them permanently in Korea itself. In a year or two, it will not be necessary even to have a stopover in Okinawa. Operation Retina employed C-141 troop-carrying aircraft. But by 1972 the giant C-5A aircraft will be in service. And by then the United States will be preparing to hand Okinawa back to Japan.

But the South Korean government strongly believes that the United States ought to continue stationing American soldiers and airmen in Korea, and that it should hang on to Okinawa as well. Both Taiwan and South Korea regard Okinawa as a military base that is vital to their future security. Prime Minister Chung Il Kwon, who during the Korean War was army chief of staff, wants to have more American troops in Korea, not fewer. He has publicly offered to let the United States have more land for more military bases in South Korea, in order that South Korea can be made into a strongpoint from which to "defend the entire Far East." Prime Minister Chung defined his offer with characteristic vigor. "Where else in Asia are you welcome?" he demanded to know of the United States. "Others say, 'Yankee Go Home.' We alone say, 'Come and establish more bases here.' "

President Park was furious that the United States failed to send the aircraft carrier *Enterprise* to bombard the North

Korean coast in retaliation for the 1968 seizure of the American intelligence ship *Pueblo*. Park also has demanded that Washington "exert political, economic, and other pressure on Japan, so that the Japanese government will realize the necessity for a regional collective defense system." The regional collective system that President Park has in mind is one that would involve Taiwan and South Korea as well as the United States and Japan, and perhaps also Australia and New Zealand, in a Pacific Treaty Organization (PATO). This was discussed when Chiang Ching-kuo, Chiang Kai-shek's son and likely successor, visited Seoul from Taiwan. But so far the United States has shown no more interest in PATO than have the Japanese.

Between 1949 and 1966, the United States gave South Korea $4.26 billions in economic aid. In 1969, South Korea received about $40 million from the U.S. in the form of grants and loans or 20 percent less than in the previous year; in addition, South Korea got $49 million worth of food under Public Law 480, as compared with $72 million under PL480, in 1968. But what President Park wants in addition to increased military aid from the United States is a pledge that American soldiers will continue to be stationed in South Korea. All the same, the South Koreans have become so self-confident that nowadays Washington is almost as afraid that the South may resume the war as that North Korea will attack again. If the South, with its 33 million population, decided to reunite Korea by conquering the North, which has only 13 million people, it is virtually certain that both Russia and China would intervene despite their present strife. Both of them look on North Korea as a highly convenient buffer state that it is in their interest to protect, even though North Korea under its present communist leadership apparently refuses to take any orders from either of them. The United States has no wish to get in a war with Russia and/or China over Korea. One Korean War was sufficient. South Korea constantly draws attention to its 50,000 troops fighting in South Vietnam on the American side, to impress the United States with Korea's steadfastness against the common communist foe. The United States has willingly supplied those troops with the very latest weapons being used in the field. But the United States appears less willing to press the very latest weapons on the 550,000 Korean troops on guard in South Korea. It has promised to do so for years, but has not yet kept all of its promises. As South Korea's almost aggressive self-confidence continues growing, voices are heard in Seoul, suggesting that it will be a good thing when the Vietnam war ends, because then it will be possible to bring home the South's two well-armed divisions for possible use against the North. Of course it is always added that this would be in the event of another full-scale attack by the North. But President Park has himself admitted that "North Korea would not dare to start an aggressive war without the support of either Communist China or the Soviet Union," and nobody in Washington or in the American embassy in Seoul believes that either China or Russia is inclined at the moment to give North Korea their support for an aggressive war. Moreover, although North Korea may at present be better armed and have superior aircraft and perhaps heavier artillery than the South, all the available evidence points to the North Korean forces being deployed for defense, not for attack.

This however does not take into consideration the apparently very odd mentality of the North Korean communist leader Kim Il Sung, who once proclaimed his country to be a "flying horse." The seizure of the *Pueblo* was an act of enormous audacity, for Kim Il Sung could not possibly have counted on the United States behaving as it did and taking no military action. On the contrary, American and South Korean intelligence seem agreed that North Korea fully expected to receive an American blow, in retaliation. But in spite of this, no special North Korean preparations to ward off such a blow could be detected. The North Korean leader was apparently willing to accept an American attack and to pay that price without flinching, so long as he could have the satisfaction of humiliating the United States by capturing its spy ship and hauling it ignominiously into one of his ports.

This is part of a behavior pattern that persuades American observers in Seoul that Kim Il Sung is not rational, therefore is dangerous. Kim is 60, and he is said to have vowed that before

1970 ends, he will have made another bid to reunite Korea by force. This will almost certainly prove to be an idle boast, on a par with Chiang Kai-shek's reiterated announcements of an early invasion of the Chinese mainland from Taiwan. All the same, the Americans in South Korea could not be sure, and were prepared for an uneasy 1970. Kim has done other odd things. He sends guerrillas from the North to land on the South's east coast. These guerrillas are invariably detected by the South's vigilant Home Guard, and are captured or commit suicide, though they sometimes manage to kill a few harmless farmers or fisherfolk first. But they manage to do no harm that would have military significance, and this is in part because the east coast is perhaps the last place anyone in his senses would choose for a guerrilla landing. It would probably be much easier for North Korean guerrillas to land elsewhere and to head for industrial targets, factories or dams, which it would be very difficult to protect from damage by saboteurs who had been trained in the art. But nothing of the sort ever seems to have been tried by the North Koreans.

In short, Kim Il Sung is a puzzle, and North Korea is an enigma. Apparently it is as much a mystery today to the Chinese and the Russians as to the Americans and to the South. Although Russia supplies the North with arms, and both Russia and China probably would defend it if it were attacked, neither has any control over its policies. Kim Il Sung quarreled with the Chinese long ago. Their reward for intervening on his side in the Korean War was to have the Chinese component of the North Korean Communist Party purged shortly after the war had ended. But the Russians do not seem to fare any better. No travel is permitted to any Soviet official in North Korea, or for that matter to any member of the International Control Commission which still feebly functions in North Korea. The North has, under Kim Il Sung, become even more of a hermit kingdom than Burma is under General Ne Win. Pyongyang has cut itself off from the rest of the world as completely as Tibet's Lhasa once did.

Nevertheless, the publicly proclaimed policy of the North remains the reunification of Korea, by force if necessary. Apparently in order to prepare the way for realization of this dream, Kim Il Sung in 1968 dispatched a murder squad to the South to dispose of President Park. The assassins did reach Seoul, and got within a thousand yards of the Blue House, as the president's palace is now called. There they were stopped. Had they succeeded in killing Park or other members of the South Korean government, there might very well have been renewed war between North and South. But on this occasion also, American and South Korean intelligence were baffled to detect any evidence that the North had prepared itself for such a contingency. No special precautions had been taken, at the demilitarized zone or anywhere else. Yet there are frequent shootings along that armistice line, in which American soldiers as well as South and North Koreans are killed.

President Park, the South Korean leader, has had an interesting career. He received his military training from the Japanese and in World War II fought for them in Manchuria. After the war, Syngman Rhee became president of South Korea and there were several plots against him by people who questioned his dictatorial methods. One plotter was Park's brother, and Park was disgraced for giving his brother sanctuary in his home. One of the military judges at the trial was the present prime minister Chung Il Kwon. When the Korean War broke out, Park was reinstated in the army. In 1960, the students of South Korea led a revolt against Syngman Rhee and became the first students in the world to overthrow a government. The army joined in the revolt. A year later, General Park staged a coup against the civilian who had succeeded Rhee, and Park subsequently was elected president. Now he has decided to seek a third term, which will require a change in the constitution. Park's excuse is that he needs a third term to complete his successful overhaul of the country's economy. The leader of the opposition, Yu Chin O, who hoped to replace Park in the Blue House in 1971, declared sternly that "peaceful transfer of power is more important than economic development." Yu Chin O heads the New Democratic Party; he is a former Seoul University professor, and author of the constitution that forbade a third term. Park heads the Democratic Republican

Party. As far as policy is concerned, it is rather hard to tell the parties apart. But President Park, since he put off his uniform, has galvanized the country and completely altered the face of the capital Seoul, where tall new buildings seem to spring up overnight and broad new boulevards appear in place of twisting lanes, as if the Army Engineering Corps had been given a completely free hand.

Park is a martinet who works hard and terrifies his ministers into doing the same. Being offered a cabinet post by Park is regarded as an onerous honor which can scarcely be refused but is bound to be no picnic. The rate of growth of the South Korean economy under Park's dynamic leadership is a phenomenal 13 percent, though in 1969 it slowed a little, to 11.7 percent. Exports have soared. "If we sell $700 million worth of goods overseas this year," Park said in March 1969, "we shall be able to export $1 billion worth next year, and $2.5 billion worth in 1975." Park regards export volume as "the best yardstick of national power." The fact is, however, that despite a terrific rise in exports, South Korea's trade deficit is an annual $1 billion, and the country's foreign debt now totals $1.7 billion.

There are other kinks in the economy. Inflation has pushed up consumer prices between 10 and 20 percent each year, and wages are so low that South Korea can undersell even Taiwan. The Japanese are back in South Korea, making deals and running factories, and the Koreans who formerly were intensely anti-Japanese, with good reason, have got accustomed to their faces again. Other foreign capital rolls in, attracted by high profits; but there is growing nervousness about the possibility of the United States and other countries shutting out South Korean goods with higher tariffs or more quotas. The country still must import food; 2,618,000 tons of grain in 1969. The farmers, who are two-thirds of the population, are too poor to buy the fertilizer that makes possible use of the new "miracle" rice and wheat strains, and also they are squeezed by the government in order to pay for steel mills and four-lane highways.

The students who overthrew Syngman Rhee are now politically quiescent but are watching Park closely. If they decide he should not have a third term, there may be renewed student ructions. Communism has been almost a dead letter in the South since the Korean War, but communist cells are said to have appeared in Seoul University, and the vigilant but brutal South Korean Central Intelligence Agency, which made murderous attacks on students in Rhee's time, does not greatly help matters by constantly accusing South Korean intellectuals whom students admire of being plotters in the pay of the North. Also, the students are well aware that though Park himself is probably completely honest, there is still a good deal of corruption in government. Park punishes it ferociously when he finds it, but all the same corruption continues to add an average 10 to 15 percent to the legitimate cost of almost all government projects. A man for the students to watch and perhaps to fear is Kim Chung Pil, formerly connected with the South Korean CIA and who had a big hand in Park's successful coup in 1961. Kim on May 30, 1968 quit politics (he was chairman of the ruling Democratic Republican Party), explaining he was going "into retreat." He is at least nominally a Buddhist. But one theory is that Kim has his eye on the presidency, not in 1971 for he hopes Park will get his third term, but in 1975 when Park is bound to leave the Blue House, assuming he is then still in it.

President Park is said to be aware that the economy has become somewhat unbalanced. He has therefore promised the farmers a better deal from now on, saying with truth that the time has come for the people who live in the towns (35 percent) to give something back to the people on the land. Unfortunately, the people in the towns not only suffer from rising prices and low wages, but have to pay high taxes on commodities in order to finance the up-keep of the huge (550,000-man) South Korean army. Meanwhile, wealthy South Koreans still manage to avoid paying any income tax. The government allots about a quarter of the budget to defense (around $250 million). But President Park points out that the same sum is now being spent on schools in South Korea.

There is no denying the intelligence as well as the toughness and tenacity of the Korean people. Girls from remote mountain villages quickly learn to put together intricate electronic components that General Electric and other large U.S. corporations are very glad to be able to get so cheaply. But where it will all end, if South Korea, Taiwan, and Hong Kong continue to undersell one another is another matter. Their present main markets, the United States and Japan, may shut out their goods in sheer self-defense. Or the Japanese may simply get Korea back, by buying into it, which they are now doing very fast. Whatever happens, the Koreans are not likely to be held back, or down. Their history is chiefly of survival against apparently unbeatable odds. If one were a Japanese or other near neighbor of Korea, one would be tempted to hope that the country remains divided. A reunited Korea of 46 million dynamic and rather ruthless people with long memories of wrongs done them by their neighbors might be a terrifying phenomenon. Even the redoubtable North Vietnamese, who have encountered Koreans in battle and ought to know, might tremble at the prospect.

# THE FLYING HORSE

KIM IL SUNG was brought home by the Russians when they entered Korea in August 1945 after the collapse of the Japanese. He claimed to have been fighting the Japanese in Manchuria. This dedicated communist—but even more dedicated nationalist as the Russians were soon to discover—eliminated all his rivals and became prime minister when the Democratic People's Republic of North Korea was proclaimed in September 1948. After the 1950 Korean War ended in the armistice signed in Panmunjom in July 1953, the border between North and South Korea was more or less where it had been, along the 38th parallel. Kim Il Sung perforce settled down for the time being to rule only North Korea. The North covers 49,000 square miles, and has a population of about 13 million people. The capital, Pyongyang, has a population of just under one million. North Korea like North Vietnam has plenty of coal and other mineral resources. Kim Il Sung has resumed the industrial and mineral development that the Japanese had begun. Perhaps half the population in consequence are employed in industry rather than in farming. Trade figures are kept a close secret, but the production of electric power, steel, cement, and coal is considerable.

In North Korean elections there is invariably a 100 percent turn out at the polls. This is generally acclaimed by the communist regime to be "a manifestation of our people's absolute trust in and loyalty to the great leader of the 46 million Korean people." The great leader of course is Kim Il Sung, and the 46 million people are the 33 million South Koreans as well as the 13 million North Koreans. Kim Il Sung claims to be their ruler too. North Korean elections are also beautifully simple. There are 457 constituencies, which are matched by exactly 457 candidates, no more and no fewer—and all the candidates who run are duly elected. What could be neater or more economical? Nevertheless, there are from time to time little turbulences within the ruling party. This party is called the Korean Workers Party, and it suffers from frequent purges, invariably conducted by the prime minister Kim Il Sung. The last reported one was at the end of 1967. Then eliminated were Pak Kum Chol, a vice president, and Yi Hyo Sung, a member of the Presidium. Out along with them went a vice premier, a secretary general, and other important communist political leaders. Their disappearance from the scene was said to be connected with a new policy of more vigorous armed interference in the South. Thus it represented a victory for the North Korean hawks. On previous occasions, Kim has purged other army commanders who came with him when the Russians returned them to North Korea and who might have challenged his power, also Chinese communists who were in North Korea during the Korean War and who apparently outstayed their welcome. Indeed, friction between Kim Il Sung and Peking has grown so great that Peking habitually now refers to him as "the fat revisionist." Kim however continues to get a good deal of military assistance from Russia. He has an air force of 500 aircraft, mostly MIG jets.

The reasoning of the North Korean hawks was well expressed by Kim Il Sung in a speech at the end of 1967, in which he said: "As the days go by the gulf between North and South Korea is growing wider in all the political, economical, and cultural spheres, and the national community of our people formed through a long history is gradually fading away." What he evidently meant was that if reunification of Korea were ever to come, it had to be soon.

One reason why Kim is unpopular in Peking is that he has on various occasions emphasized the need for one "united anti-American front." This concept of course is rejected by China, which will have nothing to do with the Soviet Union. However, Kim, quite characteristically, has also criticized the

Russians, at least obliquely, over Czechoslovakia. After the Russians invaded Czechoslovakia, Kim declared in a speech that each "socialist country should be allowed to develop independently." He was of course thinking more about North Koreans' cherished independence than about the situation of the Czechoslovakians, but no doubt Moscow got the message. In the upshot, both the Chinese and the Czechoslovakians stayed away from the celebrations of the anniversary of the Korean republic. The Russians were there, though, and seemed anxious to disclaim any intention of trying to control Kim Il Sung or to run North Korea.

Kim Il Sung makes the normal communist claims of enormous advances in education, health, production, and other spheres of public endeavor. He claims in particular to have built fine modern houses for peasants, with electric power in all of them. A bit of North Korean propaganda says: "The humming of tractors reverberates merrily over the fields of socialist cooperative farms." And blocks of apartments in Pyongyang are described as "homes of happiness built under the parental love and solicitude of the leader, deeper than the sea and higher than the mountains." There is in short a cult of personality, with Kim Il Sung as the personality. He is regularly described as "serious patriot and iron-willed genius-commander." He has never in fact been much thought of as a military leader or a Marxist theoretician either. But it does seem to be a fact that the peasants who flock into Pyongyang marvel at the town's apartment houses, and describe their capital proudly as "the pearl of the Orient." But they have to work for these benefactions. Kim Il Sung has personally defined the working day, rather quaintly, as one of 480 minutes. These minutes have to be fully used. "There must be no waste of labor. We must realize that the 480 minutes working day system is a state regulation which no one is allowed to violate. We must struggle against any practices involving the slightest waste of labor or violation of labor discipline. Work every minute, every second! Achieve maximum productivity!" The people are urged to save "even a grain of rice, a gram of iron, or a drop of gasoline." Foreign experts tend to conclude from these exclamations that there are still rather severe shortages of many things in the North.

About half of North Korea's trade is with the Soviet bloc; maybe $200 million a year with the Soviet Union. North Korea also trades with Japan and Hong Kong. It buys wheat, wheat flour, and trucks from France, and sells rice to Indonesia. Grain production is about 5 million tons, with a target of 5 to 7 million tons by the end of 1970. Other targets for 1970 include 44.5 million tons of cement, 23 or 25 million tons of coal, 1.5 million tons of chemical fertilizer, and 400 million meters of textiles. What these figures suggest is that under their very different political systems, the two parts of Korea are pushing ahead vigorously with the development of their economy. Another war between them would presumably once again destroy most of what has been built up since 1950. That may very well be a good reason to think that neither country will in fact go to war. Should they do so, however, the United States would be faced with a momentous decision. Like the American troops in Europe, the 50,000 American soldiers in South Korea are a kind of tripwire, calculated to bring the U.S. right into a conflict immediately if one broke out. That, of course, is the reason why President Park is so anxious that the Americans shall not go home. In North Korea, Kim Il Sung has no such hold on his allies. He threw out the last of the Chinese "volunteers" long ago, and the Russians have hitherto been too prudent to come in. Nor indeed has Kim Il Sung ever invited them, and there is no suggestion that the North Koreans would welcome them.

# AMERICA AND THE KOREANS

REGULAR FIGHTING BETWEEN organized armies stopped in Korea in 1953, but ever since then there have been at least two divisions of American soldiers in the South, alongside the South Korean army of about half a million men. What is the function of those 50,000 or so Americans who keep perpetual vigil in South Korea? Technically, they are still there only as part of a United Nations force; but in fact of course the United Nations armies that fought against North Korea, and against the Chinese "volunteers" who poured into the war after General MacArthur marched north, have long been disbanded, leaving the Americans as the only foreigners on guard. Why do they have to be there, when the South Korean army is so large and well-armed and would therefore seem to be at least a match for the North Korean army of Kim Il Sung?

It is not difficult to find in Seoul Americans who will explain that those young soldiers from the United States have to be retained indefinitely in South Korea as a kind of human tripwire to insure that if war breaks out once again in Korea, the United States will be involved from the start in the fighting. This is roughly the function of the 250,000 American troops who sit guard in western Europe. There the theory is that so massive an American military presence ensures that any war that breaks out in Europe need not be a nuclear war, at least in the first instance. The Russians are being saved from the temptation of trying to overrun Europe by one quick nuclear blast. Should they do so, they would perforce kill large numbers of American soldiers, which would automatically entail an American nuclear retaliation on Russia.

Alternatively, should the Russians resist the nuclear temptation but try to invade western Europe with large armies, they would again encounter a large United States armed force. And this is supposed to give them pause, more so than encountering German, French, and other European troops would do. No one any longer puts much credence in this theory, and in the United States Senate the demands for a pullout of American troops from Europe get steadily louder and more impatient.

There is not much risk of nuclear war beginning in Korea, started by either side, so the Americans in South Korea are not there to avert that. But they are still there as a tripwire. Why should they be? Why should not the United States simply have a defense treaty with South Korea, promising that if South Korea is attacked, the United States will be its ally; provided of course that American public opinion is willing to support such a treaty and the U.S. Senate ratifies it? From the Korean side, we have seen that this question is answered with a strong negative. The South Koreans want the Americans in there on their side; all the time; and physically, like children clutching a hand in the dark. This is an undignified posture which surely will not long endure.

On the American side, the answer to this question that was returned by one American official in Seoul, was that the American public cannot be trusted to keep its word, even were that word to be solemnly pledged. If North Korea, for instance, attacked the South and the Korean War were resumed, Americans back home might recall the heavy casualties of 1950 to 1953, and think twice about agreeing to join in the war on the side of the South. However, the Americans back home would really have no choice, if in the first hours of fighting young Americans already in Korea had been among the first to die. So runs the theory. The American soldiers would have fulfilled their function of human tripwire, and the United States would be irrevocably committed to avenging them.

This theory is based on frank lack of faith in the steadfastness or trustworthiness of ordinary Americans who make up what is called public opinion. It is not a very commendable theory, on moral, political, or perhaps even military grounds. Yet it is peculiarly difficult to refute. For the popular hazy notion that the American divisions in South Korea are required to defend the South, and that if they were pulled out the Korean War would at once resume, is plainly a faulty notion. Why should not the big South Korean army be able to hold its own line, especially as the South Korean government decided it had 50,000 South Korean soldiers to spare to send to fight in South Vietnam? If the popular notion were correct, it should give rise to a further disturbing question. This is as follows: If, nearly 20 years after the regular fighting stopped in South Korea, the South despite its large, well-trained, well-armed military forces is still unable to dispense with the services of 50,000 American troops, does that mean this situation must continue indefinitely and that as far as can be seen into the future, there will always be 50,000 Americans on guard in South Korea?

There is absolutely no sign of any thaw in the relations between North and South Korea. Both sides remain bitterly antagonistic to each other. The Korean armistice has never become a Korean peace. The North Korean communist leader Kim Il Sung has vowed to reunify the country by force in 1970 or at any rate in his own lifetime (he is now 60). The South Koreans have become increasingly self-confident as they have become better trained and better armed (and also as Kim Il Sung's rifts with both the Chinese and the Russians have grown). It sometimes seems almost as if the United States military role in the South is as much to restrain the South Koreans from going to war again, as to help to defend them from attack.

These obvious but frequently overlooked facts raise serious questions about American policy toward Korea. If the questions are seldom asked, it is probably because the facts have been not so much overlooked as deliberately ignored, kicked with a shrug under the rug. Or it may be that some at least of the policymakers decided, in agreement with the American official I spoke to in Seoul, that the American public cannot be trusted with facts and so have to be kept both blinkered and muzzled, like the ox whose only reason for existence is to tread out the corn in the fullness of time. But a permanent or even semipermanent American military presence in Korea is a fact that cannot go unrecognized, especially now that the question of an American military presence or nonpresence in Vietnam is being painfully faced up to.

Korea is very close to Russia, to China, and also to Japan, and is very far from the United States. This is a hard and un-softenable fact of geography. If the Korean peninsula is to be divided politically, with bitter enmity on both sides of the dividing line, the ensuing situation is one that concerns Korea and its near neighbors but not necessarily the United States, except insofar as this country is a leading member of the United Nations. Is there any suggestion that if the Korean War were to break out again, the other members of the United Nations would again rush into the fray? This is not a very credible idea. It might be more feasible that both Koreas be admitted as members of the United Nations, to fight out their battle verbally in New York rather than on actual battlefields in Korea which their armies have already tormented more than enough. The present deep schism between Russia and China indicates that these giants might either be neutral, or possibly even on opposing sides, in a new Korean conflict. Japan, meanwhile, is renewing its former close association with Korea and has an obvious self-interest in that country's future. And the Japanese are no longer an unarmed power.

These new groupings of forces demand a re-examination of the United States role in Korea; they may even suggest that the 50,000 Americans in South Korea are actually becoming rather irrelevant.

**11**

# JAPAN AND OKINAWA

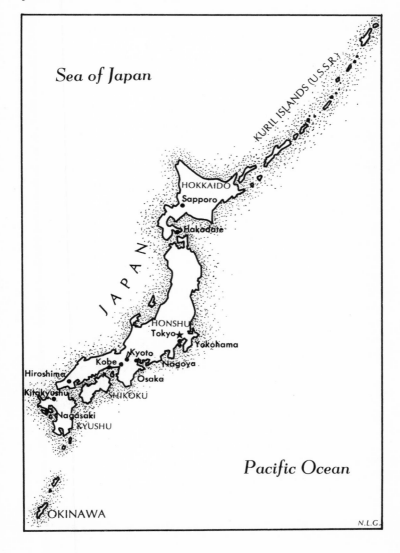

Sea of Japan

KURIL ISLANDS (U.S.S.R.)

HOKKAIDO
Sapporo
Hakodate

JAPAN

HONSHU
Tokyo
Yokohama
Kyoto
Kobe
Nagoya
Hiroshima
Osaka
Kitakyushu
SHIKOKU
Nagasaki
KYUSHU

Pacific Ocean

OKINAWA

N.L.G.

## SUN  UP  IN  ASIA

U.S. CONGRESSMEN LOVE visiting Tokyo, Japan, the world's biggest and also its most expensive city. They deny they go there for the fleshpots. Perhaps to prove serious intent, they needle the U.S. embassy in Tokyo with complaints that the Japanese are dragging their heels. Now that Japan can afford it, why won't the Japanese play a big military role in Asia? That gripe repeats Vice President Spiro T. Agnew's gaffe about "the fat Jap." It also should make war historians, and Ernie Pyle's ghost, groan. Yet in a way, the junketing Congressmen are right. Japan is the fire-bird of Asia—which may be why the Japanese love Igor Stravinsky. The world's only victim of an atomic attack so far, Japan has risen phoenix-like from the ashes of Nagasaki and Hiroshima to be the globe's third biggest industrial power. Emperor Hirohito, whom Americans once wished hanged, has got himself a brand-new palace. Yet there are still in Japan over 100 costly U.S. military installations; why can't Japan at least look to its own moat?

According to frequent public opinion polls, 45 percent of the Japanese—which means 45 million people—think the U.S. bases are harmful to Japan; only 18 percent approve them. Many voters would not only shut down the U.S. bases but thereafter wouldn't bother much about *any* defense. The Japanese constitution, mostly the work of the late General Douglas MacArthur, pledges Japan to "no threat or use of force." MacArthur's constitution is revered; a Japanese cabinet minister was forced to quit in 1968 for calling it a "foolish concubine." Japan has a 174,000 man army; but an army captain earns as little as a Tokyo cabdriver. The Japanese socialists would turn the army into a national police force, then would hope to cut it to near zero. The party envisages an unarmed, neutral, socialist Japan. Asked, "Suppose you were invaded, how would you react?" the socialists answer: "Nonviolently, like Czechs."

And yet . . .

In the summer of 1969, for the first time since World War II, the Rising Sun flag of Japan was displayed in almost all the ports of Asia, on warships of the Japanese navy that were visiting all the way from Australia and New Zealand to Pakistan and India. Japan's gray destroyers and frigates are once again sailing the Pacific, China Sea, and Indian Ocean. They may well exchange ceremonial salutes with Russian warships that are also active now in those waters. Sixty-four summers before, the Russian fleet sailed halfway round the world to lick the Japanese, whom the Tsar called "monkeys" (as Hitler did later). But instead of the Japanese being licked, it was Admiral Togo who sank the Tsar's ships, at Tsushima. That Japanese victory thrust Russia out of the Pacific Ocean, and also helped to bring on the Russian revolution. Now that both nations' fleets are again active, could they clash again? It seems unlikely. The Japanese are determined to fight no one. Their spending on arms, though it is increasing in step with their rising national wealth, at about $1.2 billion is still under 1 percent of Japan's annual gross national product. That is a smaller percentage than Luxembourg spends on its arms. However, the bursting Japanese economy depends for very survival on daily traffic through the Straits of Malacca of 400,000 tons of imported oil, iron ore, and coking coal. Therefore, Japan now proposes spending additional sums for more destroyers and submarines as well as on missile batteries for protecting the Japanese islands' smoggy, crowded cities, and closely packed industrial areas. The Tokyo metropolitan area has 11 million people; the city of Osaka has 7 million. Japanese farmers are vanishing from the land into the cities almost as fast as American ones, and fully a third of the Japanese population now lives in four vast coastal megalopoli. Japan stands first in the world as a builder of ships, television sets, and radios; second for trucks; third in steel; fourth in power production. The new, rich, "fat Jap" must think about defense. Japan isn't Luxembourg.

The Japanese also have to think about trade, for they live by exporting. The Japanese businessman, a short, brisk, black-suited figure with a black briefcase, is ubiquitous from Guam to Beirut, where the neon signs shout SONY and other Japanese brand names. Japan's biggest trade problem is with the United States, where the Japanese annually sell more than a third of their $13 billion of exports. This trade with the U.S. is the deep rich soil in which Japan's blooming prosperity is rooted. In 1968, Japan's exports to the U.S. increased by more than 34 percent, probably a record in the history of world trade, and yielding Japan a record trade surplus of $1 billion. That's the rub; for the U.S. has a grave balance of payments deficit, and Japan has more trade barriers than any other country, including import quotas that apply to over 100 American products. The Japanese are highly reluctant to open up their home market widely to American manufactures. They promise more liberalization of trade, but concessions hitherto have applied to items like bourbon whisky and chewing gum that are so American even the Japanese don't care to try to compete.

Japanese caution over trade riles visiting Congressmen every bit as much as Japanese reluctance to scrap the Mac-Arthur constitution and become America's strongly armed ally. But Japanese businessmen fear American competition with reason. Despite Japan's remarkable performance, breaking economic records and putting $3 billion in reserves while plowing back a fifth of the GNP into further industrial expansion, the Japanese economy is quite fragile. Like the country's thin, tough rice paper, the economy can stand strain, but not sharp pokes or heavy blows. The Japanese business structure is top-heavy with big corporations. Just 2 percent of the companies have 90 percent of the corporate capital and are managed by as few men as can (and often do) squeeze in one small room. Nevertheless, these top Japanese firms are not on the scale of big business in the U.S. or Europe. More than the

Europeans, Japanese fear "the American challenge," shrink in dismay from U.S. business' enormous financial power and dread a U.S. takeover. Japan's biggest car maker, Toyota Motor, bans foreigners from its board. Americans seeking to invest in Japan run a whole gauntlet of bureaucratic restrictions. Rather than import capital, Japanese firms prefer to borrow at high cost from local banks, and to pay royalties for foreign know-how. The Japanese were after all the first isolationists; for over two centuries before Commodore Perry's ships sailed to Japan in 1853, few foreigners could even visit Japan, and Japanese who dared to go abroad risked execution if they returned.

The modern Japanese, somewhat less inhibited, have built extraordinarily well on their narrow postwar platform. The Ginza shopping district of Tokyo is now smarter than New York's Fifth Avenue. But despite color TV, new expressways, a million automobiles a year, and 155-mph trains, the masses' standard of living remains low; not low for Asia, but still astonishingly low for a nation whose GNP almost equals the combined GNPs of all other Asian countries put together. The Ginza is dazzling, but Tokyo is still cram full of cold little wooden houses. The motor traffic is something to see, but the drains are sometimes something to smell. Japan in short is an affluent society run by businessmen who sacrifice everything to private enterprise and who put welfare almost last. The Japanese "establishment" has only two components, bureaucrats and businessmen. Before the war it was a four-legged stool, including the military and imperial court castes, but now the two that remain are for all practical purposes one. Graduates of Tokyo University who don't get high government jobs go on the boards of banks and corporations and intermarry with top bureaucrats. The Diet, the Japanese parliament, has been run since the war by the businessman's party, the Liberal-Democrats. There is a Diet-industrial complex. This makes the Diet a kind of pale cheese, occasionally nibbled at by inconsequential socialist or communist mice.

The liveliest element in Japanese life is the students, who rage against the establishment which presses down and suffocates them, the way low ceilings of smog strangle most Japanese cities. Of every 100 Japanese students, about 84 are apolitical, nevertheless the activists manage to intimidate the military and cow the government; Prime Minister Eisaku Sato had to confess that the students had him "at my wits' end." They kept the most prestigious universities in Japan unusable for a year. About 8 percent of the students are communists and a like number are anarchist-Trotskyists. The communists are almost humdrum, but the anarchist-Trotskyists have everywhere seized the lead by sheer unreason. "If you can understand us, that makes you the enemy," one student rebuffed Shigeharu Matsumoto, an eminent scholar who was prepared to sympathize. Almost all students and most young faculty feel heavily oppressed by older autocratic professors, who run the colleges like U.S. plumbers do their union, jealously guarding their jobs in order to be able to hand them on exclusively to their own sons and sons-in-law. Having once rebelled, led by the anarchist-Trotskyists and partly financed from Peking, the students are deadlocked into chaos by their grim feeling that if they ever give in, the vindictive old professors will inflict bitter punishments.

This Japanese generation gap mirrors wider confusions. The Diet suffers from what the Socialists call a "tyranny of the majority." There are no vigorous committees of either chamber, no Fulbrights nor even a Wilbur Mills. The Liberal-Democrats ponderously rule, the weak and divided opposition merely rages. Sometimes the face of new-style democracy is barely saved by a handful of communists and splinter-party Democratic Socialists who consent at least to remain in the chamber when government bills are being rubber-stamped after the Socialists have angrily stomped out. The Socialist Party has 50,000 members and is 10 million votes behind the Liberal-Democrats. The communists, with 200,000 members, command 2,500,000 scattered votes. The *Komeito*, Clean Government Party, is moving up fast and now virtually controls Tokyo. *Komeito* is an off-shoot of the religious sect *Soka Gakkai*, Value Creating Society, which claims 10 million followers. It is anticapitalist, antimilitary, anticommunist—but pro-Peking. The reasons why *Soka Gakkai* appeals to Japanese are its contempt for party politicians and their graft, and its insistence on higher values than profitmaking. Its president Mr. Daisaku Ikeda is a lover of the arts who can't understand why Peking persistently refuses *Soka Gakkai's* overtures.

The Japanese don't fear either China or Russia. At different times they have been alone in the ring with both, and licked them, but that isn't the reason. They aren't afraid of being attacked, but if an attack came it would be met with fatalism. Modern war is a kind of black death, nobody can win. The Japanese of all people ought to know. Meantime, they are eager to trade with Russia and with the United States, with mainland China and with Taiwan. At Asia's first world exposition, in the spring of 1970 in Osaka, part of the Soviet exhibit honors Lenin; 1970 is the centenary of his birth. The Japanese asked that the American exhibit include the machine that landed men on the moon. Any exhibit Peking cared to send would be welcome.

But this Japanese even-handedness enrages the Chinese communists. Only if Japan abrogates its security treaty with the U.S. and ends all relations with Taiwan, can there be friendly relations between Tokyo and Peking, say the communist Chinese. The Japanese ignore those fulminations, continue trading and visiting with both Peking and Taipei, and claim they can be a bridge between Peking and the west. Japan's trade with Taiwan is slightly larger than its trade with the mainland. But no group in Japan, not even businessmen, think the nationalists on Taiwan can last, whereas China represents 700 million potential customers. That is good reason for being patient with China, despite insults. Japan is not turning the other cheek to Peking through any feeling of inferiority. There may be seven times more Chinese than Japanese, but Japan's GNP is twice China's and grows faster.

The Japanese resist American pressure to play a bigger military part in Asia, but are uncomfortable that other Asians tend to shrug them off as merely "economic animals." Japan contributed $200 million to the Asian Development Bank, the same as the U.S. contributed, and talks about extending aid to both Vietnams once the war is over. But Shigeharu Matsumoto insists that what is needed much more is a community of ideas between Japanese and other Asian intellectuals. For that purpose, Asian visitors are specially welcome at International House, in Tokyo, which Mr. Matsumoto directs. He wants big Japanese companies to set up a kind of Japanese Ford Foundation to finance good works in Asia. They probably will.

The hope of middle-of-the-road Japanese is for more pragmatism at home and abroad. When the navy succeeds in showing the once hated Rising Sun flag without having rocks thrown at it, the Japanese conclude that at last the war is over. Now they are less timid about establishing relations with fellow Asians on other matters besides trade. Until now their diplomacy has been very low key, but they are about ready to pluck up heart. ("At least," says one Japanese diplomat, "Asia can't treat us worse than Latin America did Rockefeller.") At home, the hope of the modern conservatives is that the antiwar, proconstitution voters, who when all is said and done show little inclination to swell the Socialist vote, will not demand the closing down of U.S. military installations without permitting Japanese ones in their place. When he visited Washington in November 1969, Prime Minister Sato persuaded President Nixon to fix an early date (1972) for the return of the island of Okinawa to Japan. In this way, Sato hoped to be able to retire with dignity, instead of being rudely hustled from office as his brother Nobusuke Kishi was. Premier Kishi lost out over the 1960 signing of the U.S.–Japan Mutual Security Treaty, which provoked mass protests that prevented President Eisenhower visiting Japan, as well as costing Kishi his job. The Tokyo students did all they could to keep Sato from even reaching the airport to fly to America, and the Socialists, communists and anarchist-Trotskyists tried their hardest to have the security treaty killed. They have not succeeded, but their shenanigans raise the question, how long can Japan walk its tight-rope? If and when the Japanese lose their balance, will they fall far left, or extreme right? All Asia is watching, including Peking. So is Washington, of course. Modern Japan was mostly made in America.

## PROGRESS AND HARMONY

SOME PEOPLE ARE bilingual. The Japanese are linguistically poor but they are tricultural. Richard Harris observes that "here is one part of the east Asian world that can turn to the west that came bursting into its closed world a century ago and can say: "Very well, here is the answer to your technical superiority. Japan can make it and has done so."

The theme of the international exposition, Expo 70, in Osaka, Japan, is "progress and harmony for mankind." Japan has proved that it can make great progress but it is also very anxious to achieve the harmony. In the Far East, Japan is cautiously helping to create a real co-prosperity sphere. In 1968, the prime minister, Eisaku Sato, visited Burma, Malaysia, Singapore, Thailand, Laos, Indonesia, the Philippines, South Vietnam, Taiwan, Australia, and New Zealand. He was well received in these countries, most of which had been former victims or targets of Japanese imperialist and military ambition. But now, the prime minister of Singapore Lee Kuan Yew, for example, assured Sato, "we have no fear of you."

In Japan, itself, *Soka Gakkai,* the Buddhist value-creating society, and its political party offshoot, the *Komeito,* or Clean Government Party, dwell a good deal on harmony. Konosuke Matsushita, the great Japanese industrialist who provides his 40,000 workers with Zen Buddhist meditation rooms as well as with swimming pools and sports fields, says, "Company management should be directed to serving society, but this cannot be carried out unless the company has good people

. . . the development of superior production must start with the development of superior people."

Although turned in on themselves by nature and by instinct, the Japanese have sought with demoniac energy to take on as it were the entire world. Every little Japanese boy and girl now knows that Japan produces goods that go all over the world—and that they sell prodigously in the citadel of western technology, the United States.

But the Japanese also seek harmony, and not least with China, because of their guilty conscience and the sense that China, the victim of former Japanese aggression, is also the father and mother of Japanese culture. More Japanese than any other foreigners visit China. Japanese newspaper reporters covered the Great Cultural Revolution, though with difficulty, yet more extensively than any other foreign correspondents did or could have done. For the Japanese, of course, could read the Chinese newspapers and Chinese wall posters. Some Japanese newsmen and businessmen were imprisoned by the Chinese, and still languish in Chinese prisons, just because they were able to comprehend too much of what was going on behind the Chinese screen.

For the truth is that Japanese relations with communist China have never been made easy by the men in Peking. Trade statistics illumine part of the story. In 1950, China was Japan's 13th best market for exports; in 1960, China was down to 57th place, but by 1964 China was back to being 11th, and by 1966 had risen to 4th place, only to fall once again because, this time, of the Cultural Revolution. At its best, this yo-yo like progression has never made China a really huge market for Japanese exports; about $200 million worth or less than one-twentieth the value of Japan's exports to the United States.

Meanwhile, Japan's trade with Russia has approached the Chinese level very rapidly and could easily leap ahead of it. The Siberian railway system serves as a "land bridge" for cargo transport from Japan to Europe and to the Middle East. Japan has ambitious plans, encouraged by the Soviet Union, to help Russia develop Siberia—on which Japan once cast an avaricious eye. The man who has pushed this in Tokyo is Takeo Miki, a clever politician who still hopes one day to be the prime minister of Japan.

Yet, both China and Russia rank *lowest* in the esteem and affection of the Japanese people, according to opinion polls. The country that came first in the polls was not the United States either, it was little Switzerland. The Japanese greatly admire that country; and why? Because they believe that Switzerland has achieved almost perfect external and internal harmony.

China's internal upheavals and crude foreign policy—for instance, the attack on India in 1962—have greatly helped to improve Japan's image in Asia's eyes. It seems clear that the Japanese have abandoned the idea of dictating to, or ruling, foreign countries; and this sits well with the rising national-isms of Asia which will not accept to be dictated to by any-one, including a ferociously ideological China. Even the rebel-lious Japanese students draw the line at adopting the Chinese brand of communism, in Japan. They say, "We have not quit one prison to enter another prison." They mean, of course, that they did not get rid of the oppressive rule of their own militarists, only to see it replaced by oppressive communist rule on the Chinese model.

The Peking view of Japan is that Japan is still out to dom-inate Asia—and to fight China.

Peking alleges that "Japanese materialism, fostered by United States imperialism, is ferociously expanding its arma-ment and is preparing for war, so that it can play an active role as a tool of America for pushing its policy of war and aggression in Asia, and can realize its own imperialist ambi-tion to tyrannize over this continent. Stepping into the shoes of aggression of Hideki Tojo [the Japanese military leader the victorious Americans hanged] the reactionary Sato gov-ernment of modern Japan is doing its best to push Japan onto the road of militarism, and is planning to build an up-to-date army to carry out expansion and aggression abroad."

According to Peking, the Japanese intend to have hydrogen

bombs and missiles, and plan also to build several fleets of aircraft carriers, guided missiles cruisers and nuclear submarines, as well as a strategic air force. Peking contends that all this will be done by Japan at the "order of its American masters"; and Peking goes on: "Heavily battered by the Asian people, U.S. imperialism is urging Japan to share its military obligations, using Japan as a tool for pushing its policy of war and aggression for making the Asians fight the Asians." Calling President Nixon "the new U.S. imperialist chieftain," Peking says he commanded Japan to turn the Asian and Pacific Council into a military alliance, with a western Pacific, anti-China, military alliance with Japan as its backbone. Moreover, Japan, in order to realize its ambition of expansion in southeast Asia, is supposed also to have sought and to have received what Peking calls "strong support and encouragement from Soviet (revisionist) imperialism. After thrusting themselves into the Asian Development Bank, the Soviet revisionists expressed a desire to join the Asian and Pacific Council, which is composed entirely of the U.S. imperialist lackeys in Asia. For this, the chieftains of Soviet revisionism and of Japanese reaction have made frequent diplomatic contacts. All this shows that U.S. imperialism, Soviet revisionism, and Japanese reactionaries are working hand in glove and are actively conspiring in a vicious plot to form an anti-China ring of encirclement to suppress the Asian people's revolutionary movement."

Peking says that the Japanese capitalists, having made huge war profits out of supplying the United States during both the Korean and Vietnam wars, have now "penetrated on a large scale into Indonesia to plunder its petroleum and mineral and forest resources. The Japanese militarist forces have recently declared that they will defend Japan's lifeline, the Straits of Malacca. The Japanese newspaper, *Sengyo Keizai Shimbun*, stated that Japanese dependence on overseas resources has increased at the same time as the U.S. and British defense systems in southeast Asia have shown a tendency to retreat, and that Japan must therefore adopt an independent defense system, to secure the oil transport line from the Middle East to Japan."

All this, says Peking, fully shows "that the Japanese militarist forces are mainly trying to bring about a national superiority complex as an Asian power, stirring up sentiments of narrow nationalism, and to hoodwink the Japanese people into following them into embarking again on the old road of Hideki Tojo." Their attempts are, however, in vain, Peking explains, because all this "will never be tolerated by the awakening Japanese people, and by the various countries in Asia who have suffered from Japanese aggression. So long as the Japanese people, the other people of Asia, and the rest of the world, remain unified, they are bound to send the whole pack of the United States imperialists, Soviet revisionists, and Japanese reactionaries to their graves."

Japan's own view of its place in Asia is naturally very different from all this. The Japanese foreign minister Kiichi Aichi, pointed out in September 1969, in *Foreign Affairs,* that in order to understand Japan's outlook and its vision of the future, it was necessary first of all to understand the country's brief but breathless history as a modern state; and the effects of these complex events on the Japanese mind.

Mr. Aichi explained that until very recently there were people still living in Japan who had personal memory of the feudal Tokugawa era. In 1853, America's "black ships" came to open up Japan, and were met on the beach of Kurihama by a feudal levy, armed with matchlocks and pikes.

For 250 years, under the Tokugawas, Japan had been almost wholly secluded from the world. The world of the 19th century into which Japan was thrust in 1853 was one of "powerful, well-organized western states, armed with tools and weapons forged in the industrial revolution, that were engaged either in imposing their will on the weaker lands of Asia and Africa, or in reducing them outright into colonies and dependencies. Ailing China, for long the cultural and political leader of Asia, was slowly being nibbled away by the western powers. Korea, like Japan, lay dormant in seclusion, but vast areas of southeast Asia were already under western domination. Aggressive Tsarist Russia cast a long shadow over the Siberian wastes, touching the northern approaches of the

Japanese islands. All-powerful Britain had recently thrashed the Chinese empire in the opium war (an event which deeply impressed our forefathers), and its fleets dominated the seas of Pacific Asia."

The Japanese faced this challenge by embarking on a prodigious feat of modernization. By comparison with the achievements of the men of the Meiji restoration in Japan, the modernizing efforts of Kemal Ataturk of Turkey, and Reza Shah of Iran, that we have noted earlier in this book, look almost effete. The Japanese not only transformed their "matchlocks and pikes" into a formidable navy and army and were soon able to gain military victories over both China and Russia. Though almost totally lacking in natural resources, they also built up a modern economy, and played an ever growing part in world trade. Aichi says that "within 50 years of Commodore Perry's visit, Japan had obtained membership in the world's Big Five." Japan did so, unfortunately, by "transforming itself into the conquering image of the alien powers it once had feared." Vaulting ambition overreached itself, and after inflicting further defeats on China in the 1930's, Japan launched into a general war of conquest in southeast Asia, which ended in the dropping by America of the atom bomb on Hiroshima and Nagasaki, as well as the destruction by fire bombs of Tokyo and many other Japanese cities.

It was the belief of Foreign Minister Aichi that the trauma of 1945 produced changes in his country as momentous as those that were initiated by the coming of the "black ships" in 1853. For a second time the Japanese state and Japanese society were fundamentally transformed. What the Japanese people yearned for was "the modest prosperity of a middle class nation, quite content in its home island, shunning unnecessary involvement and above all renouncing war." Japan's postwar "peace constitution" not only renounced war but also provided for individual freedom and civil liberty. These innovations received wide popular support. By 1952, which marked the end of the American occupation of Japan, the rebuilt Japanese economy was beginning to compete successfully in world markets. In subsequent years, Japan joined all the major international institutions—the United Nations and its agencies, GATT and the IMF (the General Agreement òn Tariffs and Trade, and the International Monetary Fund). Today, Japan's gross national product of about $150 billion, though much smaller than America's $900 billion, is actually larger than that of any other noncommunist country in the world. Japan's per capita spending is below $1,200 and ranks only 20th in the world. But this is because wages are low so that capital investment can be high, in order for Japan's trade to expand, and also in order for the country to build more roads, houses, water mains, and other public amenities. Japan, in short, is still intent on modernizing itself—for instance by operating 155 mph trains.

Mr. Aichi rightly points out that Japan has not only achieved reasonable prosperity, "but has also enjoyed unbroken peace for the longest period since the Tokugawa era. During this time, the people have not only rebuilt their economy, but have busied themselves in the arts, and literature, and other vital areas of civilized life, enriching their great heritage." All Japanese are literate. The Japanese newspapers' daily circulations are in the millions. Tokyo is the world's largest city. By 1985, Japan's gross national product is expected to grow four times, to about $600 billion, in what economists call "constant dollars," meaning that this discounts monetary inflation and therefore is a true measure of real growth.

How did Foreign Minister Aichi see Japan's role in Asia as a rearmed power? Needless to say, his view was completely at variance with that of Peking. He emphasized, for instance, that Japan seemed to have become highly visible to Americans as an Asian power with the potential for contributing to the security of the region, but that a simple transfer of peace-keeping responsibilities in Asia, from the United States to Japan, was out of the question. Partly because of Japan's constitution which forbids recourse to war save for self-defense in the strictest sense of the term; and partly because Japanese public opinion is simply not prepared for such an undertaking. Nor, he believed, would the other nations of Asia welcome it.

That meant, he thought, that there would have to be a continuing presence of American deterrent power in Asia. American forces would remain in Okinawa even when that Pacific island reverted to Japanese rule in 1972. Japanese defense forces, of 285,000 men, could not under the Japanese constitution be sent to fight abroad. Japan's defense spending, at $1,340 million, would increase annually at the rate of 14 to 15 percent, corresponding to the growth of the gross national product. This implied that "in about 10 years Japan's defense budget might roughly correspond to Communist China's today, including Chinese outlays both for conventional armaments and for the backbreakingly expensive nuclear weapons development program."

The Japanese foreign minister said that the various countries of Asia were showing active interest in regional cooperation, and some of them were asking questions about the ability of Japan, as the leading economic power, to expand its assistance to them. He pointed out that Japan had contributed to the capital of the Asian Development Bank, and had helped to establish the Asian and Pacific Council. Japanese assistance, both private and government, to Asian countries, had reached the level of $559 million in 1968; and the government budget for aid in the 1969–1970 fiscal year had increased 42 percent, to $452.3 million. The Japanese finance minister Takeo Fukuda had told the Asian Development Bank that Japan would increase economic aid substantially, to about double in five years. About $400 million of Japanese aid goes to southeast Asian nations, and the finance minister announced a $200 million development plan, intended to help Vietnam and other nations in southeast Asia after the end of the Vietnam war. Tentatively called the Indo-China Reconstruction and Development Fund, the plan called for a total contribution of $200 million, of which $40 million was to be provided by Japan in two annual installments. The fund would provide free aid to Vietnam, including North as well as South Vietnam and the neighboring countries of Laos and Cambodia. Japan also promised Indonesia assistance, of about $110 million.

Aichi thought that economic assistance was only part of

the task, and what was also needed was a larger objective. "I believe, on the basis of our own historical experience and our view of the future, that no objective is more important than the construction in east Asia of a viable community of nations, embodying 'unity and diversity.' I believe we should help the nations of Asia to develop, aiming toward the attainment of a harmonious and stable whole." Thus the keyword is again repeated: harmonious. First, harmony at home; but also, harmony abroad, though like the average American, "the average Japanese would be far more interested in solving the knotty and multitudinous problems at home than in making the painful switch over to an outward looking frame of mind." Nevertheless, "the Japanese mind is characterized by resilience and shrewdness, and has proved itself capable of adapting . . . it's becoming clearer that Japan must deal with both its external responsibilities and its domestic challenges."

How about China? Mr. Aichi forecast what he called "increasingly complex relationships" among the two superpowers, and communist China and Japan, in the course of the 1970s. He thought that "the question of attaining a viable equilibrium in relations between nuclear-equipped Peking and ourselves will take at least another decade for a full answer." In the meantime, the regional military balance in east Asia was essentially between the United States and Communist China.

# PEOPLE AND POLITICIANS

ABOUT THE SIZE of California, Japan is divided into 46 prefectures, and the population has become stabilized at a little more than 100 million.

The imperial house of Japan claims descent from an emperor named Jimmu Tenno, who, legend says, reigned about 2,600 years ago. But Japan really enters history in relation to China. The Mongols who had conquered China and had subdued Korea in the late 13th century attempted to conquer Japan, but the armada of Kubla Khan was fortunately destroyed by a typhoon. About three centuries afterward, the Japanese characteristically attempted to turn the tables. Hideyoshi invaded Korea intending to attack China, but his attempt finally failed. The emperors of Japan were pushed into the background by powerful feudal chieftains, the Shoguns, who in 1640 turned Japan into a "hermit kingdom" by closing its ports to almost all foreign entry. The imperial house came to life again with the Meiji restoration of 1868. The present emperor of Japan, Hirohito, ascended the throne in 1926. After the country's defeat in World War II, Japan became a political democracy, while retaining the emperor as a ceremonial head of state. But it is as a rapidly expanding economy that postwar Japan has attracted most attention.

Unemployment in Japan is almost invisible. It dropped to under one-half million, or only 0.9 percent of the work force. What has emerged is a shortage of labor which is likely to seriously affect major enterprises as well as small business. The labor ministry has forecast that the demand for labor in 1970, as far as high school graduates are concerned, will be 4.4 times greater than the supply, and will increase to 6.5

times greater than the supply by 1975. The shortage of skilled labor, put another way, is estimated at 1.6 million, meaning that three out of every five firms in manufacturing report a need for more skilled workers. Partly in consequence of the labor shortage, wages go up and go up by large annual installments of as much as 20 percent. The upswings are increasing; in 1967 wages increased by over 12 percent. This swinging Japanese economy supports 174 daily newspapers with combined circulations of 46 million, and more than 20 million television sets. Many people believe that Japan has the best color television in the world.

These crowded, hard-working people are prodigious investors and savers. Investment in equipment goes up by leaps and bounds. For example, in 1968 total planned investments represented an increase of 27.6 percent over the previous year. The previous year had seen a rise of 34 percent. New investment was heaviest in oil refining and petroleum chemicals, in electric power and in general machinery. Meanwhile, the posts and telecommunications ministry had reported that deposits in postal savings banks increased by 22 percent in 1965—which was a recession year. Two years later, annual small savings had risen by 36 percent in a year.

Japan's merchant shipping fleet is the fifth largest in the world, and Japan Air Lines (JAL) ranks eighth among the airlines of the world. JAL has around-the-world service, and operates a direct Tokyo to Moscow air service jointly with the Soviet airline Aeroflot. JAL operates more than 40 flights a week between Japan and the United States. Japanese domestic airlines carry about 10 million passengers a year.

The five largest trading firms in Japan are Mitshubishi, with annual sales of about $6 billion; Mitsui, annual sales about the same; Marubeni-Iida, $4.5 billion; Itoh, $4 billion; and Nissho-Iwai, over $3 billion.

The Japanese parliament is called the Diet, and it consists of two chambers, a Lower House of Representatives, and an Upper House of Councillors. A nationwide election for the Upper House in the summer of 1968 showed a small decline in the strength of Japan's ruling Liberal Democratic Party. But the Socialist Party suffered a major setback. There are 250 seats in the Upper House. The Liberal Democrats got 137, a gain of 2; the Socialists on the other hand got 65 seats whereas formerly they had held 73. The Japanese Communist Party did best of all, going up from 4 to 7 seats. The Communist Party is generally strongly pro-Moscow and anti-Peking. The most successful candidates in the election were not professional politicians at all, but writers, comedians, and television commentators who had made a hit with their audiences irrespective of their views on politics. Thus, Shintaro Ishihara, a 35-year-old novelist, got 1 out of every 16 votes cast in the 43.3 million vote, single and nationwide constituency; this made him the country's largest vote getter. The truth is that the Japanese voters don't think much of politicians, and though they rather openly despise the Liberal Democrats, they keep on voting for them, apparently mainly in order to prevent the Socialists from getting into office. The Socialists have been trying for years to do so, but, as a former foreign minister, Shiina Etsusaburo, said in 1965, "the Socialists are the cat that can't catch the mouse."

Japan first hitched onto the western-style political party bandwagon in the 1880s. But a certain degree of cheerful cynicism apparently prevailed from the very start. Robert K. Reischauer said of the first two political parties in Japan: "These two parties, the Liberal Party and the Constitutional Progressive Party, were established by Mr. Itataki and Mr. Okuma because these two gentlemen were angry at the way in which the *samurai* (literally, feudal retainers) of Choshu and Satsuma were monopolizing all the good positions in the government. They used their parties as tools to pry open posts in the administration for themselves and for their loyal henchmen." Things haven't changed much. A former Japanese prime minister, Hamaguchi Osachi, said of the political parties before World War II: "No sooner had the people recognized the establishment of party government than they were greatly disillusioned with its evils." He complained that the people didn't take time to find out whether the fault lay with the system or with the politicians, they just lost faith and despaired of the future.

The Liberal Democratic Party was formed out of two conservative parties which merged on November 15, 1955. The party really consists of about ten separate factions, each headed by a prominent politician. Each member of each faction gets regular pay, which is quite separate from his official pay as a member of the Diet. This system can lead to amusing snafus. Once, a socialist Diet member went to the Liberal Democratic Party headquarters, and there solemnly accepted his monthly pay as a member of the faction. It wasn't really his pay at all, however. Owing to a confusing similarity of names—some Japanese names are very like one another—he was able to draw the pay that was due to a Liberal Democratic Diet member. Eisaku Sato, the present prime minister of Japan, heads a faction which has about 111 members. These are about evenly divided among Lower House members and Upper House members. Speculation in Tokyo at the end of 1969 was that in 1970 Mr. Sato would step down, and that his place as prime minister would probably be taken by Mr. Takeo Fukuda, the present finance minister.

The voters as well as the members of the factions get something out of this system. One politician has complained that when his constituents come up to Tokyo, they demand a box lunch and other goodies, and act as if these perquisites were theirs by natural right. In fact, this politician said ruefully, "They lead the politicians around by the nose." In order to keep on the right side of their constituents, Japanese politicians have to spend a good deal of money in the local community. As an example, Shoriki Matsutaro, who owns a big-circulation newspaper called *Yomiuri Shimbun,* has built an extensive newspaper plant with some of the world's most modern and expensive equipment in the small town of Takaoka, in Toyama prefecture, which is his election district. The plant loses money, but the farmers of Toyama get a wonderful newspaper service, and as a result Shoriki keeps on winning elections.

In Japan as in the United States, it costs a great deal of money nowadays to have a chance of being elected. In Japanese Lower House elections, it is said that the cost per candidate averages something like $40,000, but that there are men who spend over $80,000. According to the *Mainichi Shimbun* newspaper, there are many legislators who require election war chests of between $110,000 and $140,000. This is where the factions come in. The *Yomiuri Shimbun* newspaper says it is well known that the factions collect funds. The amount differs according to the size and nature of the faction. But even a small faction needs somewhere between $80,000 and $140,000. And a faction with more than 50 Diet men as members has regular expenses of between $280,000 and $550,000. A leader of a middle-sized faction has to collect over $500,000 for an election. As might be expected, some politicians go pretty far over the score in order to raise money. The usual charge against them, of course, is doing favors for big businessmen. Occasionally this leads to a politician who has a post in the government being fired. The prime minister, in other words, demands his resignation. However, the voters never seem to get unduly indignant about such revelations. For instance, one minister was fired for taking two businessmen with him on a trip to South Korea. At the next general election, the voters of his district returned him to the Diet with more votes than he had ever received before. Just like Massachusetts, in fact.

It is highly unlikely in Japan, as elsewhere, that a politician will get a government post on merit alone. Diet men get the money they need from their faction, and their faction sees to it that it is well represented in any government. Great pressures are brought to bear on a prime minister to make sure that he appoints members of the faction to his government; and changes in the government generally mirror changes in the strength of the factions. A major or minor reshuffle in a Japanese cabinet rarely has much to do with differences of opinion about policy. Generally, Japanese prime ministers resent and denounce the factions—*after* they have become prime ministers. "All my efforts will go to the abolition of factions," said Ishibashi Tanzan. Prime Minister Nobusuke

Kishi said, "abolition of factions is the voice of heaven." The present prime minister, Eisaku Sato, solemnly declared, "I start with myself," and "dissolved" his faction, which was called the Thursday Club. It still meets, however.

Before World War II, the Japanese economy was controlled by several huge financial combines called the *zaibatsu*. The two biggest were Mitsui and Mitsubishi. The *zaibatsu* had close ties with the conservative political party. They contributed funds to the leaders of the party. The party did the *zaibatsu* favors in return. The American occupation broke up the *zaibatsu*, but not for long. Today, behind the political parties and their factions—for the socialists have factions too—stand powerful vested interests, including Japan's steel and power kings, top bankers, and industrialists. Prime Minister Sato dissolved his Thursday Club, but he did not dissolve the Choei Society that the Tokyo gas company had built around him. The vice president of the Tokyo gas company, Mr. Hiroshi Anzai, described the group as follows: "Since Mr. Sato was not too well known among the business community, the Choei Society was formed around him. We selected a member from each of the top companies and that way put the club together. We meet and chat with Mr. Sato about once a month, in the evening. Mr. Sato seeks out the opinion of all the members of the group, but the atmosphere is light and informal." As a fact, the Choei Society is only one of many groups that Prime Minister Eisaku Sato meets regularly with. He meets with about 20 of these groups in all, and it is said that this gives him effective liaison with about 280 top Japanese executives. That is said to be a wider range of contacts with the business community than any previous prime minister has ever had.

This kind of contact has, of course, led to a good deal of criticism of both the party and the businessmen. Prime Miniser Sato himself has sighed, "Political funds are a problem. I think collecting political funds by individuals ought to be restricted, and a system should be created so that funds are centered on the parties." A retired but influential Japanese banker, Mr. Ataru Kobayashi, has criticized politicians and businessmen alike. Politics, he said, are "dirty because the politicians think that strings are attached to the money; they ought to forget who gave them the money. And the businessmen constantly remind the politicians where they got the money from, and that also is wrong. Individual political contributions ought to be done away with."

This, however, seems to be very utopian advice in Japan, or indeed anywhere else. Kikuo Nakamura, who has stood for election himself and therefore knows what goes on, thinks it is just a case of nature taking its course. In his amusing and informative book, *How the Conservatives Rule Japan,* published by Princeton University Press in 1969, Mr. Nathaniel B. Thayer quotes Mr. Nakamura as explaining why there are so many cases of bribery in elections.

*The answer is that many people look at the elections as festivals. In Japan, there are many festivals which occur regularly throughout the year. At each of these festivals, gifts of money are distributed, the celebrants gather in one of the buildings of the temple compounds to feast and drink, the children carry portable shrines through the streets and are made happy by gifts of candy. Elections are just the same. There is a steady stream of people into the candidates election headquarters to eat and to drink. They warm themselves around the braziers on the mats and excitedly gossip about past elections. Others show up promptly at mealtime, talk a bit, eat, and then go home. Election headquarters are supposed to serve only light refreshments, but that restriction is not always observed when one looks behind the scenes. More stimulating refreshments are also served. The mood of the elections is no different than that during the festivals, when people gather at the temple compounds to drink it up.*

Another Japanese politician told Mr. Thayer, "I don't want to shell out all that money on food and *sake* (wine). It's against the law, and besides, it costs me a lot of money. But hold a political rally without refreshments, and nobody shows up. Next thing you know, the voters are calling you a cheap-skate and beginning to have doubts about your ability to look after the welfare of your district."

On the face of it, Japan's electoral laws are most stringent. The things which are forbidden are door-to-door campaigning, signature campaigns, a candidate having more than one auto-mobile and more than one set of loudspeakers. The number of campaign posters is supposed to be limited. Article 140 of the public officer election law says that no person shall engage in "acts which tend to arouse enthusiasm" for the purpose of the election campaign. What happens, of course, in practice is that very little attention is paid to such regulations. Mr. Thayer points out that in the case of Article 140, for example, there was only one arrest during the last four elections. How-ever, in the 1967 elections, more than 15,000 people were rounded up in connection with charges of bribery and "in-ducement with material interests."

## THE KEYSTONE

THE UNITED STATES military forces on Okinawa, the "Keystone of the Pacific," lost their credibility in January 1968, when North Korea captured the U.S. spy ship *Pueblo*. What are they doing here, these 55,000 soldiers, airmen, sailors, and marines on Okinawa, if in a crunch they were helpless to save the *Pueblo* from ignominious seizure? Kadena air base on Okinawa covers 5,620 acres and is one of the largest Air Force installations in Asia, able to handle an almost unlimited number of aircraft of all kinds.

The 19,000 U.S. airmen, 8,000 sailors and 3,200 marines who are based in Japan cannot be dispatched on a combat mission until the Japanese government has been consulted, under the terms of the 1960 U.S.-Japan Mutual Security Treaty. But the Americans on Okinawa were under no such restriction.

The air force on Okinawa says indignantly that its planes are always in the air, and could have gone to the *Pueblo*'s rescue, but that Washington at the crucial time issued no call for action. That negative decision perhaps was reached because, by the time Washington heard that the *Pueblo* was in trouble, the spy ship was already in a North Korean port. In any event, Okinawa's credibility gap is here to stay. Washington, in consequence, yielded to demands for Okinawa's reversion to Japan by 1972, when B-52 bombers will no longer be taking off from Okinawa to blast targets in South Vietnam. Everything is now in train for what the one million Okinawans call *ittaika*, oneness, with Japan. From 1972, the American air and naval bases on Okinawa, which have cost the United States about $2 billion, will operate under the same restrictions that apply to the American bases in Japan. The United

States will defer to Japanese wishes and remove nuclear weapons from Okinawa. It has never been publicly admitted that there are any, but in fact there is a tactical missile unit as well as an Air Force strategic wing at Kadena air base, and some Japanese allege that the B-52s have on occasions patroled near China and North Korea, with hydrogen bombs in their bays.

None of Washington's concessions to Japan sits well with the U.S. military on Okinawa. Their view is that Okinawa is too valuable to be given up, or even to be restricted in its military use. First, there is its strategic locality: around 1,000 miles from either Manila or Tokyo, less than 500 miles from either Taipei or Shanghai. American military bases in Taiwan are too close to the Asian mainland; Guam, 2,500 miles deeper in the Pacific than Okinawa, is thought to be too far. Then there's the expense of a move. It would cost at least another $2 billion to create a substitute Okinawa, for instance on the South Korean island of Cheju, which has been offered to the United States for the purpose by the South Korean government. Even so, any replacement would be inadequate, for where else could the U.S. find a trained labor force of 59,000 skilled men, thoroughly accustomed to working on an American base? Lastly, the military on Okinawa argue that as things are now, the U.S. has untrammeled use of Okinawa. The island can be employed for either conventional or nuclear war. In a nuclear war, Okinawa itself would be very vulnerable, so the military are obviously thinking in terms not of a nuclear exchange, but of nuclear weapons on Okinawa that deter by their mere presence a conventional attack anywhere in the wide region that Okinawa shields. They argue that an enemy who feared that his aggression would provoke even small "tactical" nuclear retaliation from Okinawa would think twice. Remove the nuclear capability from Okinawa, however, and that deterrence is lost.

These ingenious arguments were blown to shreds by the *Pueblo* affair. Not a single plane left Okinawa to go to the spy ship's aid, and the knowledge that there are nuclear weapons on Okinawa did not deter the North Koreans. Nevertheless,

the U.S. military in Okinawa still go on patiently repeating
that when the island reverts to Japan, a nuclear advantage
will be lost. The well-known aversion of the Japanese people
to nuclear weapons ensures that Japan will not tolerate them
on the island once it is back under the Japanese flag. And
Okinawa's usefulness for conventional war will also be diminished, though the American air and naval bases are allowed
to remain. For Japan will henceforth have to be consulted
about combat use of the bases, and a Japanese prime minister
who gave his okay to an American combat mission—like un-
leashing B-52s on Asians—would probably be committing
political *hari-kiri*.

What this argument of the U.S. military boils down to is
that it is easier for the United States to defend Japan if the
U.S. is unhampered by the wishes of the Japanese people.
The real choice for the United States was not to cling stubbornly to Okinawa, but to reach agreement with the 100
million Japanese, who are now the world's third industrial
power. This choice has been made. The United States is
irrevocably committed to Okinawa reverting to Japan. The
American military men on Okinawa are not now fighting even
a rearguard action; they have lost the campaign.

Okinawa is the largest and most populated of the Ryukyu
island chain that stretches from 40 miles east of Taiwan
toward southern Japan. The islands were annexed by Japan
in 1872, and in the ensuing 73 years the islanders complained
that they were treated by Tokyo as poor relations. Their
grievances didn't, however, prevent the Okinawans passionately identifying themselves with Japan and behaving as
first-rate patriots. In the spring of 1945, one Okinawan in eight
died trying to prevent Americans occupying the island and
hauling down the Japanese flag. Some 12,500 Americans also
died in the costly battle for the island.

But Okinawa has now been under American orders for a
quarter of a century, half as long as the U.S. ruled the Philippines. The Okinawans have never ceased regarding themselves
as Japanese or ceased demanding that their island be returned
under the Japanese roof. Nevertheless, enormous changes have

meantime occurred in their way of life. They no longer are simple farmers and fisherfolk, eking out a meager uncertain livelihood on a tropical Pacific island that is frequently swept by typhoons. Their standard of living has risen to the point that there are now more automobiles to population than is the case in Japan. Eight years ago, Highway One, a four-lane road built by the U.S. on the island's east coast, was monopolized by military traffic. Highway One is now one long civilian traffic jam. The price of land has risen so high that the only way to uncork the bottleneck may be to build a new highway out on the coral shore. Ten years ago, Okinawa's per capita income per year was $145; today it is $580 and there have been few price increases, apart from land. For the past five years, Okinawa's real rate of economic growth has been 13 percent annually. Okinawan companies run by Okinawans make big money, and reinvest up to 20 percent of their profits. The 59,000 Okinawans who work on the U.S. bases draw $35.5 million in annual pay. American spending, and U.S. and Japanese economic assistance, pour more funds into the economy. The island's imports vastly exceed its exports, $379 million to $89 million. U.S. spending at a rate of about $220 million a year almost plugs the hole. The remainder of the gap is more than wiped out by $39 million in U.S. economic aid, and also $63 million in Japanese aid (Japan in 1968 offered $40 million, the Okinawans at once demanded $80 million).

The American plan has been to encourage as much home rule as will not interfere with base operations. The government of the Ryukyu islands consists of a directly elected chief executive, Mr. Chobyu Yara, who won in November 1968, and a 32-man legislature; 31 are members of four political parties, and there is one Independent. The Liberal Democratic Party has 18 seats, the Socialist Masses Party eight, the (Communist) Okinawa People's Party three, and the Japan Socialist Party two. So the 18 Liberal Democrats confront 10 Socialists and 3 Communists. But all parties want reversion to Japan, and Mr. Yara won chiefly on that issue. The Ryukyu government still has some leading strings. The United States Civil Administrator, Stanley S. Carpenter, has a whole civil administration of his own, nine departments including labor, public works and health, education and welfare; but he and they say their function is to tender advice and technical assistance to the Ryukyu government and its 13,000 Okinawan employees. The U.S. High Commissioner, Lt.-Gen. James B. Lampert, a West Pointer and engineer who is an expert on nuclear weapons and logistics, has power to overrule the chief executive and the legislature. But it is a long time since that veto was used and it will be a surprise if it is ever exercised again.

This suggests all will be plain sailing for *ittaika*. But the real problems may begin after reversion. And they may turn out to have very little to do with the U.S. bases. Once the Okinawans are back under the Japanese roof, old grievances against Japan may reassert themselves. Reversion after an interval of jubilation may be followed by growing Okinawan demands for home rule; at least for a far greater degree of autonomy than Tokyo normally accords an ordinary Japanese prefecture. The island's new class of businessmen are likely to demand (and to need) protection against Japanese competition if they are to survive. Okinawa after 25 years of American rule and large doses of the American way of life won't resemble any other Japanese prefecture. This is likely to prove ticklish for the Japanese authorities. In spite of all the pumped-up enthusiasm in Tokyo about Okinawans as soul brothers, few Japanese really regard Okinawans as truly Japanese, or as equals. And if the Okinawans demand and get better than average treatment, how are the other 46 prefectures going to feel? The northern Japanese island of Hokkaido also has a way of life that is distinct from the rest of Japan. If Naha the capital of Okinawa receives preferential treatment, Sapporo the capital city of Hokkaido will clamor for special favors too.

Japanese who concede in private that much of the fuss about the return of Okinawa has been the work of Japanese and Okinawan politicians seeking an issue, also admit that the show caught the public fancy, and that the issue is now real. The cynics however note with dry amusement that a similar bid to regain four northern islands that the Russians occupy has fallen flat. Nobody cares much about Habomei, Shikotan, Etorofu and Kunashiri, partly because nobody seriously expects the Russians to hand the islands back without demanding some impossible quid pro quo. Interest in Okinawa has been kept alive by the publicity attending the U.S. bases, visits of American nuclear submarines, and air crashes. The Russians do not publicize the Kuriles. The clamor for Okinawa is at least in part a product of American success in developing the island economically and bringing the Okinawans along politically.

Meanwhile, the Japanese are pampering the Okinawans whom they wish to welcome home. The Okinawans have learned to like California rice, and to despise the Japanese rice that Tokyo offers as part of its economic assistance to the island. Japan buys from Okinawa, at high prices, sugar and pineapples that could certainly be had cheaper elsewhere. Okinawans buy gasoline at half the price that is charged in Japan. When the Japanese get the island back, the pampering may have to continue and even be intensified. Looking forward to the day when the American bases are removed, farsighted Japanese are urging that big *zaibatsu* Japanese firms should begin now to put steel mills and other major plants on the island, to provide employment for Okinawans. This no doubt would help de-pollute Japan's own smog-filled atmosphere, but is it an economic proposition? The big Japanese companies themselves seem somewhat dubious about its practicality.

There appears little prospect that American bases on Okinawa will in due course be replaced by Japanese military bases. The Okinawan sentiment against militarism is if anything even stronger than the antiwar sentiment in Japan itself. The Okinawan Socialists are politically stronger than the Japanese Socialists. And an Okinawan Socialist expressed outright horror at the very idea that the Japanese "Self-Defense Forces" might one day replace American airmen and marines on Okinawa. "Why, they would never be allowed to land!" he exclaimed. "They would be met at the port by antiwar demonstrators crying 'Go back!'" Evidently a lot has changed since the Okinawans bravely fought to the death in defense of Japanese imperialism against the Americans, in 1945.

Japan's problems with Okinawa after *ittaika* need not unduly concern the United States. But the U.S. certainly has a continuing concern with U.S.–Japan relations. In order for the U.S. to retain Japan's goodwill, the Ryukyus are to be returned. The United States had always recognized that Japan possessed "residual sovereignty" over Okinawa.

But removal of nuclear weapons from Okinawa ought not to mean merely that they will be planted somewhere else in the vicinity. There was talk in Washington of the weapons being removed to "other sites in the Pacific area." What other sites? The islands of Micronesia, which formerly belonged to Japan and for 23 years have been administered by the United States as trustee for the United Nations? That would be a mockery of the trust. The U.S. already has a missile base at Kwajalein and this is permitted under the terms of the U.N. trusteeship, but to proceed from this to using the western Pacific islands as bases for offensive missiles (to "deter Peking") could be a long step in the wrong direction. It could also prove to be militarily worthless—why seek out remote islands as new Keystones of the Pacific, when the U.S. has all those submarines, able to move about freely with nuclear missiles on board? The true keystone of peace in the Pacific is a solid U.S.–Japan partnership, which won't be achieved, in fact is far likelier to be wrecked, by returning Okinawa to Tokyo clean of nuclear weapons, and then perversely planting the missiles elsewhere in the area.

## AMERICA AND THE JAPANESE

ALL ALONG THE trail we have been following, all the way from the Nile Delta, we have really been holding onto a thread like Theseus finding his way through the labyrinth. The thread which had to be grasped and followed, and which was always plainly in view even when it may have seemed to twist and turn, is of course *the urge to modernize,* that all of those countries we have passed through have exhibited in greater or lesser degree. It could almost be said that one large reason why the United States has interest in Asia is that Asia is trying quite hard to become like America, at least in the sense of becoming part of the 20th century, which America symbolizes for most of mankind in the atomic age. We began our exploration with a giant dam that the Egyptians are erecting with the help of the Russians, in order to further modernize their country, which is a land of 30 million people—about the same number as the population of America at the time of the Civil War. And, not inappropriately, we close these explorations in Japan, an Asian country which by a deliberate act of national will decided to modernize itself about the same time as America was recovering from its Civil War wounds. Japan, after one terrific setback that for a time seemed likely to put an end to all Japanese effort forever, has succeeded in making itself the world's third most productive economy, after the United States and Soviet Union. At the same time as it has finally succeeded beyond all reasonable expectations, in achieving and indeed going far beyond its original modernization target, Japan has also begun to regain some of the military strength that it wholly lost following its sensational defeat at the end of World War II.

Once again the gray warships of Japan sail the oceans with the Rising Sun flag fluttering over them. Japan spends well over a billion dollars a year on conventional arms, including a large 174,000 man army. A billion dollars is only a tiny fraction (perhaps 0.75 percent) of the Japanese GNP, but it is still a sufficiently large sum for Japan's military budget to rank 8th or 9th in the world. The Japanese, though they clearly have the capability, say they do not intend to make themselves possessors of nuclear weapons. They are apparently prepared to leave such dread powers to the Americans, Russians, and Chinese, who already have nuclear weapons, and also perhaps to the Egyptians and Israelis, who may be tempted to acquire them because of present quarrels with each other. The main reason why the Japanese intend to eschew nuclear weapons for themselves, and to uphold the principle of "nonproliferation" by their example, is what happened to the Japanese cities of Hiroshima and Nagasaki a quarter of a century ago. They were devastated by the first primitive atom bombs, the only cities in the world which have thus far gone through such a frightful experience. Nowadays most of the 100 million Japanese live in crowded, vulnerable coastal cities; and more and more of them seem likely to do so. It is simply not in the cards that those cities and those crowded millions of people could be successfully defended against a nuclear attack. The Japanese have therefore concluded that as their cities cannot be defended against nuclear attack, it would be suicidal for them to possess nuclear weapons. The only consequence of such possession, they felt, would be to risk attracting the lightning to Japan. However, the United States has agreed to hold a "nuclear umbrella" over Japan, which lessens the chances of a nuclear attack on the Japanese (although not, perhaps, on the Americans who are holding the "umbrella"). Short of a nuclear war, Japan's conventional forces are capable of self-defense (and are indeed called the self-defense forces). This self-defense might just conceivably extend to South Korea, with the defense of South Korea being regarded as coming within the sphere of Japan's vital national interest. But it is unlikely that the Japanese forces would range any farther afield than that; and there would indeed be strong opposition by the Socialists of Japan to the "self-defense forces" fighting anywhere. The Socialists prefer to think of the Japanese army as a kind of national guard. Meanwhile, Japan pushes strongly ahead, year by year, with the expansion of her trade with the United States, and with Europe and all Japan's Asian neighbors, and with both Russia and China.

Japan's place in the forefront of the modernization of Asia helps to define the role of the United States toward Japan. It is primarily as a trade partner that Japan should be regarded, not as a military partner and assuredly not as an ally against either Russia or China. Japan seems prepared to become an economic partner of the United States. The Japanese, admittedly under some American pressure, are now ready to make some cautious concessions to American firms that are anxious to sell in the Japanese home market which so far has been jealously guarded against them (and against all foreigners) by the skillfully woven rules and regulations of the powerful MITI, the Japanese Ministry of International Trade and Industry. The Japanese are also willing to play an increasing part in international aid, helping other Asian countries to raise their national incomes through growing productivity. As their share of this necessary task, the Japanese may be prepared to lend and invest as much as they intend to spend on military defense, between $1 and $2 billion a year. That would be a considerable contribution to foreign aid. It seems unlikely for instance that Soviet Russian economic assistance has ever amounted in practice to nearly as much as that, on an average annual basis. American aid to India is said to have totaled altogether about $7 billion in 10 years; but most of that has been in the form of PL480 food and cotton, in other words it has really been the disposal of American farm surpluses that otherwise might have proved awkward to handle. The Japanese are already at work, under United Nations auspices, building dams on the Mekong River, and the other development projects in which they are interested range widely from Siberia to Indonesian Borneo and Arab Kuwait. Although the Australians and New Zealanders have been willing in some degree to share the American burden in Vietnam, which the Japanese have not, Japan looks like it is outstripping New Zealand and Australia in the provision of economic aid to the still-developing Asian countries.

In short, the American military bases in Japan are fast becoming a rather small element in the overall United States–Japan relationship. And this is just as well, for these relations could be seriously disrupted, if the American bases were to be allowed to remain in the foreground, or even if they do not shrink into the background fast enough. As the military bases recede in importance, however, the chances will improve of Japan playing a role which is near and dear to the Japanese heart. This role is acting as a bridge between the United States and mainland China. The Japanese appear to believe that they can one day perform in this role successfully, in spite of the fact that Japan not long ago was China's chief oppressor. But Japan seems unlikely to be given the opportunity to try its skill as a bridge builder, until some time after the turmoil and confusion caused by the Great Proletarian Cultural Revolution in China has subsided. Meantime, the Chinese tend to look on Japan with intense suspicion, as the jackal-like accomplice of both "imperialist" America and "revisionist" Russia.

What have recently abated in Japan's favor are the suspicions that other Asian countries understandably harbored concerning the Japanese, who thirty years ago overran them and thrust the rule of Nippon upon them, and sought to justify these conquests by declaring that it was heaven's plan to have "all the world under one [Japanese] roof." In the end of course, the Japanese lost all their conquests as well as their own independence for a time, and were compelled to make gestures of apology and restitution. Now, however, the old spirit of conquest appears to have been replaced by a genuine Japanese willingness to help throughout Asia that process of modernization in which Japan is the pioneer, and in which all the Asian countries are anxious to have a share. This, and not the existence of American military bases on Japanese soil, is the probable key to future relations between Japan and the United States as well as between Japan and the other Asian countries.

# 12

## PEOPLE NOT DOMINOES

THIS BOOK BEGAN on the Nile and it ends in the
Pacific; patient readers have made a trip that has taken them
from Suez through the Middle East and the Persian Gulf, into
central Asia and then over the mighty Himalayas, cloud-
capped, ice-capped, and hundreds of miles long, to the tropical jungles and seas and islands of southeast Asia, and finally on
to China and Japan. We have been seeking along the way to
examine and understand the nature and extent of American
involvement with those exotic lands and peoples.

Above all, with people; not with "dominoes." These are
human beings, and their problems though very varied are all
human ones. Displaced Palestinians; emirs whose trouble is
that of Midas; Pushtuns seeking a national home; Brahmins
with the tables turned on them, who find themselves being discriminated against; Vietnamese in danger of being slaughtered
whichever way their country goes—and overseas Chinese in
the same plight, but in their case for being Chinese instead
of being Indonesians or Filipinos.

In most places the official American emphasis unfortunately
has been on the plane of dominoes, not people. American
policy has been concerning itself with global strategy, in which
whole countries are mere pawns. If the Soviet Union persists
in arming Arabs, ought the United States to arm the Israelis
to prevent the Middle East "going communist"; or would it
be more statesmanlike and in America's larger interests to try
to woo the Arabs away from the Soviet Union, even at some
cost to Israel? The same questions were asked concerning the
Pakistanis and the Indians, in their perennial quarrel over

Kashmir; nowadays the debate there has become whether the
United States should resume shipments of arms to Pakistan to
woo that country away from Communist China. In regard to
Vietnam, the argument at policy-making level has often been
on an abstract plane—would a communist Vietnam deal a blow
to American interests by becoming a ready-made tool for Chinese expansion, thus fulfilling the famous domino theory; or
in actual fact might not a communist Vietnam be a thorn in
China's side, by going Titoist, and thus turn out to be an
American asset and not a liability at all?

It cannot be said that pursuit of American interests in Asia
by those means has had good results. On the contrary, the
consequences have been often tragic and have sometimes approached catastrophe. The reason is simple. Too frequently,
the pursuit has been postulated on a myth, like the notion of
"containing" China, or the concept of "international communism" as a piece of gigantic political machinery, with its
myriad parts all perfectly correlated and working jointly to
"communize the world." There are no doubt individual communists who dream of such a machine. Unfortunately for them,
fortunately for the rest of us, it simply does not exist. Yet much
of American foreign policy makes no sense if this is admitted.

The two great driving thrusts in modern Asia have little to
do with communism and less with any sort of "international"
plan. The twin forces that are propelling and at the same time
reshaping Asia are the headlong drives of nationalism, and of
modernization. Until American policy allots those two forces
their proper place in the scheme of events, it will never understand Asia nor will it be able to achieve whatever purposes it
has in mind. In order to modernize their countries, Asian nationalist leaders will if need be accept help from any source,
including capitalist America and Soviet Russia and Maoist
China; and in fact that is what many of them have done. But
both Russia and the United States—and China to a lesser degree, only because China has less to spare—have deluded
themselves that by this means they can woo and win the
Asians to their side in their Tweedledee-Tweedledum fight for
"the world." The Russians have doled out aid to Asian coun-

tries at the not inconsiderable rate of about $250 million a year. Yet all their experiences now go to show that to the degree that Soviet aid does succeed in starting an underdeveloped country on the road to development, the chances of a communist revolution become smaller, not larger. The United States also has extended lines of aid to underdeveloped countries—in Asia, at an annual rate of about $1 billion a year, this of course *not* including Vietnam; but though the aid may have prevented a country turning communist, there is no evidence it has convinced any country that capitalism is the solution of their difficulties. On the contrary, most of them firmly believe that they will achieve modernization much faster without it. The United States has also gone out of its way to place an extra obstacle in its own path that Russia has mostly avoided more through luck and chance than anything else. The American military bases in Asian countries are a direct affront to the burgeoning nationalism that stirs strongly in all of them. The bases are at the root of most of the American difficulties with Asian countries from the Philippines to Thailand to Okinawa and Japan, and including even the South Vietnamese government. The only noncommunist country where the Russians may be said to have a military presence now is Egypt, and the predictable consequence has come to pass there; the Egyptians are becoming more and more anti-Russian, not in spite of but because of their growing dependence on Soviet military supplies.

The American military posture in Asia calls urgently for revision. It involves very large expenditures of money that comes out of the American taxpayers' hides. Most of this spending is sheer waste; much of it is positively counterproductive, in terms of what the American policy-makers imagine that they are accomplishing. With great benefit to Americans, and with hardly any pain to Asians, the American military forces in most of Asia could be cut by about two-thirds. In terms of manpower, that would be a reduction of roughly 650,000. Most of them would come home from Vietnam, of course, but there is large room for cuts in Korea, Thailand, Okinawa and Japan, and the Philippines.

Such a revision of the American military posture in Asia would by no means entail the United States turning its back on Asia, nor do the Asians wish this. The drive to modernize is a form of Asian flattery of the west, and especially of the United States. It is an admission that in some material things Asia needs to catch up with the west. Envy of western material superiority tends however to be too indiscriminate. One large service the United States can render Asia is to suggest that these countries do not seek to acquire an arms race; smog and other forms of pollution; overcrowded cities that are at the same time fast decaying; the drug habit; or urban crime.

Traveling through Asia can be a disconcerting experience for a westerner with a reasonably reflective mind. On our 1969 travels that began west of Suez and ended far east of Suez, in Tokyo, my wife and I after a while felt that however far east we went, we were still stuck fast in western goo. The whole of Asia it seemed had been recolonized, this time by Muzak and the Rolling Stones. The jet aircraft, the hotels, the restaurants, and the taxicabs all were tuned in to western pop music. The inescapable conclusion was that Asia as yet knows the west only in its most superficial aspect. This of course cuts both ways. But in an important sense the traffic is still too much one-way. John M. Steadman, for example, observes in his excellent book, *The Myth of Asia* (Simon and Schuster, 1969): "The most obvious signs of unity in Asia are, paradoxically, those of Western influence." Japanese speak to Burmese (and Indians and Pakistanis to one another) in English. The common denominator in architecture and in books as well as in music is always western style. As the westerner moves around in Asia, Mr. Steadman pertinently notes, he sees everywhere the same western-style bank, airport, hotel, office building—and supermarket, and automobile sales room. "Scenes shift as abruptly as a Chinese opera. An entire cast enters and departs, while another—just as exotically costumed —comes on-stage. . . . Yet always there remains one corner of the stage that does not change."

In short, the world west and east is nowadays one world. A commonplace, surely, if ever there was one. But in fact

Asia while it is adopting western materialism still lacks the most urgent worthwhile things. Neil H. Jacoby, a former dean of the graduate school of business administration at the University of California at Los Angeles, has drawn up a short list of what Asia could advantageously get from the west still. He suggests roads to link farms with markets; power lines; telegraphs and telephones; or what in general he calls "public capital of the infrastructural kind." To which one would surely add, dams and schools and houses and hospitals. Asia can still use western missionaries, but nowadays they tend to be disguised as bankers and bureaucrats and economic planners; the religious impulse travels from east to west rather than the other way round.

Foreign aid, as we saw, has really been a crude instrument of foreign policy, whether wielded by an American or a Russian or a Chinese hand; and the results of this hypocrisy have, not unexpectedly, benefited neither the wielder nor the subject as much as was hoped. Now "foreign aid" is distinctly unfashionable, in Moscow and in Peking as much as in Washington. Yet at no time did it ever amount to much; in the case of the United States, one-sixtieth of the federal budget, and probably a still smaller component of Soviet and Chinese government spending. Moreover, aid was largely used for alleviating domestic economic headaches. Much of the American "aid" to India and Pakistan was disposing of surplus food and cotton; and, of $8 billion of *economic* aid to East Asia over a period of 20 years, a breakdown shows all but $500 million going to Vietnam and South Korea, with Taiwan accounting for almost all that residue. Over the same 20-year period, South Korea received aid at the rate of $148 per head, but India with more than 10 times Korea's population received only $14 per head; the corresponding figures for Taiwan (population 14 million) and Indonesia (117 million) are $177 and $6. Foreign aid may or may not have a future, but if it is to have one, it had better be more evenly distributed than this, if it is to do any good.

Until the end of this century and beyond, Asia is going to be the scene of wars and revolutions, which are part of the process of modernization and of surging nationalism. These turbulences are unlikely to have much connection with the domino theory, or with international communism. No war in Asia is likely to be the spark of a third world war, save possibly a really serious military clash between Soviet Russia and Communist China; and there is no reason why the United States need be involved in any Asian war. This however does not mean the United States can be indifferent to whatever happens in Asia. There are two good reasons why it should not be. First, "no man is an island"; there is a moral duty to one's neighbors, and in today's shrinking world we are all each other's neighbor. Second, the United States is today the richest country in the world, regularly producing and consuming about half of all the world's goods, although Americans are only 6 percent of the world's population. But this wealth still is based to a large degree on oil, minerals and other raw materials that come from the underdeveloped parts of the earth, including Asia. And, if one includes with the United States the other developed countries, western Europe and Japan, these are not only the rich countries, but they are adding to their per capita incomes at a rate that is *seventeen* times faster than the underdeveloped countries. It should be perfectly obvious that the gap that already yawns between rich and poor cannot continue widening at this pace without something blowing up. The gap has to stop widening and be narrowed, and to do this calls for a conscious deliberate effort by the rich to assist the poor. This is an economic argument, or a balance of power argument, or a geopolitical argument.

There is still the moral argument, which ought to be the most powerful of all, especially in the United States which owes its very existence to a moral principle that its founders embraced. Who, really, wants to live in a world, even if one is fortunate enough to inhabit the richer part, that is divided into a tiny zone of affluence and a vast and growing sea of poverty and misery? Americans have recently made the belated discovery that there is much for them to do at home, in the way of removing misery caused by poverty. But still they cannot in good conscience turn their backs on Asia, or behave like Dives to Lazarus, especially to a Lazarus who is becoming much too proud to beg for crumbs. Doing well what has to be done, at home, is a better foreign policy than preaching to others abroad—for men respond to example rather than to teaching. But Americans also have to decide if they, and the Asians with whom they have now endured so much together, are to behave as strangers, or to be brothers.

# Index